Josephine Clifford

Overland Tales

Josephine Clifford

Overland Tales

ISBN/EAN: 9783744708777

Printed in Europe, USA, Canada, Australia, Japan

Cover: Foto ©Thomas Meinert / pixelio.de

More available books at **www.hansebooks.com**

OVERLAND TALES.

BY
JOSEPHINE CLIFFORD.

SAN FRANCISCO:
A. L. BANCROFT & CO.
1877.

Entered, according to Act of Congress, in the year 1877, by
JOSEPHINE CLIFFORD,
in the Office of the Librarian of Congress, at Washington.

COLLINS, PRINTER.

Dedicated

TO MY KINDEST

AND

MOST CONSTANT READER,

MOTHER.

PREFACE.

IN the book I now lay before the reader, I have collected a series of stories and sketches of journeyings through California, Arizona, and New Mexico. There is little of fiction, even in the stories; and the sketches, I flatter myself, are true to life — as I saw it, at the time I visited the places.

A number of these stories first appeared in the OVERLAND MONTHLY, but some of them are new, and have never been published. I bespeak for them all the attentive perusal and undivided interest of the kind reader.

THE AUTHOR.

CONTENTS.

	PAGE
LA GRACIOSA,	13
JUANITA,	53
HETTY'S HEROISM,	68
A WOMAN'S TREACHERY,	87
THE GENTLEMAN FROM SISKIYOU,	101
SOMETHING ABOUT MY PETS,	119
POKER-JIM,	137
THE TRAGEDY AT MOHAWK STATION,	153
LONE LINDEN,	161
MANUELA,	188
THE ROMANCE OF GILA BEND,	204
A LADY IN CAMP,	219
THE GOLDEN LAMB,	237
IT OCCURRED AT TUCSON,	260
A BIT OF "EARLY CALIFORNIA,"	274
HER NAME WAS SYLVIA,	282
CROSSING THE ARIZONA DESERTS,	296
DOWN AMONG THE DEAD LETTERS,	310
MARCHING WITH A COMMAND,	321
TO TEXAS, AND BY THE WAY,	354
MY FIRST EXPERIENCE IN NEW MEXICO,	367

OVERLAND TALES.

LA GRACIOSA.

IT was a stolid Indian face, at the first casual glance, but lighting up wonderfully with intelligence and a genial smile, when the little dark man, with the Spanish bearing, was spoken to. Particularly when addressed by one of the fairer sex, did a certain native grace of demeanor, an air of chivalrous gallantry, distinguish him from the more cold-blooded, though, perhaps, more fluent-spoken, Saxon people surrounding him.

Among the many different eyes fixed upon him now and again, in the crowded railroad-car, was one pair, of dark luminous gray, that dwelt there longer, and returned oftener, than its owner chose to have the man of the olive skin know. Still, he must have felt the magnetism of those eyes; for, conversing with this, disputing with that, and greeting the third man, he advanced, slowly but surely, to where a female figure, shrouded in sombre black, sat close by the open window. There was something touching in the young face that looked from out the heavy widow's veil, which covered her small hat, and almost completely enveloped the slender form. The face was transparently pale, the faintest flush of pink tinging the cheeks when any emotion swayed the breast; the lips were full, fresh, and cherry-red in color, and the hair, dark-brown and wavy, was brushed lightly back from the temples.

The breeze at the open window was quite fresh, for the train in its flight was nearing the spot where the chill air from the ocean draws through the Salinas Valley. Vainly the slender fingers tried to move the obstinate spring that held aloft the upper part of the window. The color crept faintly into the lady's cheeks, for suddenly a hand, hardly larger than her's, though looking brown beside it, gently displaced her fingers and lowered the window without the least trouble. The lady's gloves had dropped; her handkerchief had fluttered to the floor; a small basket was displaced; all these things were remedied and attended to by the Spaniard, who had surely well-earned the thanks she graciously bestowed.

"Excuse me," he said, with unmistakable Spanish pronunciation; "but you do not live in our Valley—do you?"

"This is my first visit," she replied; "but I shall probably live here for the future."

"Ah! that makes me so happy," he said, earnestly, laying his hand on his heart.

The lady looked at him in silent astonishment. "Perhaps that is the way of the Spanish people," she said to herself. "At any rate, he has very fine eyes, and—it may be tedious living in Salinos."

Half an hour's conversation brought out the fact that a married sister's house was to be the home of the lady for a while; that the sister did not know of her coming just to-day, and that her ankle was so badly sprained that walking was very painful to her.

From the other side it was shown that his home was in the neighborhood of the town ("one of those wealthy Spanish rancheros," she thought); that he was slightly acquainted with her brother-in-law; that he was a widower, and that his two sons would be at the depôt to receive him. These sons would bring with them, probably, a light spring-wagon from the ranch, but could easily be sent back for the comfortable carriage, if the lady would allow him the pleasure of seeing her safely under her sister's roof. She said she would accept a seat in the spring-wagon, and Senor Don Pedro Lopez withdrew, with a deep bow, to look after his luggage.

"Poor lady!" he explained to a group of his inquiring friends, "poor lady! She is deep in mourning, and she has much sorrow in her heart." And he left them quickly, to assist his *protégé* with her wraps. Then the train came to a halt, and Don Pedro's new acquaintance, leaning on his arm, approached the light vehicle, at either side of which stood the two sons, bending courteously, in acknowledgment of the lady's greeting. When Don Pedro himself was about to mount to the seat beside her, she waved him back, with a charmingly impetuous motion of the hand. "I am safe enough with your sons," she laughed, pleasantly. "Do you stop at my brother-in-law's office, pray, and tell him I have come."

Sister Anna was well pleased to greet the new arrival — "without an attachment." Her sister Nora's "unhappy marriage" had been a source of constant trouble and worry to her; and here she came at last — alone. Brother-in-law Ben soon joined them, and Nora's first evening passed without her growing seriously lonesome or depressed. Sister Anna, to be sure, dreaded the following days. Her sister's unhappy marriage, she confided to her nearest neighbor, had so tried the poor girl's nerves, that she should not wonder if she sank into a profound melancholy. She did all she could to make the days pass pleasantly; but what can you do in a small town when you have neither carriage nor horses?

Fortunately, Don Pedro came to the rescue. He owned many fine horses and a number of vehicles — from an airy, open buggy to a comfortably-cushioned carriage. He made his appearance a day or two after Nora's arrival, mounted on a prancing black steed, to whose every step jingled and clashed the heavy silver-mounted trappings, which the older

Spaniards are fond of decking out their horses with. He came only, like a well-bred man, to inquire after the sprained ankle; but before he left he had made an engagement to call the very next morning, with his easiest carriage, to take both ladies out to drive.

And he appeared, punctual to the minute, sitting stiffly in the barouche-built carriage, on the front seat beside the driver, who, to Nora's unpractised eye, seemed a full Indian, though hardly darker than his master. True, the people of pure Spanish descent did say that this same master had a slight admixture of Indian blood in his viens, too; but Don Pedro always denied it. He was from Mexico, he said, but his parents had come from Spain. However this might be, Nora stood in mute dismay a moment, when the outfit drew up at the door; and she cast a questioning glance at her sister, even after they were seated in the carriage; but Sister Anna's eyes seemed repeating an old admonition to Nora — "Be patient, poor child; be still." And Nora, passing her hand across her face, heeded the admonition, gathered courage, and gave herself up to the perfect enjoyment of the scene and the novelty of the expedition.

It was a late spring day — the Valley still verdant with the growing grain, the mountains mottled with spots of brown where the rain of the whole winter had failed to make good the ravages of thousands of sheep, or where, perhaps, a streak of undiscovered mineral lay sleeping in the earth. Scant groups of trees dotted the Valley at far intervals, ranged themselves in rows where a little river ran at the foot of the Gabilan, and stood in lonely grandeur on the highest ridge of the mountain. Where the mountain sloped it grew covered with redwood, and where the hills shrank away they left a wide gap for the ocean breeze and the ocean fog to roll in.

Across the Valley was another mountain, dark and grand,

with flecks of black growing *chemasal* in clefts and crevices, and sunny slopes and green fields lying at its base. And oh! the charm of these mountains. In the Valley there might be the fog and the chill of the North, but on the mountains lay the warmth and the dreaminess of the South.

Keenly the dark eyes of the Spaniard studied the lovely face, flushed, as it seemed, with the pleasure derived from the drive in the pure air and the golden sunshine.

"You like our Valley?" he asked, as eagerly as though she were a capitalist to whom he intended selling the most worthless portion of his ranch at the highest possible figure.

"Not the Valley so much as the mountains," she returned. "We have had fogs two days out of the week I have spent here, and I fancy I could escape that if I could get to the top of the mountains."

"Ah! you like the sunshine and the warm air. You must go farther South then — far South. I have thought a great deal of going there myself. There is a beautiful rancho which I can buy — you would like it, I know, — far down and close by the sea. And the sea is so blue there — just like the heavens. Oh! you would like it, I know, if you could only see it," he concluded, enthusiastically, as though this were another ranch he was trying to sell her.

But the thought of traffic or gain was very far from his heart just then, though Don Pedro was known to be an exceptionally good business man and a close financier. Many of his Spanish compeers looked up to him with a certain awe on this account. Most of them had parted with their broad acres, their countless herds, all too easily, to gratify their taste for lavish display and easy living, with its attendant cost under the new American *régime ;* or had lost them through confiding, with their generous heart, their guileless nature, to the people whose thoughts were bent on securing, by usury and knaves' tricks, the possessions of the very men whose hospitable roof afforded them shelter. "He can cope with any American," they would say, proudly, speaking of Don Pedro; and Don Pedro would show his appreciation of the compliment by exercising his business qualifications towards them, as well as towards "los Americanos."

But the haughty Don was well-mannered and agreeable; and after securing from Nora an indefinite promise that she would some time, when her ankle got strong, ride his own saddle-horse, he left the ladies safely at their door and retired, his heart and brain filled with a thousand happy dreams. He had only once during the ride pointed carelessly across the valley to where his ranch lay; but Nora had gained no definite idea of its extent.

One pleasant afternoon the two sons of Don Pedro stopped at the door. Their father had encouraged them to call, they said; perhaps the lady and her sister would bestow upon them the honor of driving out with them for an hour. Both lads spoke English with elegance and fluency (let the good fathers of the Santa Clara College alone for that), but among themselves their mother-tongue still asserted itself; and in their behavior a touch of the Spanish punctilio distinguished them favorably from the uncouth flippancy of some of their young American neighbors.

Nora cheerfully assented, and in a few minutes the whole party was bowling along,— the eldest brother driving, the younger explaining and describing the country and its peculiarities. Pablo and Roberto had both been born on their ranch, though not in the large white house they saw in the distance. That had been finished only a little while when their mother died. The *adobe* which had been their birthplace stood several miles farther back, and could not be seen from here.

"It is not on this ranch, then?" queried Nora.

"Pardon, yes; on this ranch, but several miles nearer the foothills; in that direction — there."

"And is the land we are passing over all one ranch?" Nora continued, persistently.

"We have been driving over our own land almost since we left town," replied Pablo, a little proudly. "San Jacinto is one of the largest ranchos in the county, and the Americans have not yet succeeded in cutting it up into building-lots and homestead blocks," he added, laughing a frank, boyish laugh, which seemed to say, "you are as one of us, and will not take it amiss."

Sister Anna looked stealthily at Nora, but her eyes, with a strange light in them, were fixed on the horizon, far off, where they seemed to read something that made her brow contract and lower a little while, and then clear off, as, with an effort, she turned to the boy and brought up some other topic of conversation. But her heart was not in what she said, and Sister Anna exerted herself to cover the deficiences that Nora's drooping spirits left in the entertainment.

It was sunset when they reached home, and standing on the rose-covered veranda of the little cottage a moment, Nora looked across to where the lingering gleams of the sun were kissing the black-looming crown of the Loma Prieta, with floods of pink and soft violet, and covering all its base with shades of dark purple and heavy gray. She raised her clasped hands to the mountain top.

"How glad, how thankful I could be, if from the wreck and the ruins I could gather light and warmth enough to cover my past life and its miseries, as the pink and the purple of the sunset cover the black dreariness of yon mountain."

"Come in, Nora, it is getting cold," interrupted Sister Anna; "or the next thing after having your nerves wrought up so will be a fit of hysterics."

"Which, you will say, is one more of the bad effects of Nora's unhappy marriage."

If Nora's wilfulness and Nora's unhappy marriage had been

ever so deeply deplored by her, the loss of Sister Anna's love, or Anna's sisterly kindness, could not be counted among its many bad effects. Brother-in-law Ben, too, was whole-souled and affectionate; more practical, and a trifle more far-seeing than Anna; but he never said, "I told you so." He quietly did all he could to bind up bleeding wounds.

It soon came to be looked upon as quite a matter of course that Don Pedro should be seen in his carriage with the two sisters; or, that his black steed should be led up and down before the cottage door, by one of his servants, dark of skin, fiery-eyed, and of quiet demeanor, like his master. Then, again, the sons were seen at the cottage, always courteous, attentive, and scrupulously polite. If in the privacy of their most secret communings the "Gringa" was ever spoken of *as* the Gringa, it was only in the strictest privacy. Neither to Nora, nor to any of their servants, did ever look or word betray but that in the fair young American they saw all that their widowed father desired they should see.

The retinue of the Whitehead family consisted of but a single Chinaman, who was cook, laundress, maid-of-all-work; but during Nora's stay she was never aware but that she had half-a-dozen slaves to do her bidding, so careful, yet so delicate was Don Pedro in bestowing his attentions. He soon hovered about the whole family like one of the *genii*. If Nora just breathed to herself, "How pleasant the day is — if we only had carriage and horses"— before the hour was over the Don, with his carriage, or Don Pedro's boys, or an invitation to ride from the Don, was at hand. Before she had quite concluded that fruits were not so abundant or fine in the country as in the city markets, the Don had contracted a pleasant habit of sending his servants with the choicest of all his fields and store-houses contained to the little cottage in town. Fish, fresh from the Bay of Monterey, and game, that plain and mountain afforded, came in the run of time, quite as a matter of course, to the kitchen and larder of Don Pedro's dear friend Whitehead. It was not to be refused. Don Pedro had a hundred points of law that he wished explained; had so much advice to ask in regard to some tracts of land he meant to purchase, that Brother-in-law Ben always seemed the one conferring the greatest favor.

It was a little singular, too, this friendship of the Don's for Lawyer Whitehead. As a general thing, the Spanish population of California look upon our lawyers with distrust, and have a wholesome horror of the law. Don Pedro, though liberal-minded and enlightened, was not backward in expressing the contempt he felt for many of our American views and opinions; but above all he abominated our most popular institution — the Divorce Court. Not as a Catholic only, was it an abomination to him, he said. He had often declared to see a divorced woman gave him the same shuddering sensation that was caused by looking upon a poisonous snake.

When her ankle had grown quite strong, Don Pedro solicited for Rosa the honor of carrying Nora for a short ride through the country. And Nora, mounted high on the shapely animal's back, had seemed in such pleasant mood when they left her sister's door, that she quite bewildered her escort by the sudden sharp tone with which she replied to the question he asked: what feature she admired most in the landscape before them?

"Those many little lakes," she said. "They have an enticing look of quiet and rest, and hold out a standing invitation to 'come and get drowned,' to weary mortals like myself."

He was too delicate to allow his shocked glance to rise to her face, but to himself he repeated, "Poor lady! she has much sorrow in her heart," and aloud he said:

"You are homesick, Leonora?" How much prettier it seemed to hear the sonorous voice frame the word "Leonora," than the stiff appellation of "Mrs. Rutherford," which the Don could hardly ever bring himself to utter. It was so long, he excused himself, and not the custom of his country — though, in direct contradiction to the first part of the excuse, he would slyly smuggle in an addition — Blanca, Graciosa, Querida — trusting for safety in her lack of acquaintance with the Spanish tongue.

"No," she answered honestly to his question, "I have no place to be homesick for. I am glad to be here; but —"

"Ah! but you must see the Southern country first," he interrupted, eagerly. "I am going South this winter to purchase a ranch, on which I shall make my home. I leave this ranch here to my two boys. Their mother died here, and the ranch will be theirs. But my ranch in the South will be very fine; the land is so fair — like a beautiful woman, almost."

"I shall miss you, if you leave us; particularly through the rainy winter months," she said.

"How happy that makes me!" he exclaimed, as once before; and he did now what had been in his heart to do then — he bent over her hand and kissed it warmly, heedless of the swarthy Mexican who rode behind his master.

All through the summer, with its dust and its fog and its glaring sun, did Don Pedro still find a pleasant hour, early after the fog had risen, or late after the sun had set, to spend, on horseback or in carriage, with "the one fair woman" who seemed to fill his whole heart. Sometimes, when returning from an expedition on which Sister Anna had not accompanied them, she would greet them on the veranda with uneasy, furtive eyes; and the Don, blind to everything but his passion for Nora, still did not observe the impatient answering glance.

Don Pedro was delicacy and chivalry itself. Bending low over her white fingers one day, he asked, "And how long was Mr. Rutherford blessed with the possession of this most sweet hand?"

"I was married but a year," she answered, with her teeth set, and quickly drawing back her hand.

On reaching home she reported to her sister. "Aha," she commented, "he wants to know how long you have been a widow, and whether it is too soon to make more decided proposals."

Then came the early rains, and for Nora fits of passionate crying, alternating with fits of gloomy depression. Don Pedro was in despair. Her varying moods did not escape him, and when, to crown all, her ankle, still weak from the sprain, began to swell with rheumatism, she took no pains to hide her fretfulness or sadness either from her sister Anna or the Don. In the midst of the gloom and the rain came Don Pedro one day to announce that he was about to set out for the South, to conclude the purchase of the ranch he had so long spoken of.

"And you are going, too?" she said, lugubriously.

"I beg you to give me permission to go. I am the slave of Leonora, La Graciosa, and will return soon. I will not go, if you grant me not permission; but I beg you let me go for a short time." He had sunk on his knees by the couch on which she rested, and his eyes flashed fire into hers for a brief moment; but he conquered himself, and veiled them under their heavy lashes. "Let me go," he pleaded, humbly, "and give me permission to return to you, Leonora. In my absence my sons will do all your bidding. They know the will of their father."

Nora had extended her hand, and motioned him to a chair beside her couch, and listened with a smile on her lips to all the arrangements he had made for her comfort during his absence.

"Since I have allowed you your own way in everything, I

must have mine in one particular. Of course, you will take a saddle-horse for yourself besides the spring-wagon. Now you shall not leave Rosa here for me, but shall take her along for your own use. It is absurd for you to insist that no one shall use her since I have ridden her; I shall not keep her here while you are struggling over heavy roads, in the wagon, or on some other horse."

It was, perhaps, the longest speech she had ever made to him, and it was all about himself too, and full of consideration for him — oh! it was delicious. With fervent gratitude he kissed her hand, called her Preciosa, Banita, till she declared that he should not say hard things of her in Spanish any more. He desisted for the time, on her promise that she would try to be cheerful while he was away, and not get homesick, unless it were for him; and they became quite gay and sociable over a cup of tea which Sister Anna brought them into the sitting-room — so sociable, that Nora said of the Don, after his departure:

"If any one were to tell me that a church-steeple could unbend sufficiently to roll ten-pins of a Sunday afternoon, I should believe it after this."

But in a little while the fits of dejection and the fits of crying came back again. Sister Anna did her best to break them up; she rallied her on breaking her heart for the absent Don; she tried to interest her in her surroundings, so that she should see the sungleams that flashed through the winter's gloom.

"See this beautiful cala that has just opened in the garden," she would say, with an abortive attempt at making her believe that her ankle was strong and well.

"I cannot get up, miserable creature that I am," came back the dismal response.

"Oh, that lovely cloth-of-gold has grown a shoot full half a yard long since yesterday; come and see."

"I cannot."

"Yes, you can; come lean on me. Now, isn't this sunshine delightful for December?"

Nora drew a deep breath; after a week's steady rain, the sky was clear as crystal, and the sun laughed down on hill and valley, blossoming rose and budding bush.

"See how the violets are covered with blue, and the honeysuckle has just reached the farthest end of the porch. Oh, Nora, how can any one be unhappy with flowers to tend, and a home to keep?"

"Ah! yes. You are right, sister; but it is your home — not mine."

Anna laid her arm around her as though to support her. She knew her sister's proud spirit and yearning heart, and she only whispered, as she had so often done, "Be patient, poor child; be still."

But that short, passionate plaint had lightened Nora's heart; after a week's sunshine the roads were dry enough to ride out once more with Don Pedro's sons, and when steady rain set in once more after that, she tried to show her sister that she could take an interest in "home" — though it was not her own.

A month had worn away, and as long as the weather permitted the regular running of the mails, Pablo and Roberto brought greetings from their father once a week; but when the roads grew impassable, they too were left without news. Not an iota did they fail of their attention to Nora, however; whatever dainties the ranch afforded were still laid at her feet, or rather on her sister's kitchen table; and the roads were never so bad but that they paid their respects at least twice a week.

"You have no cause to complain," said Sister Anna.

"No," replied Nora, with a yawn; "but I wish the Don would come back."

3

And he did come back.

"I am so glad you have come," she said, frankly, meeting him on the threshold.

"I can read it in your eyes," he exclaimed, rapturously. "Oh, how happy that makes me!" And if Sister Anna's head had not appeared behind Nora's shoulder, there is no telling what might have happened.

He had brought the spring with him; mountain and valley both had clothed itself in brightest green, in which the bare brown spots on the Gabilan Range were really a relief to the satiated eye. In the deep clefts of the Loma Prieta lay the blackish shade of the *chemasal*, and only one degree less sombre appeared the foliage of the live-oak against the tender green of the fresh grass. Again did Nora all day long watch the sun lying on the mountains — a clear golden haze in the daytime; pink and violet, and purplish gray in the evening mist.

"Is it not beautiful?" she asked of Brother-in-law Ben, one evening, as he came up the street and entered the gate.

"You are just growing to like our Valley, I see; it is a pity that you should now be 'borne away to foreign climes.'"

"And who's to bear me away?" she asked, laughing, as they entered the house.

"Let me call Anna," he said; "we will have to hold family council over this."

In council he commenced: "Don Pedro has this day requested that I, his legal adviser, go South with him, to see that all papers are properly made out, all preliminaries settled, before he fairly takes possession of his land."

"Well?" queried Anna.

"Well, my dear, so much for his counsellor Whitehead. But to his friend Benjamin's family he has extended an invitation to accompany us on this trip, presuming that his friend's wife and sister-in-law would be pleased to see this much-praised Southern country."

"We'll go, of course," assented Anna, artlessly.

"Certainly, my dear — of course;" affirmed easy-going Ben. "But, my dear, I hope you both understand all the bearings of this case."

Nora's head drooped, and a flush of pain overspread her face, as she answered, chokingly, "I do."

"Then, my dear, since Don Pedro has never mentioned Nora's name to me, except to send message or remembrance, had I not better tell him —"

"No, no!" cried Nora, in sudden terror. "Oh, please not; leave it all to me."

"Certainly, Mrs. Rutherford," he assented, still more slowly; "I am not the man to meddle with other people's affairs — unasked," he added, remembering, perhaps, his business and calling.

"Don't be angry with me, Ben," she pleaded; "you have always been so kind to me. What should I have done without you two? But you know how I feel about this — this miserable affair."

"All right, child," he said, pressing her hand. "I should like to give you a piece of advice, but my lawyer's instinct tells me that you will not take it, so that I am compelled to keep my mouth shut — emphatically."

They set out on their Southern trip, a grand cavalcade; Don Pedro on a charger a little taller, a little blacker than Nora's horse; in the light wagon Anna and her husband, and behind them a heavier wagon containing all that a leisurely journey through a thinly populated country made desirable. For attendance they had Domingi, the Don's favorite servant, two *vaqueros*, and an under-servant, all mounted on hardy mustangs. Never did picnic party, intent on a day's pleasuring, leave home in higher spirits. The fresh morning air brought the color to Nora's cheeks, and her musical laugh rang out through the Valley; and when they passed one of the little lakes, all placid and glistening in the bright sun, Nora turned to her companion with a smile: "I don't think those lakes were meant to drown one's self in, at all; they were made to cast reflections. See?" and she pointed to herself, graceful and erect, mirrored in the clear water.

"Oh, Graciosa," murmured the Spaniard.

How bright the world looked, to be sure; flowers covered the earth, not scattered in niggardly manner, as in the older, colder Eastern States, but covering the ground for miles, showing nothing but a sea of blue, an ocean of crimson, or a wilderness of yellow. Then came patches where all shades and colors were mixed; delicate tints of pink and mauve, of pure white and deep red, and over all floated a fragrance that was never equalled by garden-flowers or their distilled perfume.

When twilight fell, and Don Pedro informed them that they would spend the night under the hospitable roof of his friend, Don Pamfilio Rodriguez, Nora was almost sorry that, for the complete "romance of the thing," they could not camp out.

"We will come to that, too," the Don consoled her, "before the journey is over. But my friend would never forgive me, if I passed his door and did not enter."

"But so many of us," urged Nora, regarding, if the truth must be told, the small low-roofed *adobe* house with considerable disfavor.

"There would be room in my friend's house for my friends and myself, even though my friend himself should lie across the threshold."

Nora bowed her head. She knew of the proverbial hospitality of the Spanish — a hospitality that led them to impoverish themselves for the sake of becomingly entertaining their guests.

Of course, only Don Pedro could lift Nora from her horse; but Sister Anna found herself in the hands of the host, who conducted her, with the air of a prince escorting a duchess, to the threshold, where his wife, Donna Carmel, and another aged lady, received them. Conversation was necessarily limited — neither Don Pamfilio nor Donna Carmel speaking English, and Brother Ben alone being conversant with Spanish.

The ladies were shown into a low, clean-swept room, in which a bed, draped and trimmed with a profusion of Spanish needlework and soft red calico, took up the most space. Chairs ranged along one wall, and a gay-colored print of Saint Mary of the Sacred Heart, over the fire-place, completed the furnishing. Nora pleasantly returned the salutation of the black-bearded man who entered with coals of fire on a big garden-spade. Directly after him came a woman, with a shawl over her head and fire-wood in her arms. She, too, offered the respectful "*buénos dias,*" and she had hardly left when a small girl entered, with a broken-nosed pitcher containing hot-water, and after her came another dark-faced man, the *mayordomo*, with a tray of refreshments and inquiries as to whether the ladies were comfortable.

Nora dropped her arms by her side. "I have counted four servants now, and Don Pedro told me particularly that his friend, Pam — what's-his-name — was very poor."

"Spanish style," answered Anna, with a shrug of the shoulder. "But it is very comfortable. How cold it has grown out-doors, and how dark it is. I wonder if we shall be afraid?"

"Hush! Don't make me nervous," cried Nora, sharply, shivering with the sudden terror that sometimes came over her.

"Be still," said Anna, soothingly; "there is nothing to be afraid of here."

After a while they were called to supper, where, to their surprise, they found quite a little gathering. Neighbors who spoke English had been summoned to entertain them, and after supper, which was a marvel of dishes, in which onions, sugar, raisins, and red pepper were softly blended, and which was served by three more servants, they got up an *impromptu* concert, on three guitars, and later an *impromptu* ball, at which Nora chiefly danced with the Don.

In spite of the biting cold next morning, all the male members of last night's company insisted on escorting our friends over the first few miles of the road. They came to a stream which they must cross, and of which Don Pamfilio had warned them, and the Don insisted on Nora's getting into the wagon with her sister. The *vaqueros* with their horses were brought into requisition, and Nora opened her eyes wide when, dashing up, they fastened their long *riattas* to the tongue of the wagon, wound the end of the rope around the horn of the saddle, and with this improvised four-horse team got up the steep bank on the other side in the twinkling of an eye.

Reaching San Luis Obispo directly, they delayed one whole day, as Nora expressed herself charmed with what she saw of the old mission church, and what remained of the old mission garden. A group of fig-trees here and there, a palm-tree sadly out of place, in a dirty, dusty yard, an agave standing stiff and reserved among its upstart neighbors, the pea-vine and potato.

"Oh! it is pitiful," cried Nora, hardly aware of the quotation. "Even this proud avenue of olives, towering so high above all, has been cut up and laid out in building-lots."

"The advance of civilization," Brother Ben informed her; and, in reply, Nora pointed silently into a yard, where a half-grown palm-tree stood among heaps of refuse cigar-ends and broken bottles. The house to which the yard belonged was occupied as a bar-room, and one of its patrons, a son of Old Erin, to all appearances, lay stretched near the palm, sleeping off the fumes of the liquor imbibed at the bar.

They laughed at Nora's illustration, and decided to move

from so untoward a spot that very afternoon, even if they should have to use their tent and camp out all night.

More flowers, and brighter they grew as our friend travelled farther South. On the plain the meadow-lark sang its song in the dew and the chill of the morning, and high on the mountain, in the still noonday, the lone cry of the hawk came down from where the bird lived in solitary grandeur. Wherever our friends went they were made welcome. Not a Spanish house dare the Don pass without stopping, at least for refreshments. He had *compadres* and *comadres* everywhere, and whether they approved of his intimate relations with the "Gringas" or not, they showed always the greatest respect, extended always the most cheerful hospitality.

At last they approached Santa Barbara, its white, sun-kissed mission gleaming below them in the valley as they descended the Santa Inez Mountains. Stately business houses and lovely country-seats, hidden in trees and vines—the wide sea guarding all. But they tarried not. Don Pedro announced that he had promised to make a stay of several weeks at his particular friend's, Don Enrico del Gada. He was proud to introduce them to this family, he said. They would become acquainted with true Castilians—would be witness to how Spanish people lived in the Southern country; rich people—that is—. They had always been rich, but through some mismanagement (through the knavery of some American, Nora interpreted it), they were greatly in danger of losing their whole estate. A small portion of their rancho had been sold to a company of land-speculators, and now they were trying to float the title to this portion over the whole of the Tappa Rancho.

"Pure Castilian blood," the Don affirmed; "fair of skin, hair lighter than Nora's tresses, and eyes blue as the sky. Such the male part of the family. The female portion— mother and daughter—were black-eyed, and just a trifle darker; but beauties, both. The daughter, Narcissa (Nora fancied that a sudden twinge distorted the Don's features as he spoke the name), was lovely and an angel; not very strong, though — a little weak in the chest."

All the evening the De Gadas formed the subject of conversation, so that it is hardly surprising that morning found Nora arrayed with more care than usual, if possible, and looking handsome enough to gratify the heart of the most fastidious lover.

A two hours' ride brought them to the immediate enclosure of the comfortable ranch house, and with a sonorous "*buenos dias caballeros!*" the Don had led his party into the midst of a ring formed by the host, his son, and other invited guests. Some of them had just dismounted, and the spurs were still on their boots; some had red silk scarfs tied gracefully around the hips, and all were handsome, chivalrous, picturesque-looking men. Don Enrico advanced to assist Anna, while Don Manuel, his son, strode toward Leonora's horse and had lifted her from the saddle before Don Pedro could tell what he was about. Such clear blue eyes as he had! All the sunshine of his native Spain seemed caught in them; and his hand was so white! Nora's own could hardly vie with it.

His head was uncovered when he conducted her to the veranda, where the ladies were assembled. His mother, a beauty still, dark-eyed, full-throated, and with the haughty look and turn of the head that is found among the Spanish people; the sister a delicate, slender being, large-eyed, with hectic roses on her cheeks. Nora detected a strange glimmer in her eye and a convulsive movement of the lips as she addressed a question in a low tone to her brother, after the formal introduction was over.

"You must excuse my sister," he apologized to Nora, "she speaks no English. She wanted to know whether you had ridden Rosa. Long ago she tried to ride the horse, but could not, as she is not strong. When Don Pedro was here last she wanted to try again; but he would not consent. I suppose she is astonished at your prowess."

Nora watched the darkened, uneasy eyes of the girl; she thought she knew better than the unsuspecting brother what had prompted the question.

The Del Gada family, their house, their style of living, was all the Don had claimed for them. The first day or two were devoted mainly to out-of-door entertainments; the orange-groves, the vineyards, the almond-plantation on the ranch were visited, and a ride to the mission of Santa Barbara, whose Moorish bell-towers haunted Nora's brain, was planned and undertaken.

The warm light of the spring-day shed a soft glimmer over crumbling remnants of the monuments that the patient labor of the mission fathers have left behind them — monuments of rock and stone, shaped by the hands of the docile aborigines into aqueducts and fountains, reservoirs and mill-house; monuments, too, of living, thriving trees, swaying gently in the March wind, many of them laden with promises of a harvest of luscious apricot or honey-flavored pear. The hands that planted them have long fallen to dust; the humble *adobe* that gave shelter to the patient toiler is empty and in ruins, but the trees he planted flourish, and bear fruit, year after year; and from the shrine where he once knelt to worship his new-found Saviour, there echoes still the Ave and the Vesper-bell, though a different race now offers its devotion.

A day or two later, winter seemed to have returned in all its fury; the rain poured ceaselessly, and swelled the creeks till their narrow banks could hold the flood no longer; the wind tore at the roses, hanging in clusters of creamy white and dark crimson, on trellises and high-growing bush, and scattered showers of snow from almond and cherry trees. The fireplaces in the Del Gada mansion were once more alive and cheerful with a sparkling fire. It made little difference to the company assembled at the ranch; it gave Nora and Sister Anna an opportunity of seeing more of the home-life of the family, and impressed them with the excellence of the haughty-looking woman at the head of the establishment. No New England matron could be a more systematic housekeeper, could be more religiously devoted to the welfare of her family and servants. "And the romance of it all," Nora often repeated. Night and morning the far-sounding bell on the little chapel in the garden called the members of the house to worship; and Donna Incarnacion, kneeling, surrounded by her family and servants, read in clear tones the litanies and prayers. Once a week the priest from the neighboring mission visited the house, and then the large drawing-room was fitted up with altar and lights and flowers, and neighbors, high and low, of all degrees, attended worship.

This, however, did not prevent the family from being as jolly as Spanish people can well be, in this same drawing-room, when Mass was over, and "the things cleared away." Of cold or rainy nights the company resorted to this room, where they had music, conversation, refreshments. But everything had a dash of romance to Nora's unbounded delight. Refreshments were brought in on large trays, borne by dusk, dark-clad women; trays loaded with oranges, pomegranates, figs, the product of the orchards surrounding the house; and wine, sparkling red and clear amber, pressed from grapes gathered in the vineyard that crept close up to the door. It was not only California, but the South, of which Don Pedro had always spoken with such enthusiasm.

"And how enthusiastic he does grow sometimes," said Nora one evening, in the large drawing-room where they were all assembled.

Manuel, who performed on the piano as well as the flute,

had just finished a piece of music which Nora had taken from her trunk for him to play, and she had insisted on turning the leaves for him. Don Pedro sat near, and Nora looking up, had caught his eye. "See the enthusiasm in his face," she said to Manuel. "How fond all of you Spaniards are of music."

"You are mistaken in two points, Donna Leonora," the young man replied. "Don Pedro is no Spaniard, he is a Mexican; and he has not grown enthusiastic over the music — he has seen and has been thinking only of you."

Nora's cheeks burned at something in Manuel's voice; but a grateful feeling stole into her heart. To tell the truth, she had felt a pang of something like jealousy of late, when Narcissa, who, from speaking no English, was thrown on Don Pedro's hands, seemed to take up more of his attention than necessary.

When the weather cleared off, our party began to talk of moving on; Don Pedro's new possession was only one or two days' journey from here, below San Buenaventura. There was to be a Rodeo on the Del Gada ranch, not so much for the purpose of branding young cattle, as to give the different rancheros an opportunity of selecting their own that might have strayed into the mountains and found their way into the Del Gada herds. Nora was for attending the Rodeo; she could hardly form an idea of what it was; but she was sure, as usual, that it must be something "highly romantic."

They were warned that they must get up early in the morning, and seven o'clock found them already on the ground — a little valley, shut in by mountains more or less steep. A small creek, made turbulent by the rains, ran through the valley, where an ocean of stock seemed to roll in uneasy billows. It was all as romantic as Nora's heart could wish. The countless herds of cattle gathered together and kept from dispersing by numbers of *vaqueros*, who darted here and there on their well-trained horses, leaped ditches, flew up the steep mountain-sides after an escaping steer, dashed through the foaming torrent to gather one more to the fold, and seemed so perfectly one with their horse that from here might have sprung the fable of the old Centaurs.

Eyes sharper than eagles had these people, master and man alike; out of the thousands of that moving herd could they single the mighty steer that bore their brand, or the wild-eyed cow whose yearling calf had not yet felt the searing-iron. Into the very midst of the seething mass would a *vaquero* dart, single out his victim without a moment's halt, drive the animal to the open space, and throw his lasso with unerring aim, if a close inspection was desirable — a doubt as to the brand to be set aside. If a steer proved fractious, two of the Centaurs would divide the labor; and while one dexterously threw the rope around his horns, the other's lasso had quickly caught the hind foot, and together they brought him to the earth, that he had spurned in his strength and pride but a moment before.

Manuel himself could not resist the temptation of exhibiting his skill; and when his father and one of the neighbors — of about fifty miles away — both claimed a large black bull, almost in the centre of the herd, he dashed in among the cattle, drove his prey out on a gallop, flung his lasso around the animal's hind feet, and brought him to the ground as neatly as any *vaquero* could have done.

He saw Nora clap her hands; he saw, too, how every ranchero of the county had his eyes fixed on her, as she sat proudly, yet so lightly, on the showy black horse; and sadly he owned to himself that he would risk life and limb any time, to gain the little hand that wafted him a kiss. But what was he? A beggar, perhaps, to-morrow, if the suit went against them.

Meantime the sun grew hot, and they all dismounted and left the wagons, and lunch was discussed; the *élite*, Americans and Spaniards alike, assembling around the Del Gada provision wagon, while the *vaqueros* were well satisfied with a chunk of bread, a handful of olives, and a draught of wine, as they leisurely drove the cattle separated from the Del Gada herd to their respective territory.

Then came the parting day. Donna Incarnacion stood on the veranda, as on the day of their arrival, proudly erect, conscious of herself and the dignity she must maintain. Beside her stood her daughter, the spots on her cheeks larger and brighter, but a pained, restless expression in the eager eyes, and printing itself sharply in the lines about the mouth. Her mother seemed not to note the girl's evident distress.

Nora, Mr. and Mrs. Whitehead, and the Don had made their adieux; and Manuel, mounted and ready to escort them, together with some half dozen others, turned once more to the veranda to ask his sister some question. Like a flash the truth broke on him as he caught the eager, straining glance that followed Don Pedro's form, and with a little passionate cry he urged his animal close to Nora's side.

"It is not my heart alone you have left desolate behind you, Leonora. My sister's, too — oh! my poor Narcissa! Now I know why my mother said that she would not live to see spring again; now I know why she prays to the saints for a 'still heart,' night and morning. Oh, Leonora, think no more of the dagger you have planted in my breast; think of poor Narcissa, and pray for her as you would for one already dead — for the love of a Spanish girl is deep and abiding, and cannot be outweighed by gold and leagues of land and fine clothes."

It was well that Don Pedro came up; Nora was almost fainting in her saddle. He did not catch the import of Don Manuel's words, but, if never before, he recognized in him now a bold and dangerous rival. The confusion attending a general breaking-up had covered this little by-scene, and when the party escorting them turned back, it would have been impossible to discover that one or two hearts throbbed wildly at the parting words.

When they rode into San Buenaventura, with its dingy little mission church fronting on the main street, Nora was not half so much interested as she had been. They were right in the midst of the mission garden. The obtrusive frame houses of the fast-crowding American population had been set up in it; the streets had been laid out through it; the ugly, brick-built court-house stood away down in the lower part of it, where the blue ocean washed the shore, and murmured all day of times long past to the tall-growing palms, that stood desolate and alone.

It made her sad, she said to the Don, when he expressed his surprise at her silence, to see the stately olives of a century's growth spread their great branches over flimsy little shops; to see the neglected vines trailing their unpruned lengths over rubbish-piled open lots, which a paper placard announced "for sale."

When night came, she retired to her up-stairs room at the hotel, put the light out, and gazed long hours on the placid ocean.

"Let us get on as soon as possible," said Sister Anna, in confidence, to her husband the next morning. "This place seems to have a singular effect on Nora. She says she could not sleep last night, for thinking whether she had a right to barter herself away, body and soul, truth and honor, perhaps, for a grand home and a great deal of money."

So they "got on." Don Pedro was happy to gratify every wish of the ladies, and very willing to enter upon his own territory, which lay so near. The earth looked so smiling to Don Pedro when, together with Nora, a little in advance of the wagons, he crossed the border of his own domain. All the morning they had passed droves of cattle on the road, and flocks of sheep, and the *vaqueros* tending them had still saluted Don Pedro as their master. Shortly they encountered the *mayordomo* of the new ranch, and after a short parley with him, the Don turned to Nora with an apology for discussing business affairs in an unfamiliar tongue in her presence.

"Let us make a compromise," suggested Nora; "do you take me down yonder to that piece of white pebble-beach, by the gray rock, and you may come back and talk to all the *vaqueros* and *mayordomos* in the land."

The *mayordomo* wended his way to where he saw the wagons halting in a grove, and Nora and the Don pursued their own way. It was quite a distance before they had reached the exact spot that Nora said she had meant — they were out of sight of the rest. The ocean, grand and solemn, lay before them, grassy plains around them, groups of trees and sloping hills in the near distance, and far off the mountains in their never-changing rest.

Lightly Don Pedro sprang to the ground, and detaining Nora one moment in her saddle, he said, impressively: "Now you set foot upon your own land, a territory named after you, 'La Graciosa.'"

Then he lifted her tenderly to the ground, and she sprang lightly away from him, and lavishly praised the beauty of his new possession.

"And it is all like this," he continued, "for miles and miles, good and beautiful, like the one for whom I named it."

"What a flatterer you are," she said, forced at last to take notice of the name. He clasped her hand, but she uttered a little shriek, "Oh! that wicked horse of yours has bitten my poor Rosa." A snort from the black mare seemed to corroborate the accusation, and Nora had gained time — to fight her battle out, and make peace with herself.

"Please get rid of that tiresome *mayordomo* of yours, and

come back to me. I want to stay here alone with Rosa and decide whether your ranch has been well named." She could not prevent the kiss he imprinted on her slender hand, but she drew it back impatiently.

"You will stay here till I return, Leonora?" he asked, earnestly.

"Yes, yes," she said, a little fretfully, and waved him off.

He had made fast her horse to the stump of a scrub-oak, that had lived its short, mistaken life here close by the sea; and Nora, when the sound of the other horse's hoofs had died away, stroked the animal's mane approvingly, and patted her neck. Then she turned and walked slowly around the abrupt gray crag, and stopped; she was alone at last. She raised her hand, and looked from under it out on the sunlit sea. The waves came up with a long, gentle swirl, till the light foam splashed against the foot of the crag, then receded, leaving a strip of white, glistening pebble exposed. She watched it silently, then turned her face to let her eyes sweep the plain, the clumps of trees, and the rolling hills.

"'For miles and miles,' he said," she soliloquized, "and that is not all his fortune. And *he* has nothing if the suit goes against them. American cunning matched against Spanish recklessness. But what have I to do with that boy? All I have wanted and prayed for is a home and an honored name; it is within my reach now; why should I let an idle dream stand in my way?"

She stood where the ocean washed up to her feet, and when she looked down she thought she saw two deep-blue eyes, wild with suppressed passion, flashing up from there. She turned, for she thought she heard behind her, in the sighing of the wind and the shriek of the sea-mews, the cry of a tortured heart. But she banished these fancies and forced her thoughts into other channels. She thought of her past life, of the wish she had had, even as a child, to travel — to see strange lands.

She thought of the Pyramids of Egypt, and that her wish to see them could now, perhaps, be gratified — in his company. Well, was it not romantic, after all, to marry the dark-eyed Don, with the haughty bearing and the enormous wealth? She had a lady friend once, a city acquaintance, who had married a wealthy Spaniard. But she had been divorced after a year's time. Divorced! what an ugly sound the word had. Was Don Pedro near? Had his ear caught the sound? No; thank God, she was alone.

And then her thoughts strayed again to the old Gada mansion, and the broken-hearted girl she had left there. "She will die," he had said; and she fell to wondering whether Father Moreno would anoint those wistful eyes with the consecrated oil, in her last hour, and mutter that "they had looked upon unholy things," and touch the little waxen ears "because they had listened to unchaste speech." What a mockery it seemed, in the case of the young innocent girl. "When *I* die —" She stooped suddenly to dip her hand into the water, and dashed it into her face and over her hair. "*Mea culpa!*" she murmured, striking her breast, "*mea culpa! mea maxima culpa!*"

And once more she pressed her hand across her face, for the gallop of approaching hoofs fell on her ear, and directly "Leonora!" rang out in sharp, uneasy tone.

She answered the call, and Don Pedro, panting, but with a happy smile, reached out his hand to draw her away from the wet sand.

"I felt as though I had lost you. What would life be without you, Graciosa?"

"You would have my god-child left," she replied, laughing.

"It would be worthless without the sponsor. I have acquired it for you. Do you accept it?"

"With you into the bargain?" she smiled gayly as she said it. She hated romance and sentimentality all at once, and when the Don kneeled at her feet to kiss both her hands, she said, with a laugh:

"There will be but one Graciosa, after all, unless you take me to my friends and the lunch-basket. I am almost starved."

"I am your slave," he avowed; "you have but to command."

He lifted her into the saddle, with trembling hands and beaming eyes. "Oh, Graciosa! Rightly named," he cried.

"Meaning me or the ranch?" asked Nora, mischievously; and, with a touch of the whip, she urged Rosa ahead, and threw a kiss over her shoulder to the Don. His eyes followed her proudly awhile, ere he spurred his horse to overtake her, and they joined Sister Anna laughing and happy as she could wish to see them.

They camped out that night, as there was no house on that part of the ranch, though there was one to be erected near the spot where they had joined Sister Anna, for Nora said she liked the view there. Early next morning they left camp, expecting to reach Los Angeles before sunset.

All day the road led along the mountain-chain, in the San Fernando Valley — a soft, warm day, made to dream and reflect. The clear blue haze hung, as ever, on the mountain-ridge, and the plain at the foot was white and odorous with the wild "Forget-me-not" of California. They looked to Nora as though passionate eyes had been raining tears on them till the color had been blanched out; and when Don Pedro gathered a handful and brought them to her, she said, "Don't, please; it hurts me to see you break them off. Throw them away."

"How strange you are," he said, but he obeyed, and did not assert his authority till some hours later, when they reached the crossing of the Los Angeles River. — Had he not said he would be her slave?

The river rushed by them muddy and wild, spread far

beyond its allotted limits — an ugly, treacherous-looking piece of water. It was deep, too; and while Don Pedro was giving orders in regard to arranging the contents of the baggage wagon, Sister Anna was trying to persuade Nora to come into their wagon while fording the stream. Nora demurred; but the Don riding up decided the question at once.

"You must go in the wagon, Leonora," he announced, with somewhat pompous authority. "I will not have you exposed to such danger. The river is wide at present, and your head will get light. Mr. Whitehead and I will go on horseback, but you must go in the wagon."

A rebellious gleam shot from Nora's eye, but Sister Anna listened with flushed face, as to something new, but very pleasant to hear. It proved an ugly crossing, and while the servants were rearranging the baggage, the Don strayed a little apart with Nora, and found a seat under a clump of willows.

"It *is* hard to go down into the floods when there is so much of life and sunshine all around," and with a little nervous shiver she nestled closer to the Don's side. Impelled by a feeling of tenderness he could not control, the stately Don threw his arms around the supple form and pressed the first kiss on her pale lips.

She shrank from him; had any one seen them? There was no need to spring up; she knew he would not attempt to repeat the caress.

The City of the Angels lay before them — a dream realized.

Whatever there was unlovely about the older, *adobe* built portion of the place was toned down by the foliage of waving trees; and warmed into tropical beauty by the few isolated palms, which some blessed hand set out long years ago. Our friends did not pass through the heart of the city, but wended their way to the house of a wealthy Spanish family, which lay among the gay villas and stately residences of the modern portion of the city. Large gardens enclosed them, in many cases surrounded by evergreen hedges of supple willow and bristly osage. Tall spires arising from a sea of green, and imposing edifices, marked the places where the Lord could be worshipped in style. The American element is strong in Los Angeles.

Senor Don Jose Maria Carillo had been looking for his guests, and met them with much state and ceremony on the highway, conducting them grandly to the gate-posts of his garden, where they were received by Donna Clotilda and a retinue of servants. Even the children, with their governess, were summoned from the school-room to greet the guests, and Spanish courtesy and Californian hospitality were never better exemplified than in the case of our friends.

"Oh, Annie, only look!" exclaimed Nora, clasping her hands in admiration, and pointing through the French window at the back of the double parlors.

The house was an *adobe*, two stories high, which the father of the present inmate had built, and of which the son was properly proud. He would not have it torn down for the world, but it had been modernized to such an extent as to rival in comfort and elegance any of the newer American houses, though the Spanish features were still predominant. The particular feature that had attracted Nora so strongly as to lead her into making the hasty, unceremonious exclamation, was a *remada*, a kind of open roof built of heavy timber beams, at the back of the house, and extending over several hundred feet of the ground. It was covered with the grape, among whose shading leaves and graceful tendrils the sunlight glinted in and out, playing in a thousand colors on clustering vines with bright flowers, that clung to the pillars supporting the roof. Beyond stretched an orange-grove, where yellow fruit and snowy blossoms glanced through the glossy leaves.

"It is beautiful, is it not?" asked a voice at her side. She had stepped to the open French window, regardless of all etiquette, and Don Pedro led her across the sill into the covered garden.

"Your own home shall be like this, Leonora, only finer and grander; you shall have everything that your heart can wish."

"You are very good." It was not the conventional phrase with her; she meant what she said, for her eyes were raised to his, and tears trembled in the lashes.

It was a charming retreat. Donna Clotilda spoke English, though none of the servants did, except a ten-year old Indian girl, who was detailed to wait on the guests. There was a round of visiting and going through the city, where every one admired Nora, and looked from her to the little Don. And Don Pedro was proud and happy, and always sought new opportunities of passing through the crowded thoroughfares, on foot, on horseback, or in carriage.

"My dear," he said, one day, "I would know how handsome you are from looking at the people who meet us, even though I had never seen your face."

"Yes?" said Nora, a little absent and dispirited, as she sometimes was.

"Yes; one man, standing at the corner there, behind those boxes — you did not see him — opened his eyes very wide and looked hard at you, and then pushed his hat back till it fell to the ground. Then he saw me, and felt ashamed, and turned quick to pick up his hat."

"What a striking appearance mine must be!" laughed Nora, restored to good-humor, for the time.

It has often seemed to me that all Spanish people, of whatever degree, throughout California, are either related or intimately acquainted with each other. Thus Nora heard from the Del Gadas occasionally; nay, even from the Rodriguez, away back in the Salinas Valley, did they hear news and greeting once. Narcissa del Gada was dying, the Don told her; and the twinge that had distorted his features when he first mentioned her name again passed over them.

But all the time of our friends was not given to pleasuring; many a long morning did Brother Ben and the Don pass together at the Court-House, the Hall of Records, and other places where titles are examined and the records kept. A ranch of twenty or thirty thousand acres is well worth securing, so that through no loophole can adverse claimant creep, or sharp-witted land-shark, with older title, spring on the unwary purchaser.

In the meantime spring was growing into summer; the sun began to burn more fierce, and Nora, always fond of outdoors, had made the *remada* her special camping-ground. She sat there one morning, after having declined to go on a shopping expedition with Sister Anna. It had seemed rather ungracious, too; but Brother Ben had come to the rescue, as usual, and had taken Nora's place. Now she sat here, pale and listless, her hands idly folded, her eyes wandering among the shadows of the orange grove.

There had been an arrival at the house, she thought, for she heard the tramp of a horse as it was led around to the stables; but she took no heed. After a while she heard the noise of one of the long windows opening, and soon she heard steps behind her. Then a low voice said "Leonora!" and Manuel, pale and haggard, stood before her.

All her listlessness vanished in an instant, and she would have flown into his arms, but for something that seemed to make him unapproachable.

"Narcissa is dead," he said, monotonously, "and since coming to town I have learned that I am a beggar; we are all homeless — outcasts."

"Oh, Manuel!" she cried, laying her hand on his arm, "my poor, poor boy. Come with me into the open air — this place chokes me. And now tell me about Narcissa." She drew him out into the sunshine, and back again to the fragrant shadows of the orange grove. She sought a rustic seat for them, but he threw himself on the sod beside it.

"Wrecked and lost and lonely," he groaned, "it is well that Narcissa is dead; and yet she was our only comfort."

"Poor Manuel!" she repeated, softly; "my poor boy." Her fingers were straying among the sunny waves of his hair, and he caught her hand suddenly, and covered it with a frenzy of kisses.

"Leonora!" he cried, all the reckless fire of his nation breaking into flames, "come with me, and we will be happy. You do not love your wealthy affianced, you love me. Be mine; I will work and toil for you, and you shall be my queen. Oh, Nora, I love you — I love you — I love you."

Poor Nora! why should stern reality be so bitter? "Foolish boy," she said, disengaging her hand, "you are mad. What if Don Pedro—"

"Ah, true; I had forgotten — you are an American. Go, then, be happy with your wealthy husband; Manuel will never cross your path again."

"Manuel!" she cried, and she stretched out her arms towards the spot where he had just stood, "come back, for I love you, and you alone." But a rustling in the willow-hedge only answered to her passionate cry, and she cowered on the garden-bench, sobbing and moaning out her helpless grief.

The rustling in the willow-hedge behind her grew louder, so that even she was startled by the noise.

"Ho, Nell!" The words fell on her ears like the crack of doom, her face grew white to the very lips, and a great horror crept into her eyes. She turned as if expecting to meet the engulfing jaws of some dread monster, and her eyes fell upon the form of a man, whose slovenly dress and bloated features spoke of a life of neglect and dissipation — perhaps worse.

"Why, Nell, old girl," he continued, familiarly, "this is a pretty reception to give your husband. I'm not a ghost; don't be afraid of me."

"Wretch!" she cried, trembling with fear and excitement. "How dare you come here? Go at once, or I shall call for help."

"No, you won't. I'm not afraid. Come, you can get rid of me in a minute. The truth is, I'm d——d hard up; got into two or three little unpleasantnesses, and got out only by a scratch. I want to get away from here — it's unhealthy here for me — but I've got no money. Saw you down town with that pompous Greaser the other day; know him well; he's got lots of money; and I thought that, for love and affection, as they say in the law, and in consideration of our former relations, you might help me to some of his spare coin."

"You miserable man," she cried, beside herself, "is it not enough that you blasted my life's happiness? Must I be dragged down to the very lowest degradation with you? Oh, Charlie," she added, in changed, softened tones, "what would your mother say to all this?"

"And my daddy the parson," he laughed, hoarsely. "Yes, we know all that. But here, Nell," he went on, while a last glimmer of shame or contrition passed over his once handsome face, "I don't want to hurt you, my girl; you've always been a trump, by G——; I am willing you should become the respected wife of Don Pedro Lopez, but I must have money, or money's worth. That cluster-diamond on your finger; tell the Greaser you lost it. Or pull out your purse; I know it is full."

"Nothing," she said, slowly and determinedly, "nothing shall you have from me — a woman you have so wronged and deceived —"

"Stop, Nell; I haven't time to wait for a sermon. Give me what you've got— Oh, here's h— to pay and no pitch hot," he interrupted himself; "there's the Don, and he's heard it all."

He spoke true; Don Pedro stood beside them, frozen into a statue. At last he breathed.

"Yes, heard all. And I would have made you my wife — you a divorced woman. Oh, Santa Maria! She divorced of such a man — for I know you, Randal,". he continued, lashing himself into a fury — " horse-thief, stage-robber, gambler. It was you who killed my friend Mariano Anzar after robbing him at cards — murderer! You shall not escape me as you escaped the officers of the law. *Hombres!* catch the murderer!" he shouted towards the house, as he made a dart at the man, who turned at bay, but halted when he saw that the Don was not armed.

"Stop your infernal shouting and don't touch me," he said, in a low, threatening voice. But the Don was brave, and his blood was up; he sprang upon the man, shouting again; they closed and struggled, and when the man heard footsteps swiftly approaching, he drew back with an effort, and hissing, "You *would* have it so, idiot," he raised his pistol and fired.

Before the smoke cleared away he had vanished, and the people who came found Don Pedro stretched on the ground. His life was almost spent, but his energy had not deserted him. He gave what information and directions were necessary for the prosecution of his murderer, and Manuel, who was among the excited throng, threw himself on his horse to head the fugitive off. The others lifted the wounded man tenderly from the ground, bore him gently into the house, and frowned with hostile eyes upon Nora; it had taken possession of their minds at once that, in some unexplained manner, the Gringa was the cause of all this woe.

Nora followed them like an automaton; she saw them carry him through the open door-window into the back parlor, and lay the helpless figure on a lounge. A messenger had already been despatched for priest and doctor, and the servants, who were not admitted into the room, lay on their knees outside.

Then the priest came, and Nora, in a strange, dazed way, could follow all his movements after he went into the room. The odor of burning incense crept faintly through the closed doors, and she wondered again — did the priest touch the white lips and say, "for they have uttered blasphemies." The fingers were stiffening, she thought; would the priest murmur now — "for with their hands do men steal;" the eyelids were fluttering over the glazed eyes; the cleansing oil was dropped upon them, for "they had looked upon unholy things."

She saw it all before her, and heard it, though her eyes were fast closed; and her ears were muffled, for she had fallen, face down, by one of the pillars supporting the *remada*, and the thick-growing tropical vine, with its bright, crimson flowers, had buried her head in its luxuriant foliage, and seemed raining drops of blood upon the wavy dark brown hair.

Thus Manuel found her when he returned from the pursuit of the fugitive. He raised her head, and looked into large, bewildered eyes. "What is it?" she asked; "have I been asleep? Oh, is he dead?"

"The wretched man I followed? Yes; but my hand did not lay him low. The sheriff and his men had been hunting him; he attempted to swim the river at the ford; the sheriff fired, and he went down into the flood."

Nora's eyes had closed again during the recital, and Manuel held a lifeless form in his arms, when Sister Anna and her husband came at last. They had heard of the shooting of

Don Pedro in the city, and the carriage they came in bore Nora away to the hotel. Manuel did not relinquish his precious burden till he laid the drooping form gently on the bed at the hotel. Then the doctor came, and said brain-fever was imminent, and the room was darkened, and people went about on tip-toe. And when the news of the death of Don Pedro Lopez was brought down to the hotel, Nora was already raving in the wildest delirium of the fever.

Weeks have passed, and Nora has declared herself not only well, but able to return home. Manuel has been an invaluable friend to them all, during these weeks of trial, and Nora has learned to look for his coming as she looks for the day and the sunshine.

To him, too, was allotted the task to impart to Nora what it was thought necessary for her to know — the death of Don Pedro and the finding of the body of the other, caught against the stump of an old willow, where the water had washed it, covered with brush and floating *débris*. But he had glad news to impart, too; the report of an adverse decision from Washington on the Del Gada suit had been false, and circulated by the opposing party in order to secure better terms for withdrawal.

One morning Nora expressed her wish to leave Los Angeles, and Mr. Whitehead did not hesitate to gratify her wish. An easy conveyance was secured, the trunks sent by stage, and a quick journey anticipated. Manuel went with them only as far as San Buenaventura, he said, for it was on his way home. But when they got there, he said he must go to Santa Barbara, and no one objected. At Santa Barbara Nora held out her hand to him, with a saucy smile:

"This is the place at which you were to leave us; good-by."

"Can you tolerate me no longer, Nora?"

"You said at San Buenaventura you would try my patience

only till here. How long do you want me to tolerate you, then?"

"As long as I live. Why should we ever part? Be my wife, Nora," and he drew her close to him, pressing his lips on hers; and she did not shrink away from him, but threw her arm around his neck, to bend his head down for another kiss.

"But you would never have married me — a poor man," he says, bantering.

"Nor would you have married me — a divorced woman," she returns, demurely.

JUANITA.

"EVERY man in the settlement started out after him; but he got away, and was never heard of again."

I had listened quietly to the end, though my eyes had wandered impatiently from the face of the man to the region to which he pointed with his finger. There was nothing to be seen out there but the hot air vibrating over the torn, sandy plain, and the steep, ragged banks of the river, without any water in it — as is frequently the case at this season of the year. The man who had spoken — formerly a soldier, but, after his discharge from the army, station-keeper at this point — had become so thoroughly "Arizonified" that he thought he was well housed in this structure, where the mud-walls rose some six feet from the ground, and an old tent was hung over a few crooked *manzanita* branches for a roof. There was a wide aperture in the wall, answering the purpose of a door; and a few boards laid on trestles, and filled in with straw, which he called his bunk. He had raised it on these trestles, partly because the snakes could n't creep into the straw so "handy," and partly because the *coyotes*, breaking down the barricade in the doorway one night, hunting for his chickens, had brought their noses into unpleasant proximity with his face while lying on the ground. He had confided these facts to me early in the morning, shortly after my arrival, continuing his discourse by a half-apology for his naked feet, to which he pointed with the ingenuous confession that "he'd run barefooted till his shoes would n't go on no more." He held them up for my inspection, to show that he had them — the shoes, I mean, not the feet—a pair of No. 14's, entirely new, army make.

We had arrived just before daybreak, my escort and I having made a "dry march"—which would have been too severe on Uncle Sam's mules in the scorching sun of a June day—during the night. The morning, flashing up in the East with all the glorious colors that give token of the coming, overpowering heat, brought with it also the faint, balmy breath of wind in which to bathe one's limbs before the sun burst forth in its burning majesty. Phil, the ambulance-driver, and my oracle, said I could wander off as far as I wanted without fear of Indians; so I had ascended the steep hill back of the station, and, spying what looked like a graveyard at the foot of it, on the other side, I had immediately clambered down in search of new discoveries. I knew that there had formerly been a military post here: it is just so far from the Mexican border that fugitives from the law of that country would instinctively fly this way for refuge; and just near enough the line where the "friendly Indian" ceases to be a pleasant delusion, to make the presence of a strong military force at all times necessary for the protection of white settlers. But there are none; and Uncle Sam, protecting his own property "on the march" through here as well as possible, allows the citizen and merchant to protect himself and his goods the best way he can. Why the camp had been removed, I cannot tell—neither, perhaps, could those who occupied it—but I am pretty sure they were all very willing to go. I've never seen the soldier yet that was n't glad of a change of post and quarters.

There were quite a number of graves in this rude burying-ground (I don't like that name, on the whole; but it seemed just the proper thing to call this collection of graves), and among them were two that attracted my attention particularly. The one was a large, high grave, with rather a pretentious headstone, bearing the inscription:

"To the Memory of James Owens,
Who came to his death May 20, 186–."

The other seemed smaller, though it was difficult to determine the exact dimensions, on account of the rocks, bones, and dry brush piled on it. It is the custom of the Mexicans in passing by a grave to throw on it a stone, a clump of earth, or a piece of brush or bone, if they have nothing else, as a mark of respect: so I concluded at once that some one of that nationality lay buried here. One, too, who had some faithful friend; for there was a look about the grave that spoke of constant attention and frequent visits to it.

On my return, having done justice to the breakfast the station-keeper had prepared (and for which he had killed one of his chickens, in order to "entertain me in a lady-like manner," as he said to Phil), I questioned him about the American whose grave I had seen out there. Before he could answer, a shadow fell across the doorway, and I half rose from the ambulance-cushion I was occupying, when I saw an Indian, a young fellow of about twenty, stand still in front of it, half hiding the form of an aged crone, on whose back was fastened a small bundle of fire-wood, such as is laboriously gathered along the beds and banks of water-courses, in this almost treeless country. The Indian stooped to lift the load from the woman's back; and she turned to go, without even having lifted her eyes, either to the ambulance that stood near the doorway, the soldiers that lounged around it, or myself. The station-keeper seized an old tin-cup, filled it with coffee, piled the remains of the breakfast on a tin-plate, and disappeared in the doorway. Returning, he answered me, at last:

"The grave you saw was dug for a man that lived here while I was yet a soldier in the —— Infantry at this camp. He had brought a Spanish woman with him, his wife, with whom he lived in one of those houses, right there, on the bank of the river. He had sold some horses to the Government, at Drum Barracks, and was sent out here with them; and seeing that it was quite a settlement, he thought he'd stay. *She* was a mighty fine-looking woman — a tall, stoutish figure, with as much pride as if she had been a duchess. Among the Mexicans in the settlement was a man who, they said, had been a brigand in Mexico, had broken jail, and come here, first to hide, and then to live. It warn't long till he began loafering about Owens' place; and one night, while Owens was standing in his door, smoking, there was a shot fired from the direction of the hill, behind this place, and Owens fell dead in his own doorway. There was no doubt in anybody's mind who the murderer was, for his cabin was empty, and he could be found nowhere about camp. The soldiers, as well as the other fellows, were determined to lynch him, and every man in the settlement started out after him; but he got away, and no one ever heard of him again."

"And the woman?" I asked.

"Oh, nobody could hurt her; and she raved and ranted dreadful for awhile. But she turned up absent one morning, about a week after we had put him under the ground, and her husband's watch and money had gone with her."

"But," said I, impatiently, "where is the settlement you speak of? I have not found a trace of it yet."

"Well, you see, they were *adobe*-houses that they built, and the rains were very heavy last year, and the Gila commenced washing out this way; the banks caved in and carried the rubbish away. They hadn't been occupied for some time; but the house where Owens lived is just right across there — if you go near the bank you can see where he built a good, solid chimbley, like they've got at home. The camp used to be down the flat apiece. I had my house there last year; but it washed away with the rain: so I built up here, where there's better shelter for my chickens. They're my only friends, besides Bose, and I've got to be choice of 'em. I don't see a white face for months, sometimes, since the war is over, and it keeps me company kinder, to see the places where the houses used to be."

"And the other grave — that with the bones and rocks piled on it?"

The man threw a look toward the doorway, and put his hands in his pockets.

"That's Juanita's grave. She was an Indian girl."

He walked out of the door; and, as I had nothing better to do, I too stepped out, thinking to go as far to look for the ruins of that "chimbley" as the blazing sun would permit. The first I saw when I came out of the doorway was the old Indian woman, sitting on the ground in the shade of the house, her back against the wall, her knees drawn up, her elbow resting on them, the doubled fist supporting the face, while the other hand hung listlessly across them. The face was aged and wrinkled, the hair a dirty gray, and the eyes seemed set — petrified, I had almost said — with some great, deep sorrow. Beside her stood the tin-cup, untouched and unnoticed; the tin-plate had been almost emptied of its contents; but a drumstick in the hands of the young Indian, and a suspicious glossiness about his mouth and chin, seemed to mark the road the chicken had taken. The station-keeper stood by the woman, and said something to her in a jargon I could not understand; but she took no more notice of him or what he said than if it were a fly that had buzzed up to her. She moved neither her eyes nor her head, looking out straight before her. I walked as far as the banks of the river, failed to discover the remains of the "chimbley," and turned back to the house. The station-keeper was not to be seen; the Indian boy paused from his labors to take a look at me; but the woman seemed to be a thousand miles away, so little did she take heed of my presence.

It was nearly noon, and I concluded to pass the rest of the day in sleep, as we were to leave the station at about ten in the night, when the moon should be up. The "whole house" had been given up to me, and a comfortable bed arranged out of mattress and wagon-seats, so that I felt comparatively safe from prowling vermin, and soon went to sleep. I awoke only once, late in the afternoon; the station-keeper was saying something in a loud voice that I could not understand, and, directly, I saw two pair of dusky feet passing by the space that the blanket, hung up in the doorway, left near the ground. After awhile I raised the blanket, and saw the Indians trudging along through the sandy plain, the woman following the tall, athletic form of the man, the yellow sun burning fiercely down on their bare heads, scorching the broad, prickly leaves of the cactus, and withering its delicate, straw-colored, and deep-crimson flowers. I dropped the curtain, panting for breath: it was too hot to live while looking out into that glaring sunshine.

Later, when I could sleep no more, and had made my desert toilet, I stood in the doorway, and saw the two Indians coming back as in the morning: the woman with a bundle of fire-wood on her shoulders, the man walking empty-handed and burdenless before her. I turned to the station-keeper, and pointing to the bundle she had brought in the morning, and which lay untouched by the wall, I said, indignantly:

"It seems to me you need not have sent the poor woman out in the blazing sun to gather fire-wood, when you had not even used this. You might have waited till now."

"She—she would have been somewhere else in the blazing sun; she was just going—" And he stopped—as he had spoken—in haste, yet with some confusion.

I cast a pitying look on the woman, which, however, she heeded no more than the rose-pink and pale-gold sunset-clouds floating above her, and then wandered slowly forth toward the hill, which I meant to climb while the day was going down.

When I reached the top, the light, flying clouds had grown heavy and sad, and their rose hue had turned into a dark, sullen red, with tongues of burning gold shooting through it — the history of Arizona, pictured fittingly in pools of blood and garbs of fire. But the fire died out, and a dim gray crept over the angry clouds; and then, slowly, slowly, the clouds weaved and worked together till they formed a single heavy bank — black, dark, and impenetrable.

Just as I turned to retrace my steps, my eyes fell on a group of low bushes, which would have taken the palm in any collection of those horribly dead-looking things that ladies call phantom-flowers. So pitilessly had the sun bleached and whitened the tiny branches, that not a drop of life or substance seemed left; yet they were perfect, and phantom-bushes, if ever I saw any. How well they would look on those graves below, I thought, as I approached to break a twig in remembrance of the strange sight. But how came the red berries on this one? I stooped, and picked up — a rosary; the beads of red-stained wood, the links and crucifix of some white metal, and inscribed on the cross the words, "*Souvenir de la Mission.*" How had it come there? Had ever the foot of devout Catholic pressed this rocky, thorny ground? Of what mission was it a gift of love and remembrance? Surely it had not lain here a hundred years — the gift of love from one of the Spanish *padres* of the Arizona Missions to an Indian child of the church! Or had it come from one of those California Missions, where the priests to this day read masses to the descendants of the Mission Indians? Yonder, in the west, with the purplish mists deepening into darkness in its cleft sides, was the mountain which to-morrow would show us "Montezuma's face," and here lay the emblem of peace, of devotion to the one living God. Perhaps the station-keeper could solve the mystery; so I hastened back through the gloom that was settling on the earth, unbroken by any sound save the distant yelping of a *coyote*, who had spied me out, and followed me, as though to see if I were the only one of my kind who had come to invade his dominion.

"See what I have found!" I cried exultingly, when barely within speaking distance of the station-keeper, who stood within the doorway.

In a moment he was beside me, calling out something in his Indian-Spanish, which seemed to electrify the woman, who still sat by the *adobe* wall. Springing up with the agility of a panther, she was by my side, pointing eagerly to my hand holding the rosary.

"What does she want?" I asked, in utter consternation.

"The rosary; give her the rosary" — the barefooted man was speaking almost imperiously — "it's hers; she has the best right to it."

"Gladly," I said; but she had already clutched it, and turned tottering back to the mud-wall, against which she crouched, as though afraid of being robbed of her new-found treasure.

The man turned to me in evident excitement: "And you found it! Where? She has been hunting for it these years —day after day—in the blazing sun and streaming rain; and *you* found it. Well, old Screetah's eyes are getting blind — she's old — old."

"But her son might have found it, if he had looked; for I found it just up on the hill there," I suggested.

"He's not her son; only an Indian I kept to look after her, kinder; for she's been brooding and moping till she don't seem to notice nothing no more. But now she's found it, maybe she'll come round again, or go on to Sonora, where, she says, her people are."

"How came she to lose it, then, if it was so precious?"

"She did n't lose it — but, I forget everything; supper's been waiting on; if you 'll eat hearty, I 'll tell you about those beads after a while. The moon won't rise till after ten, and you 've good three hours yet."

I was so anxious to hear about the beads, that I would not give the man time to wash dishes; though he insisted on putting away the china cup and plate, which he kept for State occasions, when he saw my disposition to let Bose make free with what was on the table — table being a complimentary term for one of the ambulance-seats.

In the days when this had been a military post, garrisoned by but one company of the —— Infantry, the station-keeper had been an enlisted man, and the servant of Captain Castleton, commanding the camp and company. Young, handsome, and generous, the men were devoted to their captain, though as strict a disciplinarian as ever left the military school. The little settlement springing up around the camp was chiefly peopled by Indians and Mexicans, and only two or three Americans. When Captain Castleton had been here just long enough to get desperately tired of the wearisome solitude and monotony of camp, and had put in motion whatever influence his friends had with the authorities at head-quarters to relieve him of the command of the post and the inactive life he was leading, an Indian woman and her daughter came into the settlement one evening, and found ready shelter with the hospitable Mexicans. That she was an Indian was readily believed; but that the girl with her belonged to the same people, was not received with any degree of faith by those who saw her. She was on her way back to Sonora, she said, to her own people, from whence she had come with her husband, years ago, along with a pack-train of merchandise, for some point in Lower California. From there she had gradually drifted, by way of San Diego, into California, up to Los Angeles, and on to some Mission near there, where she had lived among the Mission Indians, after her husband's death, and where Juanita had been taught to read, write, and sing by the Mission priests.

At last Screetah had concluded to go back to Sonora, and had drifted downward again from Los Angeles, to Temescal, to Temacula, to Fort Yuma, and through the desert, till, finally, some compassionate Mexicans had carried her and the girl with them through the last waterless stretch to this place. The girl, with her velvety eyes and delicately turned limbs, soon became the favorite and the adored of every one in camp and settlement; and, though that branch of her education to which her mother pointed with the greatest pride — reading and writing — had never taken very deep root in the girl's mind, she sang like an angel, and looked "like one of them pictures where a woman's kneeling down, with a crown around her head," while she was singing. Indeed, the religious teachings of the good priests seemed to have sunk deeply into the gentle heart of Juanita, and her greatest treasure—an object itself almost of devotion — was a rosary the priest had given her on leaving the Mission. It had been impressed on her, that "so long as these beads glided through her fingers, while her lips murmured *Aves* and *Pater-nosters*, night and morning, so long were the angels with her. Did the angels take the rosary from her—which would happen if Juanita forgot the teachings of the priests, and no longer laid her heart's inmost thoughts before the Blessed Mother — then would she lose her soul's peace and her hopes of heaven; and she must guard the sacred beads as she would her own life."

There was no point of resemblance between Juanita and the old Indian woman; and the girl, though warmly attached to her, declared that she was not her mother, only her nurse or servant. Her mother, she said, had been a Spanish Doña, and her father a mighty chief of his tribe, whose head had been displayed on the gate of some Mexican fortress for weeks after it had been delivered to the Government by some treacherous Indian of his band. Juanita's personal appearance, the fluency with which she spoke Spanish, her very name even, seemed to confirm her accounts, dim and confused as the recollections of her earliest childhood were; nevertheless, she had "Indian in her," as the man said, for she proved it before she died.

But to return to the time of their arrival in camp. Screetah seemed in no hurry to resume her journey through the burning desert; and, as Captain Castleton said, he would no doubt have retained her by force rather than let her drag the poor child through the waterless wastes into sure destruction. He had given them an old tent after they had been with their Mexican friends for nearly a week; and when these same Mexicans left the camp, the two women were given possession of their house. Here it became a source of never-ending delight to the old Indian that all the choice things by which she set such store, and which among her "civilized" Indian friends had been so scarce, as coffee, sugar, and bacon, were served out to her as though they rained down from the sky. But to do Screetah justice, the sweetest side of bacon and the biggest bagful of sugar never gave her half the pleasure that she felt when one of the soldiers gave to Juanita a lank, ragged pony, which, on a scout, he had bought, borrowed, or stolen from an Indian at the Maricopa Wells. Her time was now pretty equally divided between the rosary and the pony, which, in time, lost its ragged, starved appearance, under her treatment, and retained only its untamable wildness, and the unconquerable disposition to throw up its hindlegs when running at full tilt, as though under apprehension that the simple act of running did not give an adequate idea of its abilities. At first, Captain Castleton, highly amused, would call for his horse when he saw Juanita battling with her vicious steed on the plain near camp, in order to witness the struggles of " the wild little Indian" near by. But, after awhile, they would ride forth together, and dash over the level ground or climb up to the highest point of the hill — Juanita's voice ringing back to the camp almost as long as she was in sight, chanting some wild anthem, in which seemed blended the joyous strains of the heavenly band and the wild song of the savage when he flies like an arrow through his native plains.

Old Screetah's low-roofed *adobe* had assumed quite an air of comfort through the exertions of some good-natured soldiers, and more particularly through the manifestations of Captain Castleton's favor. From a passing pack-train, laden with Sonora merchandise, he had bought the matting that covered the mud-floor; the sun-baked pottery-ware was Screetah's greatest boast, as it came from the same province — her birthplace; and the bright-colored Navajo blanket had been bought with many a pound of bacon and of coffee — articles more precious far in this country than the shining metal which men risk their lives to find here. No wonder that the captain passed more of his time in Screetah's hut than in his white wall-tent, where the sun, he said, blinded him, beating on the fly all day long; and where the slightest breeze brought drifts of sand with it. That Juanita seemed to live and breathe only for him had come to be a matter of course. Among the Mexicans it was accepted that at a certain phase or change of the moon there had been some words spoken, or some rite performed, by old Screetah, which, according to their belief, constituted Indian marriage; and both seemed happy as the day is long.

Like a thunderbolt from the clear sky it struck him one day, when the mail-rider brought official letters advising him of the change that had been made in his favor. He was directed to proceed at once to Drum Barracks, there to await further orders! It was, perhaps, the first time that he experienced the curse of having his most ardent wishes gratified. For days he wandered about like the shadow of an evil deed — restless from the certainty of approaching judgment, and fainting with the knowledge that he was powerless to ward off the coming blow. It was hard to make Juanita understand the situation, and the necessity of parting; but when she had once comprehended that she was to be abandoned — a fate which, to her, meant simply to be thrust out on the desert and left to die — the Indian blood flowed faster in her veins, and rose tumultuously against the fair-faced image that her heart had worshipped. What was life to her with the light and warmth gone out of it? He was leaving her to die; and die she would.

When the little cavalcade, ready and equipped for the march, was about to leave the camp, Juanita was nowhere to be found. For hours the captain sought her in every nook they had explored together, and called her by every endearing name his fancy had created for her. Juanita's pony was gone from his accustomed place, and he knew it would be useless to await her return. Captain Castleton was not a coward; the searching glances he sent into every *cañon* they passed, and among the sparse trees on their road, were directed by the burning desire to meet the dearly loved form once more; but they would not have quaked had the arrow Juanita knew so well to speed, sank into his heart instead.

Days passed ere Juanita returned; and, though Screetah grovelled at her feet with entreaties not to leave her again, and the soldiers showed every possible kindness and attention to the girl, she was seldom seen among them. Sometimes, at the close of day, she was seen suddenly rising from some crevice in the hill, where she had clambered and climbed all day; but oftener she was discovered mounted on her pony, her long, black hair streaming, her horse in full gallop, as though riding in pursuit of the setting sun. No word of complaint passed her lips; no one heard her draw a sigh, or saw her shed a tear;

and none dared to speak a word of comfort. But when Screetah tried to cheer her, one day, she held out her empty hands, saying, simply, "I have the rosary no more!" Then Screetah knew that all hope was lost, and she pleaded no more, but broke the beautiful, sun-baked pottery, tore the matting from the floor, and crouched by the threshold from noon to night, and night till morning, waiting quietly for the silent guest that she knew would some day, soon, enter there with Juanita.

One day, she came slowly down from the hill and entered the dark *adobe*, where Screetah sat silent by the door.

"A little cloud of dust is rising on the horizon," she said to the old Indian, "and I must prepare;" and Screetah only wailed the death-song of her race.

Though Juanita had returned on foot, she had ridden away on the pony the day before, and the soldiers started out to look for the animal, thinking it had escaped from her, or had been stolen by some marauding Indian. But they found the carcass not far from camp — with Juanita's dagger in the animal's heart. The next day she went to the top of the hill again, and when night came, she said, "The cloud grows bigger." On the third day, when Juanita lay stretched on the hard, uncomfortable bed, denuded of all its gay robes and blankets, a sudden excitement arose outside, such as the signs of anything approaching camp always create. A hundred different opinions were expressed as to what and who it could be. Nearer and nearer came the cloud of dust, and a cry of surprise went up, as the horse fell from fatigue on the edge of the camp, and the rider took his way to old Screetah's hut.

What passed within those dark, low walls — what passionate appeals for forgiveness, what frantic remorse and bitter self-accusations they echoed — only Screetah and the dying girl knew. The old Indian was touched, and tried to plead for him; but Juanita seemed to heed neither the man's presence nor the woman's entreaties. She died "with her face to the wall," and the words of forgiveness, which he had staked life and honor to hear, were never uttered by those firmly-closed lips.

With the day of Juanita's death commenced the old Indian woman's search for the rosary, and she tore her hair in desperation when they laid the girl in her narrow cell before she had found it. Day after day, the search was continued. Was it not the peace of Juanita's soul she was seeking to restore? After awhile the camp was broken up, by orders from district head-quarters, and a forage-station established. Our friend, whose term of service had expired, was made station-keeper, and, one by one, the people from the settlement followed the military, till, at last, only he and old Screetah were left of all the little band that once had filled the dreary spot with the busy hum of life.

HETTY'S HEROISM.

"BUT, father, you don't really mean to watch the old year out, do you? It's only a waste of candles, and the boys won't want to get up in the morning."

"Mebbee so, mother; but New Year's Eve don't come every day; so let's have it out." And old man Sutton tipped back his chair, after filling his pipe, and looked contentedly up at the white ceiling of the "best room."

Johnny, the younger son of the family, whistled gleefully, threw more wood on the blazing pile in the fire-place, and then, resuming his oft-forbidden occupation of cracking walnuts in the best room, said:

"Don't the wind howl, though? Just drives the rain. Golly, ain't it nice here?"

"You're not to say bad words," broke out his mother, sharply. "Father, why don't you correct the boy? Such a night as this, too, when —"

"What's that?" interrupted the oldest son, springing from his seat, and showing a straight, manly form and clear, deep eyes, as he stood by the door in a listening attitude.

"Coyotes, brother Frank; the ghosts don't come round this early, do they?" laughed the younger.

"Hush, Johnny! It's some one crying for help — a woman's voice!"

"Tut, tut! where would a woman come from this time o' night, and not a house within miles of us?"

"A woman's voice, I'll stake my head," insisted Frank, after a moment's silence in the room.

The mother had laid down her glasses. "Wonder if the boy thinks Lolita is coming through the storm to watch the old year out with him?" She laughed as at something that gave her much pleasure, though the rest did not share her merriment.

They were all three listening at door and window now, and when Frank threw the one nearest him quickly open, there came a sound through the din and fury of the rain-storm that was neither the howling of the wind nor the yelp of the coyote.

"Now what do you say?" asked Frank; and he had already passed through an inner apartment, and in a moment stood on the porch again, swinging a lantern and peering out into the dark and rain, listening for that cry of distress. It came in a moment — nearer than they had expected it.

"Help! help! oh, please come and help!"

"The d—l!" was old man Sutton's exclamation; not that he really thought the slender little figure perched on the back of the tall horse was the personage mentioned — it was only a habit he had of apostrophizing.

The horse had stopped short and was breathing hard, and the prayer for help was frantically repeated by the rider. "Come quick, and help the poor fellow; I've been gone so long from him — oh! *do* come!"

"What poor fellow — and where is he?" asked the old man, in bewilderment.

"The stage-driver — and he's lying near the old Mission, with his leg broken. The horses shied in the storm and overturned the stage, and I was the only passenger, and I crept out of it, and the driver couldn't move any more, and told me to unhitch the horses and come this way for help, and — oh! *do* come now!" She ended her harangue, delivered with flying breath and little attention to rhetoric or interpunctuation.'

"And you came those nine miles all alone, gal?" asked the old man.

"Oh, I think I must have come a hundred miles," she replied, with a wild look at the faces on the porch and in the open doorway; "and it is so cold!" She drew the dripping garments closer about her, while father and son consulted together, with their eyes only, for a brief moment. Then the old man said she must be taken in, and they must get the wagon ready, and waken Pedro and Martin.

Without a word Frank gave a lantern to Johnny, lifted the girl from the horse and carried her into the room, brushing the drenched hair back from her face, when he sat her down, as he would have done a child's. But she pleaded excitedly, "Indeed I cannot stay — let me go back, and you can follow."

"So you shall go back, my gal," said Mr. Sutton, "as soon as the wagon is ready. See how she's shivering, mother; get her some hot tea, and give her your fur sack — for she'll go back with us or die."

"My fur sack?" repeated the old lady, incredulously; "my best sack — out in this rain!"

"Best sack be ——," he shouted, angrily; "I'll throw it in the fire in a minute!" And the best sack quickly made its appearance, in spite of the threat of speedy cremation.

The tea was brought by Johnny, hastily drank, and then the girl repeated her wish to move on. Frank's own cloak was thrown over "the best fur sack"— not, I fear, so much from a desire to save this garment as from the wish to keep the shrinking form in it from shivering so painfully.

It was New-Year's day — though the light had not yet dawned before the sufferer was comfortably lodged at the Yedral Ranch, and Hetty, as well as the Sutton family, slept later into the morning than usual. The sun had risen as serenely cloudless as though no storm had passed through the land but yesternight; and Father Sutton, thinking he was the first one up, was surprised to encounter Hetty with Johnny, her new-found cavalier. He hailed her in his unceremonious fashion: "I'm glad to see you up bright and early, gal — make a good farmer's wife some day. Did you come down this way to live on a ranch?"

"No, sir; I came to teach school. Your name is among those of the gentlemen who engaged me."

"The ——! Are you the new school-marm? Then you're Miss —"

"Hetty Dunlap is my name."

He held out both hands. "A happy New-Year to ye, Hetty Dunlap — and happy it'll be for all of us, I'm thinking; for a gal that's got so much pluck as you is sure to know something about teachin' school. Here, Johnny, how d'ye like your teacher?"

Now, Johnny had drawn back with some slight manifestation of disfavor when Hetty's true character came to light. But she laid her hand on his shoulder in her shy yet frank manner, and said quickly:

"I had already selected Johnny as a sort of assistant disciplinarian. I am so little that I shall want some one who is tall and strong to give me countenance;" which at once restored the harmony between them. They went in to breakfast together, during which meal it was decided by Father Sutton that Hetty was to live in his family, though "the Price's" was the place where, until now, the teachers had made their home, being nearest to the school.

"But then," said the old man, "if the Rancho Yedral can't afford a mustang for such a brave little rider every day of the year, then I'll give it up;" and he slapped his hat on and left the house.

"Yes," Frank commented rather timidly, "you are brave — a perfect heroine. And yet you are so very small." She was standing in just the spot where he had brushed the hair out of her face last night, and perhaps his words were an apology.

"True," she assented, "I am small; not much taller than my sister's oldest girl, and she is only twelve."

"You have a sister?"

"Yes, in the city; and she has six children." Her voice was raised a little, her nut-brown eyes looked into his with an unconscious appeal for sympathy, and her delicate nostrils quivered as in terror — which the bare recollection of the little heathens seemed to inspire her with.

"And did you live at her house? — have you neither father nor mother living?"

"Neither. How happy you must be — you have so kind a father and so good a mother —"

The "good mother" came in just then, shaking her best sack vigorously, and lamenting, in pointed words, the "ruination" of this expensive fur robe — calling a painful blush to Hetty's cheek as well as Frank's. The young man tried vainly to make it appear a pleasant joke. "Indeed, mother, you ought to look upon that piece of fur as a handsome New-Year's gift — you have my promise of a new fur sack as soon as I go to the city. And isn't my word good for a fur sack?" he asked, laughingly.

"Yes," said the good mother. "I know your extravagance well enough; but, to my notion, you can afford such things better after you've married Lolita, than before."

Frank bit his lips angrily, and turned away — but not before Hetty had seen the hot red that flushed his cheek.

Toward noon there was loud rejoicing on the porch, and Hetty, looking from her window, saw Mrs. Sutton welcoming a tall, dark-eyed girl of about twenty, whose companion — her brother, to all appearance — seemed several years her senior.

This girl, Lolita Selden, the daughter of an American

father and a wealthy Spanish mother, was a fair specimen of the large class represented by her in California. Generous and impulsive, as all her Spanish half-sisters are, neither her piecemeal education, nor the foolish indulgence of the mother, had succeeded in making anything of her but an impetuous, though really kind-hearted woman. In the brother's darker, heavier face, there was less of candor and sympathy, and his figure — though he had all the grace and dignity of the Spaniard — was lacking in height and the breadth of shoulder that made Frank Sutton look a giant beside him.

It was some time before our heroine was introduced to the pair; not, indeed, till dinner was on the table, though Frank had repeatedly hinted to his mother that Hetty might not feel at liberty to make her appearance among them without being formally invited — to which he received the cheering response that "he was always botherin'."

When they met, it was hard to say whether Hetty was more charmed with Lolita's stately presence and simple kindness, or Lolita with Hetty's heroism. The brother, too, seemed lost in admiration of Hetty's heroic conduct or Hetty's pretty face — a fact which escaped neither Frank nor his mother, for she commented on it days afterward. "What a chance it would be for a poor girl like this 'ere one, if she could make a ketch of young Selden, and he married her!"

"What! that black-faced Spaniard?" but Frank's generous heart reproached him even while he spoke, and his mother took advantage of his penitence and charged him with a message to Lolita, that needed to be delivered the same day. When, therefore, after school-hours, Frank returned bringing with him both Hetty and Lolita — the latter was visiting her new friend at the school-house — the mother was well pleased, and spoke more kindly than she had yet spoken to the new teacher.

"Old man" Sutton, too, had many a pleasant word for

both young girls; and altogether Hetty soon realized that home could be home away from her sister's house and the six plagues it held.

Spring came into the land, dressing in glossier green the grayish limbs of the white-oak in the valley, opening with balmy breath the blossoms of the buckeye by the stream, and covering with gayest flowers the plain and the hillside; while in some shady nook the laurel stood, shaking its evergreen leaves in daily wonderment at the dress changes and the youthful air all nature had put on. The wild rose creeping over the veranda of the Yedral Ranch shed its perfume through the house, and cast its bright sheen upon the very roof-tree, a passion-vine, in sombre contrast, rearing its symbolic blossom cheek to cheek with the rosy flower-face of the gay child of Castile.

Long since had the stage-driver left the Yedral Ranch, grateful for kind treatment received, his head and heart full of a firm conviction on two points: The first, that there was just one man good enough to be Hetty Dunlap's husband, and that that man was Frank Sutton: the second, that there was only one woman good enough to be Frank's wife, and she Hetty Dunlap.

He had resumed his old post, and many a pleasant word and startling bit of news did he call out to Hetty and her friends when they were down by the "big gate," as he drove by very slowly, so as to enjoy conversation as long as possible. George was a deal pleasanter when Hetty was there by herself, or at least without Lolita; and once, when, by chance, Hetty and Frank were there alone together, he called down, regardless of the staring passengers in the coach, "That's the way I like to see things; two's good company, and three's none. Don't see what you want to be luggin' that Spanish gal round with you for, Frank; she ain't none o' your'n nohow, and never will be, nuther."

Before the flush had died on her face, Hetty found her arm drawn through Frank's, and as they slowly bent their steps homeward, the mind of each seemed absorbed in the contemplation of some intricate puzzle, on the solving of which depended their whole future welfare. Then Frank raised his merry, twinkling eyes and charged her with being hopelessly enamored of George, the stage-driver, defying her to say that she had not just then been thinking of him, as he knew by her absent looks.

"I — I was only looking down that way, and thinking there is no lovelier spot on earth than Yedral Ranch." She stopped abruptly; what she was saying now to cover her confusion, she had said a few days ago, from the fulness of her heart, to Lolita, strolling along this same road; and the Spanish girl had answered impulsively, "Yes; and you shall always make your home here when I —" Then she had stopped, crimson in the face, and Hetty had not urged her to finish the sentence.

But Frank, with quickly altered tone, asked softly, "Do you like it so well, Hetty — really and truly? And have you not wanted often to go back to the city?"

"To the city?" she repeated, with a little shiver; "no—no!"

The call of a partridge from behind the nearest *manzanita* bush warned them that young Johnny was there, and the next moment he appeared before them — his mother's ambassador to Hetty. "Would she be kind enough just for once to help with the cake? His mother had burnt her right hand, and she could not stir the batter with her left."

"And could not you have done it 'just for once' as well?" asked Frank, impatiently; at which question Johnny opened his eyes wide.

"She didn't ask me," he said; and then they all went silently to the house.

To do Mrs. Sutton justice, she was loud in her praises of

Hetty's obliging disposition, and Hetty's proficiency in cake-baking, that evening at tea; and particularly to Julian Selden, who was there with his sister, did she untiringly sing Hetty's perfections. This seemed to have the effect of making the young Spaniard bolder and more desirous of pushing his suit, for the very next evening they came home from Hetty's school *a partie carrée*—Lolita, her brother, Hetty and Frank.

The facts of the case were that, following a suggestion of Frank's, Johnny, on Julian's second attempt to escort Hetty home, had kept close by her side during the whole ride, much more to Hetty's delight than Julian's. In consequence, Julian had been wise enough to bring Lolita with him; and Frank, though chagrined, was better pleased to find them both at Hetty's school than one alone.

Through the spring and far into the summer they met almost daily in this way; and sometimes, though Mother Sutton's invitations to Lolita and her brother to "come every day — every day," were loud and vociferous, the brother and sister would return to their own home after a protracted ride, leaving Hetty and Frank to find their way back to Yedral Ranch alone. Hetty thought she could see a cloud on Mrs. Sutton's brow whenever this happened; and dear as those rides were to her, she avoided them whenever she could. Unhappily (Frank did not consider it so), while out alone together one day, Hetty's saddle-girth broke, and though she sprang quickly to the ground, Frank's nerves were so unstrung, he declared, that he could not at once repair the damage, but had to convince himself, by slow degrees, that she really was not hurt or frightened. Consequently, it was later than usual when they reached home; and Mother Sutton, darting a quick look to see that the door had closed behind Frank, who had explained the cause of delay, muttered something about "cunning minxes, who had neither gratitude nor shame," and then tramped out of the room, leaving Hetty with cheeks burning and eyes strangely bright under the tears rising in them.

Next morning she made much ado over a sprained ankle, which was not so painful as to keep her at home, but just bad enough to cause her to ride slowly to school with Johnny and home again before school-hours were fairly over. I fear that she was a "designing minx," for, if she managed, by keeping her room to evade Frank's questioning glance and Mother Sutton's hostile looks, she managed no less to escape an honor which, according to this good lady's statement, corroborated by Lolita's more than usual tenderness, Julian Selden had meant to confer upon her. But she could not stay in her room forever; and Father Sutton dragged her out of it one day, challenging her to tell the truth ("and shame the devil"), by acknowledging that something had hurt her beside the sprained ankle. Had Mrs. Sutton shown no spite openly against "the gal" before, it broke out now, in little sharp speeches against women "tryin' to work on the sympathy of foolish young men. Her boys, she knew, could n't never be ketched that way by no white-faced —"

"Will yer be still now!" thundered the old man, taking the pipe from between his lips and pointing with it to Hetty, who at this moment was really the white-faced thing the old lady had meant to call her.

"Johnny," said Hetty, next morning, on their way to school, "I think—I 'll go home when vacation begins, and—"

"Why, what d' you mean?" asked the boy, startled out of all proper respect.

"Just what I say;" and she enumerated her reasons for considering it her duty to return to her lonely sister and the six pining children; and it was a matter of doubt whether Johnny's lips quivered more during the recital, or Hetty's. But when the school-house was reached, Johnny was a man again; and if he did blubber out loud when he told his elder brother of it, late in the evening, down by the big gate, nobody but Frank heard him, and *his* lips were rather white when next he spoke.

"You asked me for that Mexican saddle of mine some time ago, Johnny. You are welcome to it."

"I don't want no Mexican saddle," replied Johnny, in a surly tone, and without grammar; but looking into his brother's face, he said, "Thank you, Frank. I'd say you're 'bully,' only Hetty said it wasn't a nice word."

In the course of the week Father Sutton, in his character as such, and as school director, was made acquainted with Hetty's intention. In both characters he protested at first, but yielded at last. He walked out with "the gal" one evening, as though to take her over the ranch for the last time, and then artfully dodged away when Frank — by the merest accident — came to join them. Left alone with this young man, Hetty trembled, as she had learned to tremble under his mother's scowling looks and half-spoken sentences. He spoke quietly, at first, of her going away; but her very quietness seemed after a while to set him all on fire.

"Hetty," he cried, "are you then so anxious to go — so unwilling to stay, even for a day, after the school closes? Is there nothing — is there no one here you regret to leave behind you?"

Poor little Hetty! How they had praised her for her heroism once. There was no praise due her then, as she had protested again and again. Now she was the heroine, when she answered, though with averted face and smothered voice, "Nothing — no one;" adding, quickly, "you have all been so kind to me that naturally I shall feel homesick for the Yedral Ranch, and shall be so glad to see any of you when you come to the city."

Frank had heard "the tears in her voice," and though he

turned from her abruptly, it was not in anger, as she fancied.

"Father," he said, a day or two later, "I don't know but I'll take a run over the mountains, now harvesting is over, and there seems nothing particular for me to do."

"Please yourself and you'll please me, Frank," was the answer. "Got any money? You kin git it when you want it."

Then there was nothing more said about the journey, and Frank, making no further preparations, seemed to have forgotten all about it.

When Hetty was lifted into the little wagon that took herself and trunk to the big gate, she repeated her hope of sooner or later greeting the members of the Sutton family in San Francisco.

"Not soon, I'm afeard, Miss Hetty; me an' father and Johnny never goes to the city, and as for Frank — I reckon he'll want to git married first, and bring Lolita 'long with him."

Martin, who was driving, probably knew the meaning of the fire in the old man's eye, for he whipped up the horse and drove off, as though "fearing to miss the stage," as he explained at the turn of the road.

Altogether, George showed neither as much surprise nor pleasure as Hetty had faintly expected him to evince. When they reached the first town he came and stood by the open coach window, after the customary halt, drawing on his gloves first, and then pointing out, with great exactitude, where the old *adobe* tavern had formerly stood, on the opposite side of the street.

During this interesting conversation, some tardy passengers came out of the hotel, with hasty steps, and mounted to the top of the stage with much hurried scrambling. Then George left Hetty's window, mounted his throne, and drove on.

We need not say how Hetty's heart sank with the sinking sun; and only when George came out of the station-house where they had taken supper, ready and equipped for the night's drive, did a light rise in her eyes.

"I thought you stopped at this station," she said, as he again leaned at her window, while the same hasty steps and confused scrambling on the top of the stage fell, half unconsciously, on her ear.

"Well — yes. As a general thing, I do. But me and Dick's changed off to-night, so 't I can see you into the cars to-morrow morning."

"How tired you will be," she remonstrated.

"Well — mebbe so. Howsomever, Miss Hetty, you didn't stop to think whether you 'd be tired when you started out to find help for me, last New-Year's eve." And Hetty blushed, as she always did, when her heroism was spoken of.

George's eyes did look heavy the next morning; but he still kept the lines, lounging up to the coach-window about the time the stage was ready to start, and always pointing out something of interest on these occasions. Once, indeed, when she fancied that her ear caught the sound of a familiar footfall on the porch of the tavern they were about to leave, he was so anxious she should see the owl just vanishing into the squirrel-hole, on the opposite side of the road, that he laid his hand on her arm to insure her quick attention, just as she was about to turn her head back in the direction of the porch. Then came the usual climbing and scrambling overhead, and directly George mounted, too, and drove on.

The shrill whistle of the locomotive seemed to cut right through Hetty's heart; and the loneliness she had never felt away down the country, now suddenly took possession of the girl's soul. No one could have been more attentive than George; the best seat in the cars was picked out for her; the daily papers laid beside her, and then — then she was left alone. George only, of all her down-country friends, had made the unconditional promise to visit her in San Francisco. She was thinking of this after he had left her, and she sat watching the cars filling with passengers for the city — travellers gathered together here from watering-place and pleasure-resort, from dairy-ranch and cattle-range. Was there another being among these all as lonely as she? And she turned her face to the window, and looked steadily over toward the hills, yellow and parched now, in the late summer — so fresh and green from the winter's rains when she had last seen them. It looked as if her life, too, were in the "sere and yellow;" the heavy, throbbing pain that was in her heart and rising to her throat — would it ever give place again to the bright fancies she had indulged in when coming this way — oh! how many weeks ago? She tried to count; but counting the weeks brought the events of each in turn before her, and she desisted; she must keep a calm face and a clear eye.

She heard the cry of the fruit-venders outside, and saw their baskets laden with fruits, tempting and delicious, raised to the car-windows, where passengers had signified their wish to purchase. Mechanically, her eyes followed the movements of the young man in front of her. Grapes, with the dew still on them; apples, with one red cheek, and peaches with two; plums, larger than either, and far more luscious, were transferred from the heavy basket into the lap of the lady beside him — evidently his new-made wife — who said, "Thanks, dear," with such a happy, grateful smile, that Hetty grew quite envious. She tried to think it was of the fruit; but pending the decision she laid her head on the back of the seat in front of her, and before she thought of what she was doing, the tears were trickling down her cheeks. Then her shoulders began to jerk quite ridiculously, and she was ready to die of shame, when a light hand was laid on them, and her name was spoken.

F

"Hetty!" the voice said again; but she did not raise her head, only answering, "Yes," as she would have done in a dream.

"Hetty!" once more, "see what I have brought you." Apples, and peaches, and plums — all these things were showered into her lap, and when she raised her head, she looked at them steadily a moment, and then said, with a long breath, "Oh, Frank!" before she turned to where he sat. As she stretched out both hands to meet his, the fruit, now forgotten, fell plump, plump, to the floor, and rolled all over the cars; and when the train moved slowly away from the depot a little later, Hetty, looking up at the lady in front of her, said to herself, that she envied her no longer — neither the apples nor—. She made a full stop here; perhaps because of George's sudden appearance, and the hilarity in which he and Frank indulged.

"Oh, Miss Hetty!" he laughed; "I couldn't make you see that owl this morning, could I?"

"No; but I think I must have been as blind as an owl myself, not to have seen whom you were hiding," she answered, taking the contagion.

Again shrieked the locomotive, but not with the "heart-rending" cry of a while ago; and George, bringing their hands quickly together in his parting clasp, sprang from the cars and left Frank and Hetty there.

Loud was the anger of good Mrs. Sutton on discovering that Frank had accompanied Hetty to San Francisco. In vain Father Sutton disclaimed all fore-knowledge of the young man's intention, and asserted that Frank had never mentioned a tour to the city. Mrs. Sutton said she knew the old man was in league with him. At the end of a week Frank returned without so much as bringing the fur sack as a peace-offering. In course of time he reconciled his mother to some extent by again carrying messages to Lolita, and sometimes bringing Lolita herself in return, just as in Hetty's time.

Autumn came; and still, to the determined schemer's dissatisfaction, Frank had not yet secured the prize she so coveted for him. The season brought with it many cares as well as pleasures to the ranchero. At a *rodeo*, looked upon by the young people generally as a pleasant entertainment, Frank was the admired of many eyes, as his lasso unfailingly singled out the animal "in demand," among the dense herds moving in a circle. The horse he rode was full of fire, and more impetuous, if possible, than his rider; and Lolita, who was among the guests at the Yedral Ranch, had never thought Frank so handsome and so well worth winning before.

To Hetty the white walls and the spacious rooms of the grammar-school, to which she had returned, seemed a prison and a wilderness in one. Her sister's house, with the six young Tartars, was more like Bedlam than ever; but Hetty had grown older and firmer, and she declared, to her sister's amazement, that unless she could withdraw herself from the mob unmolested, at her option, she should seek a home with more congenial associates. The sister opened her eyes wide, as if only now discovering that Hetty was full-grown; and she assented silently.

First, after her return, letters from Frank lighted up her life at intervals. But when the early rains of autumn, after an Indian summer full of sunny days and glorious memories of vanished springs, turned to the settled melancholy of " a wet winter," these letters ceased, leaving in Hetty's existence a blank that nothing else could fill. Christmas came, with its vacations and merry-makings, and beside the dull, deep pain in Hetty's heart, there was still the unselfish wish to give others pleasure, though she herself could never again feel that glad emotion. From morn to night her deft hands flew, sewing, stitching, sketching — busy always, yet never for herself.

It was very near Christmas now—so near that Hetty, eager to have all things ready for the joyous eve, had sat down to her work without the usual care for neat appearance. Perhaps it was because her curls were a little neglected, and her collar was not pinned on with the usual precision, that her face looked worn this morning; her eyes were languid, and the flush on her cheeks could not cover the deficiency of flesh which became painfully visible.

Thus she sat, stitching, ever stitching. The silent parlor, with its covered furniture and light carpeting, seemed the right place for ghosts to flit through, and peer, mayhap, with dull, glazed eyes into the fire, as Hetty caught herself just now. But she drove back the ghosts—are they not always our own memories, woven out of unfulfilled wishes, useless regrets, and profitless remorse?—and hastily resumed her work. The ringing of the door-bell seemed so much the doing of one of these ghosts, that she paid no attention to it, but kept on stitching, quietly stitching. Directly the parlor-door was thrown open, and the Mongolian servitor, looking with calm indifference on the little streams of muddy water oozing at every step from the boots of the new-comer, returned to the kitchen, heedless, to all appearances, of the scream with which Hetty flew to meet the stranger.

"George!" she cried, "oh! George!" and she clasped the damp arm of the man, gotten up on the grizzly-bear pattern, as though there could be no pleasure greater than this in all the world.

Though a man, George was wise enough to know that he was not indebted to his personal attractions for this affectionate greeting; but taking both her hands in his, he said, "Yes, Miss Hetty, I've come to tell you all about it."

At the fall *rodeo* on the Yedral Ranch, Frank's horse had fallen, covering its rider with its weighty body. He recovered from a death-like swoon with wandering mind; and the spine

being injured, according to the doctor's statement, it seemed doubtful that he would ever leave his bed, except as imbecile or cripple. Reason returning, Frank felt that his friends' fears of his remaining a cripple were not without foundation, and a hopeless gloom settled on his spirit. Many a time, when George had made "fast time" and spent the half-hour gained at Frank's bed, did Hetty's name rise to his lips; but it was never pronounced. Only this: looking up out of deep sunken eyes, one day, quite recently, Frank had said to him, "George, I shall get well, and not be a cripple. If only —"
"It's all right," had been George's answer; and he had hurried from the house as though charged with the most urgent commission.

After an hour's conversation, Hetty had only one question to ask. Looking up with shy eagerness, she almost said below her breath, "And Lolita?"

For answer, George took the flushed face between his hands. "You've grown mighty thin, Miss Hetty," he simply said. Then he continued, with great *nonchalance*, "Lolita got stuck after the new schoolmaster — they've got a man in your place. But come, Miss Hetty, you 'peared to me last New-Year's eve like an angel, in my distress; suppose you do as much now for Frank Sutton. We can get down there on New-Year's eve, and give you lots of time to spend Christmas here first. What d'ye say?"

No lover could have pleaded more earnestly. All her objections were overruled, and when at last she said, almost breathlessly, "Oh, but his *mother*, George!" he answered, with all his honest heart: "It's my firm belief, Miss Hetty, that you were cut out for a real hero-ine; and a hero-ine you've got to be to the end of the chapter — which I don't say but the last trial of your hero-ism will be greater than the first."

And sure enough, on New-Year's eve, came the rumbling

of wheels and the tramp of horses' hoofs close up to the veranda of the ranch-house on the Yedral. None of the inmates seemed startled, though none had expected company. Without a word Father Sutton sprang to the door — alas! that the old man was swifter of foot now than the young giant of a year ago — caught the lithe figure that sprang from the stage in his arms and set her down, as Frank had done, in the middle of the room. But she was not cold, dripping wet now, only blinded by the light one moment, and the next on her knees by the lounge, where a pale, haggard man lay stretched. He half raised himself to catch her in his arms, and for a wonder did not sink back with the moan that had become so painful to his father's ears. For once Hetty had cast aside all timidity, and she looked up brightly into Father Sutton's face, while one arm circled Frank's neck and the other hand lay unresistingly in his.

"Hey!" shouted the old man; "now we know whose gal you are; I used to call you mine once. Mother, get some supper; I reckon she is wellnigh starved and perished with the cold. Lively, Johnny! bring some more wood; Hetty'll stay for good, and you'll get time enough to hang 'round the gal to-morrow."

And what a bright to-morrow it was! Such a New-Year's day had never dawned on Yedral Ranch before. Every one seemed to have found a treasure, even to Mrs. Sutton. Together with Hetty's trunk had come a large, promising-looking box, and when Father Sutton presented this to his better-half, she almost screamed —

"Oh, I know! it's my new fur sack!"

A WOMAN'S TREACHERY.

"HOW much you resemble Mrs. Arnold!" exclaimed the Doctor's wife, after an hour's acquaintance, the day we reached Fort ——. It was not the first time I had heard of my resemblance to this, to me, unknown lady remarked on. A portion of the regiment of colored troops to which Doctor Kline belonged, and which we met on their way in to the States, as we were coming out, had been camped near us one night; and a colored laundress, who had good-naturedly come over to our tent to take the place of my girl, who was sick, had broken into the same exclamation on first beholding me. Captain Arnold belonged to the same regiment, and was expecting, like all the volunteers then in the Territory, to be ordered home and mustered out of service, as soon as the body of regular troops, to which my husband belonged, could be assigned their respective posts. Their expectations were not to be realized for some time yet; and when I left the Territory, a year later, a part of these troops were still on the frontier.

Fort —— was not our destination; to reach it, we should be obliged to pass through, and stop for a day or two at, the very post of which Captain Arnold had command — which would afford me excellent and ample opportunity for judging of the asserted likeness between this lady and myself. I must explain why we were, in a measure, compelled to stop at Fort Desolation (we will call it so). It was located in the midst of a desert — the most desolate and inhospitable that can be imagined — in the heart of an Indian country, and just so far removed from the direct route across the desert as to make it impracticable to turn in there with a command, or large number of soldiers; for which reason, troops crossing here always carried water-barrels filled with them. A small party, however, such as ours was then, could not with any safety camp out the one night they must, despite the best ambulance-mules, pass on the desert.

With most pardonable curiosity, I endeavored to learn something more of the woman who was so much like me in appearance; and I began straightway to question Mrs. Kline about her. The impression of a frank, open character, which this lady had made on me at first, vanished at once when she found that Mrs. Arnold was to be made the subject of conversation between us.

"Is she pretty?"

"Yes — quite so." Ahem! and looked like me. But my mother's saying, that there might be a striking resemblance between a very handsome and a very plain person, presented itself to my memory like an uninvited guest, and I concluded not to fall to imagining vain things on so slight a support.

"What kind of a man is Captain Arnold?"

"The most good-natured man in the world."

"Oh!" Something in the manner of her saying this in praise of Captain Arnold made me think she wanted to say nothing further; so I stopped questioning.

We left the Doctor and his wife early the next morning, and reached Fort Desolation at night-fall. The orderly had preceded us a short distance, and, when the ambulance stopped at the Captain's quarters, Mrs. Arnold appeared on the threshold, holding a lantern in her hand. She raised it, to let the light fall into the ambulance; and as the rays fell on her own face, I could see that she looked like — a sister I had. The Captain was absent, inspecting the picket-posts he had established along the river, and would return by morning,

Mrs. Arnold said; and she busied herself with me in a pleasant, pretty manner. She could not resemble me in height or figure, I said to myself, for she was smaller and more delicately made; nor had any one in our family such deep-blue eyes, save mother — we children had to content ourselves with gray ones.

The night outside was dark and chilly; but in the Captain's house there were light and warmth, and it was bright with the fires that burned in the fireplaces of the different rooms — all opening one into the other. I was forcibly struck with the difference between the quarters at Fort —— and Mrs. Arnold's home at Fort Desolation. Comforts (luxuries, in this country) of all kinds made it attractive: bright carpets were on the floors here; while at the Doctor's quarters at Fort ——, one was always reminded of cold feet and centipedes, when looking at the naked *adobe* floors. Embroidered covers were spread on the tables and white coverlets on the beds; while at the Doctor's all these things were made hideous by hospital-linen and gray blankets. Easy-chairs and lounges, manufactured from flour-barrels, saw-bucks, and candle-boxes, were made gorgeous and comfortable with red calico and sheep's-wool; but the crowning glory of parlor, bed-room, and sitting-room was a dazzling toilet-set of china — gilt-edged, and sprinkled with delicate bouquets of moss-roses and foliage.

"Where *did* you get it?" I asked, in astonishment — *not* envy.

"Is n't it pretty?" she asked, triumphantly. "The Captain's quartermaster, Lieutenant Rockdale, brought it from Santa Fé for me, and paid a mint of money for it, no doubt."

At the supper-table I saw Lieutenant Rockdale, who commanded the post in the Captain's absence, being the only officer there besides the Captain; and, as he messed with them altogether, I need not say that the table was well supplied with all the delicacies that New York and Baltimore send out to less highly favored portions of the universe, in tin cans. Lieutenant Rockdale was a handsome man — a trifle effeminate, perhaps, with languishing, brown eyes, and a soft voice. He seemed delighted with our visit, and took my husband off to his own quarters, while Mrs. Arnold and I looked over pictures of her friends, over albums, and at all the hundred little curiosities which she had accumulated while in the Territory. The cares of the household seemed to sit very lightly on her; a negro woman, Constantia, and a mulatto boy, of twelve or thirteen, sharing the labor between them. The boy seemed to be a favorite with Mrs. Arnold, though she tantalized and tormented him, as I afterwards found she tormented and tantalized every living creature over which she had the power.

I had noticed, while Constantia and Fred were clearing off the table, that she had cut him a slice from a very choice cake, toward which the child had cast longing looks. Placing it carefully on a plate, when he had to leave it for a moment to do something his mistress had bidden him, in the twinkling of an eye she had hidden it; and when the boy missed it, she expressed her regret at his carelessness, and artfully led his suspicions toward Constantia. Hearing him whimpering and sniffling as he went back and forth between dining-room and kitchen, his childish distress at losing the cake seemed to afford her the same amusement that a stage-play would, and she laughed till the tears rolled down her cheeks. Later, he was summoned to replenish the fire; and, knowing the little darkey's aversion for going out of the house bare-headed (he had an idea that his cap could prevent the Indian arrows from penetrating his skull), she hid the cap he had left in the adjoining room, and then laughed immoderately at his terror on leaving the house without it. The next morning, she led me out to the stables to show me her horse — a magnificent, black animal, wild-eyed, with a restless, fretful air. Crossing the space in front of the house, she called to a soldier with sergeant-chevrons on his arms—a man with just enough of negro blood in his veins to stamp him with the curse of his race.

"Harry!" she called to him, "Harry, come hold Black for me; I want to give him a piece of sugar." She opened her hand to let him see the pieces, and he touched his cap and followed us. He loosened the halter and led the horse up to us, but the animal started back when he saw Mrs. Arnold, and would not let her approach him. Harry patted his neck and soothed him, and Mrs. Arnold holding the sugar up to his view, the horse came to take it from her hand; but she quickly clutched his lip with her fingers, and blew into his face till the horse reared and plunged so that Harry could hold him no longer. Laughing like an imp, she called to Harry:

"Get on him and hold him, if you cannot manage him in that way: get on him anyhow, and let Mrs. —— see him dance."

The mulatto's flashing black eyes were bent on her with a singularly reproachful look; but the next moment he was on the horse's back, the horse snorting and jumping in a perfectly frantic manner.

When Mrs. Arnold had sufficiently recovered from her merriment, she explained that the horse had not been ridden for a month; the last time she had ridden him he had thrown her—she had pricked him with a pin to urge him on faster.

About noon the Captain arrived; and I found him, as Mrs. Kline had described, "the most good-natured man in the world," and, to all appearances, loving his wife with the whole of his big heart. He was big in stature, too, with broad shoulders, pleasant face, and cheerful, ringing voice. The shaggy dog, who had slunk away from Mrs. Arnold, came leaping up on his master when he saw him; the horse he had ridden rubbed his nose against his master's shoulder before turning to go into his stable, and Constantia and Fred beamed on him with their white teeth and laughing eyes from the kitchen-door. Later in the afternoon, he asked what I thought of his quarters, and told me how hard his colored soldiers had worked to build the really pretty *adobe* house in strict accordance with his wishes and directions. But I could not quite decide whether he was more proud of the house or of the affection his men all had for him. Then he told me the story of almost every piece of furniture in the house; and, moving from room to room, we came to where their bed stood. Resting beside it was his carbine, which the orderly had brought in. Taking it in his hand to examine it, he pointed it at his wife's head with the air of a brigand, and uttered, in unearthly tones:

"Your money, or your life!"

With a quick, cat-like spring, she was by the bed, had thrust her hands under the pillow, and the next instant was holding two Derringers close to his breast. Throwing back her head, like a heroine in velvet trousers on the stage, she returned, in the same strain:

"I can play a hand at that game, too, and go you one better!"

She laughed as she said it — the laugh that she laughed with her white teeth clenched — but there was a "glint" in her eye that I had never seen in a blue eye before.

When once more on the way, my husband asked me how I liked Mrs. Arnold. "Very well," said I; "but —," and I did not hesitate to tell him of the peculiarities I had noticed about her. He himself was charmed with her sprightliness, so he only responded with, "Pshaw! woman!" after which I maintained an offended (he said, offensive) silence on the subject.

Not quite four months later, my husband was recalled to Santa Fé, and we again crossed the desert, with only three men as escort. I had heard nothing from either Mrs. Arnold or the Captain in all this time, for our post was farther out than theirs; indeed, so far out that nothing belonging to the same military department passed by that way. It was midsummer, and the dreary hills shutting in Fort Desolation, and running down toward the river some distance back of the place, were baked hard and black in the sun; the little stream that had meandered along through the low inclosure of the fort in winter time was now a mere bed of slime, and the plateaux, which had been levelled for the purpose of erecting the Captain's house and the commissary buildings on them, could not boast of a single spear of grass or any other sign of vegetation. The Captain's house lay on the highest of these plateaux; lower down, across the creck, were the quartermaster and commissary buildings (here, too, were Lieutenant Rockdale's quarters); and to the left, on the other side of the men's quarters, was the guard-house — part *jacal*, part tent-cloth.

How *could* any one live here and be happy? Black and bald the earth, as far as the eye could reach; black and dingy the tents and the huts that strewed the flat; murky and dark the ridge of fog that rose on the unseen river; murky and silent the clefts in the rocks where the sun left darkness forever.

It might have been the fading light of the waning day that cast the peculiarly sombre shadow on the Captain's house as we drew up to it; but I thought the same shadow must have fallen on the Captain's face, when he appeared in the door to greet us. Presently Mrs. Arnold fluttered up in white muslin and blue ribbons; and both did their best to make us comfortable. How my husband felt, I don't know; but they did not succeed in making me feel comfortable. Perhaps the absence of the bright fire made the rooms look so dark, even after the lights had been brought in — there was certainly a change. Supper was placed on the table, but I missed Constantia's round face in the dining-room. In answer to my question regarding her, I was told she had expressed so strong a desire to return to the States that she had been sent to Fort ——, there to await an opportunity to go in. Lieutenant Rockdale's absence I noticed also. He did not mess with them any more, I was informed.

My attention was attracted to a conversation between Captain Arnold and my husband. The guard-house, he told him, was at present occupied by two individuals who had made their appearance at Fort Desolation several days ago, and had tried to prevail on the Captain to sell them some of the government horses, and arms and ammunition, offering liberal payment, and promising secrecy. They were Americans; but as the number of American settlers, or white settlers, in this country is so small, it was easy for the Captain to determine that these were not of them, and their dress and general appearance led him to suspect that they belonged to that despicable class of white men who make common cause with the Indian, in order to rob and plunder, and, if need be, murder, those of their own race. Of course they had not made these proposals directly and openly to the Captain — at first representing themselves as members of a party of miners going to Pinos Altos; but they soon betrayed a familiarity with the country which only years of roaming through it could have given them. He had felt it his duty to arrest them at once, but had handcuffed them only to-day, and meant to send them, under strong escort, to Fort ——, where their regimental commander was stationed, as soon as some of the men from the picket-posts could be called in.

It was late when we arose from the supper-table, and the Captain and my husband left us, to go down to the guard-house, while Mrs. Arnold led me into the room where their bed stood. This room had but one window — of which window the Captain was very proud. It was a *French* window, opening down to the ground. Throwing it open, Mrs. Arnold said:

"What a beautiful moon we have to-night; let us put out the candle and enjoy the moonshine"—with which she laughingly extinguished the light, and drew my chair to the window.

From where I sat I could just see the men's quarters and the guard-house, though it might have been difficult from there to see the window. We had not been seated long when I fancied I heard a noise, as though of some one stealthily approaching from somewhere in the direction to which my back was turned; then some one seemed to brush or scrape against the outside wall of the house, behind me. "What's that?" I asked in quick alarm. It had not remained a secret to Mrs. Arnold that I was an unmitigated coward; so she arose, and saying, "How timid you are!—it is the dog; but I will go and look," she stepped from the low window to the ground outside, and vanished around the corner of the house. Some time passed before she returned, and with a little shudder, sprang to light the candle.

"How chilly it is getting," she exclaimed; and then continued, "it was the dog we heard out there. Poor fellow; perhaps the cook had forgotten him, so I gave him his supper."

Rising from my seat to close the window on her remark about the cold, I stepped to the opposite side from where I had been sitting; and there, crossing the planks that lay over the slimy creek, and going towards the commissary buildings, was a man whose figure seemed familiar: I could not be mistaken—it was Lieutenant Rockdale. No doubt the man had a right to walk in any place he might choose; but, somehow, I could not help bringing him in connection with "the dog, poor fellow," for whom Mrs. Arnold had all at once felt such concern.

Soon the gentlemen returned, and we repaired to the parlor, where a game of chess quickly made them inaccessible to our conversation. The game was interrupted by a rap at the front door, and Harry, the sergeant whom Mrs. Arnold had compelled to mount her black horse that day, appeared on the threshold. In his face there was a change, too; his eyes flashed with an unsteady light as he opened the door, and ever and again, while addressing the Captain—whose thoughts were still half with the game—his looks wandered over to where Mrs. Arnold sat. We were so seated that the Captain's back was partly toward her when he turned to the sergeant; and he could not see the quick gesture of impatience, or interrogation, that Mrs. Arnold made as she caught the mulatto's eye. Involuntarily, I glanced toward him—and saw the nod of assent, or intelligence he gave in return.

The sergeant had come to report that the prisoners in the guard-house had suddenly asked to see the Captain: they had disclosures to make to him. When Captain Arnold returned, his face was flushed.

"The villains!" he burst out. "They had managed to hide about five thousand dollars in United States bank-notes about them, when they were searched for concealed weapons, and they just now offered it to me, if I would let them escape. Not only that, but from something one of them said, I have gained the certainty that they are implicated in the massacre of the party of civilians that passed through here about two months ago: you remember, the General ordered out a part of K company, to rescue the one man who was supposed to have been taken prisoner. The wretches! But I'll go myself, in the morning, to relieve the men from picket-duty, and select the best from among them to take the scoundrels to Santa Fé!"

When about to begin my toilet the next morning, I gave a start of surprise. Was *that* what had made the house look so dark and changed? Before me stood a large tin wash-basin

— of the kind that all common mortals used out here — and the beautiful toilet-set of china, with its splendors of gilt-edge and moss-roses, had all disappeared — all save the soap-dish and hot-water pitcher, which were both defective, and looked as though they had gone through a hard struggle for existence.

When our ambulance made the ascent of the little steep hill that hides Fort Desolation from view, I saw three horses led from the stable to the Captain's house — the Captain's horse and two others. He was as good as his word, and before another day had passed, the two men penned up in that tent there would be well on their way to meet justice and retribution. A solitary guard, with ebony face and bayonet flashing in the morning sun, was pacing back and forth by the tent; and walking briskly from the commissary buildings toward the men's quarters, was Harry, the mulatto sergeant.

From the first glance I had at Mrs. Kline's face, when we reached Fort ———, I knew that the mystery of the change at Fort Desolation would be solved here. Constantia was there, and acting as cook in Dr. Kline's family. She was an excellent cook, and we did ample justice to her skill at suppertime. The gentlemen leaving the table to smoke their cigars, Mrs. Kline and I settled down to another cup of tea and *médisance*. From what Constantia had stated on coming to Fort ———, it would seem that in some way Captain Arnold's suspicions had been aroused in regard to the friendship of Lieutenant Rockdale for his wife. About two months ago, he one day pretended to start off on a tour of inspection to the picket-posts; but returned, late the same night, by a different road. Stealing into the house through the kitchen, he had, rather unceremoniously, entered the bed-room, where he found Lieutenant Rockdale toasting his bare feet before the fire. Raising his carbine to shoot the man, Mrs. Arnold had sprung forward, seized his arms and torn the gun from him. In the confusion that followed, the toilet-set referred to, and other articles of furniture, were demolished: but Constantia, who had crept in after the Captain, to prevent mischief, if possible, gave it as her opinion that Mrs. Arnold "had grit enough for ten such men as him an' de leftenant."

"If you did but know the ingratitude of the creature," continued Mrs. Kline, "and the devotion her husband has always shown her!" And she gave me a brief sketch of her career: Married to Arnold just at the breaking out of the war, and of poor parents, she had driven him almost to distraction by her treatment, when thrown out of employment some time after. At last he went into the Union forces as substitute — giving every cent of the few hundred dollars he received to his wife, who spent it on herself for finery. Later, when for bravery and good conduct he was made lieutenant in a negro regiment, she joined her husband, and finally came to the Territory with him. In their regiment, it was well known that he had always blindly worshipped his wife; and that she had always ruled him, his purse, and his company, with absolute power.

Before retiring for the night, we debated the question: Should we remain the next day at Fort ——, or proceed on our journey? The mules needed rest, as well as the horses, for the quartermaster could not furnish fresh mules, which we had rather expected; still, my husband was anxious to reach Santa Fé as soon as possible — and we left the question of our departure where it was, to settle it the next morning at breakfast. The news that came to Fort ——, before the next morning, made us forget our journey — for that day, at least. Captain Arnold had been murdered! The big, true-hearted man was lying at Fort Desolation — dead — with his broken eyes staring up to the heaven that had not had pity on him — his broad breast pierced with the bullet that a woman's treachery had sped!

Before daybreak, a detachment of six men had come in

from Fort Desolation to Fort ——, to report to the commander of their regiment that Captain Arnold had been assassinated, and Sergeant Henry Tulliver had deserted, taking with him one horse, two revolvers, and a carbine. Captain Arnold had started out the morning before, with only two men, to call in the picket-posts. An hour later, the two men had come dashing back to the fort, stating that they had been attacked, and Captain Arnold killed, by the two white men who had been confined in the guard-house. It was ascertained then, for the first time, that the prisoners had made their escape. A detachment of men was sent out with a wagon, and the Captain's body brought in — the men, with their black faces and simple hearts, gathered around it, with tears and lamentations, heaping curses on the villains who had slain their kind commander.

Suddenly a rumor had been spread among them that Harry, the sergeant, had set the prisoners free; and instantly, a hundred hoarse voices were shouting the mulatto's name — a hundred hands ready to take the traitor's life. Vainly Lieutenant Rockdale — who, after the Captain's departure, had at once repaired to his house — tried to check the confusion, that was quickly ripening into mutiny: the excitement only increased, and soon a crowd of black soldiers moved toward the men's quarters, with anything but peaceful intentions. Perhaps Harry's conscience had warned him of what would come, for while the mob were searching the quarters, a lithe figure sprang over the planks across the creek, ran to the stables below the Captain's house, and the next moment dashed over the road, mounted on a wild-looking, black horse.

Could they but have reached him — the infuriated men, who sent yells and carbine-balls after the fugitive — he would have been sacrificed by them to the *manes* of the murdered man; and perhaps this effect had been calculated on, when the fact of his having liberated the prisoners had been brought to their ears.

"How did it come to their ears?" I asked of the Doctor, under whose care one of the six men, overcome with fatigue and excitement, had been placed. It seems that Mrs. Arnold had expressed her conviction of the sergeant having liberated the prisoners to Lieutenant Rockdale in little Fred's hearing, and the boy had innocently repeated the tale to the men.

In the afternoon of the same day, the detail had been made of the men who brought the news to Fort ——; but when the detachment had been only an hour or two on the way, they found the trail of the escaped prisoners. The men could not withstand the temptation to make an effort, at least, to recapture them. They knew them to be mounted, for the two horses which Sergeant Tulliver had that morning separated from the herd were missing; but the trail they followed showed the tracks of *three* horses, which led them to suppose that Harry had found the men and joined them.

But the trail led farther and farther from the road, and fearing to be ambushed, they turned back, leaving the man who had been driven from the companionship of his brethren by a woman's treachery, to become one of the vultures that prey on their own kind.

THE GENTLEMAN FROM SISKIYOU.

IN Gilroy, when the sun lies hot and yellow on the roofs of the frame-built houses and the wide meadows, waving with grain or cropped short by herds of grazing cattle, the eye turns instinctively to the mountains, where the dreamy mid-day atmosphere seems to gather coolness from the dark woods that crown its summit.

"Over that way lie the Hot Springs," says one or the other, pointing out the direction to the stranger who comes for the first time to Santa Clara Valley.

If he wait till the early train of the Southern Pacific Railroad comes in from San Francisco, he will see any number of passengers alighting at the depot, whose dress and belongings speak of a residence in a place somewhat larger and wealthier than the pretty little town of Gilroy. After a comfortable dinner at either of the two hotels, carriages, stages, and buggies are in readiness to convey those in search of either health or pleasure on to the Springs.

It is too early in the season yet to feel much inconvenience from the dust; and the drive through the precincts of what is called Old Gilroy is a charming trip. The modest but cheerful houses are just within sight of each other, separated by orchards, grainfields, vineyards; a grove of white oaks here and there, a single live oak, and clumps of willow and sycamore, make the landscape as pleasing as any in the country. Nearer the first rise of the mountain, the view of grainfields, fenced in by the same dry board fence, would become monotonous were it not for the ever-fresh, ever-beautiful white oak that stands, sentinel-like, scattered through the golden fields, its lower branches sometimes hidden in the full-bearing garbs.

First we hardly notice that the road ascends; but soon, as the foot-hills leave an open space, we can see a vast plain lying beneath us, and then the climb begins in good earnest. "Round and round" the hill it seems to go — a narrow road cut out of the long-resisting rock — the wounds which the pick and shovel have made overgrown by tender, pitying vines, that seek to hide the scars on the face of their fostering mother. Trees high above us shake their leafy heads, and the wild doves who have their nests in the green undergrowth, croon sadly over the invasion of their quiet mountain home. Vain complainings of tree and bird! When the eyes of man have once lighted on nature in her wild, fresh beauty, they are never withdrawn, and they spare not the bird on her nest, nor the tree in its pride.

Here opens a mountain valley before us, and, nestled in the shadow of sycamore and alder, a cosy, home-like cot. The peach and grape-vine cluster by the door; and where a rude tumble-down fence encloses the fields, the Rose of Castile, the native child of California, creeps picturesquely over the crumbling rails, and fills the air with its own matchless fragrance. Bees are drawing honey from geranium and gilli-pink, and the humming-bird, darting through space like a flash one moment, hangs the next, with a quivering, rapturous kiss, in the petals of the sweet-breathed honeysuckle.

Then the road winds higher, and the hills and rocks above grow steeper, bearing aloft the laurel tree and manzanite bush, the madrone tree and the poison ivy. There is not an inch of ground between the wheels of the stage and the steep declivity; and once in a while a nervous passenger of the male gender turns away with a shudder, while the female hides her eyes in her veil or handkerchief, never heeding the sight of the bare, bald crags, and the pine-covered heights far above and in the dreamy distance.

As we enter the heart of the *cañon*, the rocky, vine-clad walls on either side seem to reassure the nervous passenger and the half-fainting lady; and the grade being very easy for quite a while, there is no more lamentation heard till the horses dash full-speed through a laughing, glittering mountain stream, the head-waters of the Cayote, throwing its spray merrily in at the open window. Again and again the brook is crossed, as it makes its quick, flashing way through blackberry clumps and wild grape-vines, glancing up at sycamore and buckeye tree as it hastens along. Suddenly the driver strikes one of the shining white rocks on which the water breaks into foam, and then a general commotion ensues in the stage, and before the passengers have settled back in their original places, a soft, sad music seems to float toward us on the air — the rustling of the gray-green pines that overhang the last rise in the road, and shade so romantically the white cottages clinging to the mountain-side, and built on the plateau that is crowned by the hotel and gardens of the Gilroy Hot Springs.

The stage halts, and after shaking hands with the dozen friends one is sure to find, and partaking of the dinner, which is consumed with ravenous appetite after the drive of two or three hours, it is still early enough for a walk to the Springs before the balmy moonlit night sets in. The terrace-like walk, partly cut out, partly filled in on the steep mountain-side, is overhung by hills rising again on hills; tiny cottages peering out here, there, and everywhere, from out manzanite, laurel and pine trees. Beneath, the mountain falls off into a deep, narrow valley, clothed in luxuriant green, a towering mountain rising on the other side.

There are thousands of silver trout in the streams in the valley; there is an abundance of game in the wild, rugged, but beautiful mountains back of and above the Springs. As in some cases, however, a horrid, vicious-looking lamprey-eel has been found on the rod, instead of a speckled-back trout, so in other cases have brave hunters returned from the chase with blanched faces and reports of startling sights of huge bears and California lions, instead of the tamer game they had expected to bag.

"But it is delightful here for all that!" is the almost involuntary exclamation of those who, on some bright June morning make their way slowly, slowly—drinking their fill of nature, sunshine, and mountain air—to the bubbling, hissing, seething Springs.

We hear this same remark just now from the midst of the group of ladies who are making their way around the gentle curves of the terrace-walk to the Springs; and as the words come from the lips of one who is to figure as the heroine of our short but veracious story, we must take a closer look at her, as she sweeps by, moving along with the rest, yet always a little apart from them. She is carelessly swinging her hat by the strings, and the sun, now and again, as they round some curve in the road, kisses the auburn of her curls into ripples of golden bronze. The *nonchalance* expressed in air and carriage was affected, it was said, and that she always knew what was going on around her, without ever asking any questions.

"That gentleman has been devouring you with his eyes this last half hour. I noticed him up at the house as we were getting ready to start—and now he is here before us;" and fat, motherly Mrs. Bradshaw laughed as only such large-framed, large-hearted people can laugh.

"I hope he finds me more palatable than the beefsteak we had this morning—it was horribly tough."

"Are you speaking of the gentleman from Siskiyou?" asked the tall lady with glasses, who was Miss Kingsley, and popularly supposed to be getting up a book on "The Resources of California."

"No, of the beefsteak," quickly replied she of the auburn curls. Mrs. Bradshaw nudged her very perceptibly, to which admonition she made answer, *sotto voce*, "I hate old maids and blue-stockings."

Miss Kingsley had drawn herself up to her stateliest height: "I had meant to inquire whether Mrs. Bradshaw was alluding to the gentleman from Siskiyou?"

"Yes, dear; did n't you see how he kept his eyes fixed on Mrs. Clayton, before he turned away when he saw us laughing?"

"I did not observe. My opinion, however, if I may venture to express it, is that Mrs. Clayton, with all her talent for subjugating mankind, will hardly succeed in bringing that gentleman to her feet. This piece of rock, I think, could be inspired with the tender passion just as soon."

"Oh! did he refuse that valuable information in regard to the resources of California?" asked Mrs. Clayton, with mingled indignation and concern.

Mrs. Bradshaw was bubbling over with laughter, while the rest of the ladies shared her mirth more or less openly, according to the degree of friendship entertained for Miss Kingsley.

When the party rounded the last bend near the spring, a tall, spare man, conspicuous in a generous expanse of white shirt-bosom, and low, stiff-brimmed hat, hastily laid down the drinking-cup, and moved out of sight, making the circuit of the bath-houses in his anxiety to avoid the advancing column of fair ones. Uncle George was on hand, as usual, smilingly filling glasses and dippers with the boiling waters, trying between whiles to answer the numerous questions propounded, mostly in regard to the retreating form disappearing among the manzanita on the hillside.

"It's the gentleman from Siskiyou." The words were

addressed to Mrs. Clayton, who was blowing little puffs of wind into the glass in her hand, and seemed to have no interest in common with the eager, laughing crowd about. "He and his pardner are both here; they own placer-mines on Yreka Flats, and came here because the gentleman's liver is affected. They're a funny couple — never speak to no ladies, and ain't sociable like, only among themselves. His pardner — there he is now, going up after him," pointing to a low-built, square-shouldered man, with black, bushy eyebrows — "waits on him like a woman, and no two brothers could n't be more affectionate. His pardner told me his own self that when they first came together, eighteen years ago, he got into a row at Placerville — used to be Hangtown, then — and they were firing into him thick and fast after he was down, when Mr. Brodie stepped in, picked him up and carried him to their cabin, and nussed him till he was well again. You see he limps a little yet; but then Mr. Brodie was the only doctor he had, and he says it's a wonder to him he has any legs left at all, he was so riddled with shot."

Sufficient water having been drank, the ladies wended their way back, scattering as they approached the hotel building — generally spoken of as "the house" — which contained parlor, dining and assembly rooms. Some sought their cottages, others climbed the hill-sides, while still others visited the little stream rushing along through the green depths that the stage-road overhung. Some had escorts, others went alone, or formed groups of three or four; and all gave themselves up to the enjoyment of that perfect freedom which makes the stay at these California watering-places a recreation and a holiday.

As the heat of the sun became more oppressive, the stragglers returned; and the closed window-blinds of the cottages spoke of an unusually warm day for the season. This, however, did not forbid the ushering in of the next day with an extra heavy fog, which dripped from the eaves like rain, and made more penetrating the wind that came in surly gusts and rudely swept back the end of the shawl thrown Spanish-fashion over Mrs. Clayton's shoulder. Her right hand grasped a bottle filled with water from the Springs; and the left, hidden until now under the shawl, was bound up in a white cloth. The wind had carried her hat away, too; and after looking helplessly around, she deposited the bottle on the bench nearest her, and gave chase to the runaway. But the hat was suddenly held up before her, and the bottle taken from the bench. It was the gentleman from Siskiyou, who stammered something she did not understand, and to which she replied sweetly and plaintively, "Thank you, ever so much. I am so helpless with that hand. I sprained it some weeks ago, falling from a carriage, and did not know how bad it was till the doctors sent me here. I must have hurt it again yesterday; and now I've got to go about like a cripple." The voice was like a child's; and a half sob seemed to rise in her throat as she spoke the last words, and a tell-tale moisture shone in her eyes.

He had awkwardly set the bottle back on the bench; and when she prepared to move on, he bent over to seize the bottle and carry it for her. In his nervousness he did not heed that she, too, was stooping forward; and only when their heads came in contact did he realize how near he had stood to her. A deep scarlet overspread his sallow face, while Mrs. Clayton said, "Oh, will you carry the bottle for me? Thanks. I wanted to bathe my hand, and was afraid to go more than once through the fog and wind."

They reached the cottage, where he deposited the bottle on the door-steps, and withdrew with a somewhat awkward, but perfectly chivalrous bow.

After breakfast, when the ground was still too wet to walk out, Jenny, sitting in the low rocking-chair by the open door, was startled by footsteps crunching under the window; and a moment later Mr. Brodie placed a bottle at her feet.

"I thought it might be better for your wrist to have the water hot to bathe it in; that's just from the spring, and I walked fast." In spite of the unvarnished speech, there was something about the man that made it plain to her why people involuntarily spoke of him as "the gentleman," when his partner was always spoken of merely as his partner.

It was only common politeness that she should allow him to sit on the door-step, while she immersed the soft, white hand; and the bottle of hot spring water was repeated, till she declared the ground dry enough to walk down to the spring with him. Any number of necks were stretched from parlor-doors and windows, when the shy, bashful gentleman from Siskiyou was seen escorting Mrs. Clayton; but falling in with a train of ladies at the Springs, they all walked back together. Mr. Brodie, unnoticed apparently by Jenny, and uncomfortable among so many of the "contrary sex," quietly slipped away under the shadow of a clump of young trees, where he was joined directly by his partner, who had watched him uneasily all the morning.

It was a warm, cloudless day, a few weeks later, and Mrs. Clayton had not joined the picnic party—because, Ben. Brodie said to himself, with a flutter of his unsophisticated heart, *he* had felt too unwell in the morning to go. Going down to the Springs alone, Jenny met his partner, and asked pleasantly whether Mr. Brodie had yet recovered from his attack of last night.

"Thank you, Miss, he's better; but it's my opinion as how he'd get well much quicker if he left these Springs and went down to 'Frisco for a spell."

"But, Mr. Perkins, his liver is affected; and these waters are said to be very beneficial."

"Yes, Miss, it *was* his liver; but I think as how it's in

the chist now; and "—doggedly aside —" mebbee the heart, too; and he'll never be himself again while he's up here."

"Oh, you must not see things so black. See, there comes Mr. Brodie now."

"Yes—" something like an oath was smothered between the bearded lips, and the shaggy eyebrows were lowered portentously—"so I see. Ben, did n't I tell yer to stay in the house, and I'd fetch yer the water?"

Whenever Si Perkins addressed Jenny as "Miss"— which was almost invariably his custom — it made her think of a short conversation between Mr. Brodie and herself, soon after their first acquaintance. He had asked her, with an assumed indifference, but a nervous tremor in his voice, "And you are a widow, Mrs. Clayton?" upon which she had turned sharply and said, snappishly, "Would I be away up here all alone if I had a husband?" It flashed through her mind again, as she saw the partner's darkened brow and working lips when Mr. Brodie answered, "It's all right, Si; I wanted to come;" and he laughed a short, confused laugh that stood for any number of unexpressed sentiments — particularly when Jenny was by.

"Shall we walk up toward the garden?" he asked of Jenny.

"I think there is shade all the way up," she replied, throwing an uneasy look on Si Perkins's scowling face. "You may light your cigar, if you feel well enough to smoke." Mr. Brodie turned to his partner to ask for a match, and the next moment left him standing alone in the sun, as though he had no more existence for him.

They halted many times on their way to the garden. It was in an opposite direction from the Springs; but here as there the road had been partly cut out on the mountain-side — partly filled in — so that it formed a terrace overhanging the dense forest-growth in the ravine below, while on the banks and mountain-tops above grew pines and madrones, the manzanite shrub and treacherous gloss of the poison-oak making the whole look like a carefully planted park. The "garden" was a little mountain valley, taking its name from an enclosed patch, where nothing was grown, but where the neglected fields were kept fresh and green by the little rivulet flowing from the cold spring at the foot of an immense sycamore. Farther on were groups of young oaks, and under these were benches; but Jenny preferred sitting in the shade of the pines on the clean, sweet grass. The birds, never molested here, hovered fearlessly about them, singing and chirping, the blue and yellow butterflies keeping time to the music.

For quite a while Mr. Brodie had been watching Jenny's lithe figure darting hither and thither, trying to take the butterflies prisoners under her hat; her eyes sparkled, and she shouted merrily whenever she had secured a prize, which, after a moment's triumph, she always set free again.

"Come and sit down," called Mr. Brodie to her, "or you will hurt your hand again, and all my three weeks' doctoring will be thrown away."

"It hurts me now," said Jenny, ruefully, "for I struck it against that tree."

She held up the offending hand, and he inspected it narrowly, looking up suddenly into her eyes, as though to read in them an answer to something he had just thought. But it was hard to read anything there, though Jenny had the sweetest eyes in the world—laughing and sad by turns, and of warm liquid light. What their color was, it was hard to determine. They had been called black, hazel, gray; never blue. Her smile was as unfathomable as her eyes; and you could read nothing of her life, her history, her character, from either brow or lip. Her hand alone—it was the right one—as it rested on the sward beside her, might have told to one better versed in such reading than Ben Brodie, how, like Theodore Storm's "Elizabeth," it had, "through many a sleepless night, been resting on a sore, sick heart."

He raised the hand tenderly, not understanding its secret, and asked, stroking it as we do a child's, "What was my partner saying to you as I came up a while ago?"

"He wants you to go to San Francisco, away from here. Would you go and leave me here alone, when you know how lonesome I should be without you?"

She heard his low, nervous laugh, as he moved uneasily, and held the hand tighter; but when she looked up into his face, expecting an answer, it came in his usual abrupt, or, as Jenny said, "jerky" style.

"No, of course I wouldn't go. I'll stay as long as you want me to. I — I — like you — pretty well."

Jenny's paling cheek blazed up crimson, and she looked fairly aghast as she repeated mechanically, "'Like you pretty well.' Thank you. *Like* me, indeed!" She had drawn away her hand, like a pettish child, and she muttered, a wicked smile breaking over her face, "I don't believe the man *could* love any one if he tried. But I'll find out;" and she turned again to where he sat, disconsolate at the loss of her hand.

Her quicker ear caught the crackling of dry twigs before he could speak again, and a shrill scream burst from her lips. He was on his feet in an instant, and flung his arms about the trembling form before his eye could follow the direction of hers.

"The bear!" she stammered; "the grizzly — there, there!" and the story of the huge grizzly having been seen in the mountains those last weeks flashed through his mind.

"Be still!" he said, as she glided from his arms to the ground; "he cannot hurt you till he has killed me." He stooped to pick up a fallen branch, and as he did so his eyes came on a level with a large black calf, rolling over and over in the tall grass. He flung the stick from him with a disgusted "Pshaw!" and Jenny dropped her hands from her eyes when his laugh fell on her ear. She joined in the laugh, though hers sounded a little hysterical; and then insisted on returning immediately, and his promise to keep the tragi-comic *intermezzo* a profound secret.

Days passed before Jenny would venture out again; and poor Mr. Brodie wandered about like one lost, dreading to visit the cottage, because of a sudden indescribable reserve of the fair tenant, yet held as by invisible hands in the nearest neighborhood of the place. One day, sitting with blinds closed and a headache, ready for an excuse to all who should come to tempt her out, Jenny missed the tall form passing shyly by the door half a dozen times per diem. The next morning she met Si Perkins — by the merest accident, of course, on her part — coming from the spring with a bottle of water.

"Is Mr. Brodie sick?" she asked, quickly.

"Yes, Miss; he was took bad night before last; but he's better," he added, anxious to prevent — he hardly knew what.

"Very well; you may tell Mr. Brodie that I am coming to see him and read to him this afternoon." She spoke determinedly, almost savagely, as though she anticipated finding Si Perkins at the door with drawn sword, ready to dispute the entrance.

She was shocked to find Mr. Brodie so pale and thin as he lay on the bed that afternoon; and Si Perkins, in a tone that seemed to accuse her of being the cause, said, "I told you it was his chist, Miss; he's getting powerful weak up here in the mountains, and yit he won't go down."

She was an angel while he was too sick to leave his room, sitting by him for hours, reading to him in her soft child's voice, and speaking to him so gently and tenderly that he felt a better, and oh! so much happier a man when he first walked out beside her again.

Then there came a day when Ben Brodie stopped at the cottage of his kind nurse, and with the air of a culprit asked Jenny to come with him, "away up into the mountains." The light that flashed in her eyes a moment was quenched by something that looked strangely like a tear, as she turned to reach for her hat. It was early afternoon, and most people were still in their cottages, with blinds, and perhaps eyes too, closed. The two walked slowly, or climbed rather, resting often and looking back to where they could see the white cottages blinking through the trees. The wind blew only enough to rustle the pine branches, without stirring the sobs and wails that lay dormant in those trees. Jays and woodpeckers went with them, and many a shining flower was broken by the way. At last Jenny stopped and looked around.

"Don't let us go farther — who knows but what we may encounter another bear?" she said roguishly; and he prepared a soft seat for her under the pines, by pulling handfuls of grass and heaping it up in one place.

She smiled to herself as she watched him; his awkwardness had left him, and for the comfort of one whom he only "liked pretty well," he was taking a great deal of pains, she thought. When she was seated, and had made him share the grass seat, the restraint suddenly returned, and he fell to stroking her hand again, and stammered something about her wrist being better.

"Yes," she affirmed, "and I mean to return to the city in a day or two."

He blushed like a girl. "May I go with you?" he asked; and then jumped at once into the midst of a "declaration" — which had evidently been gotten by heart — winding up by asking again, "and now may I go with you to San Francisco, Jenny? and will you marry me?"

Her eyes had been fixed on the lone bare crag away off across the valley; and the color in them had changed from light gray to deep black, and had faded again to a dull heavy gray.

"You may go to San Francisco, of course, though I shall not see you there. And 'I like you pretty well,' too;-but you must not dare to dream that I could ever marry you."

A little linnet in the tree above them had hopped from branch to branch, and now sat on the lowest, almost facing them. When Jenny's voice, stone-cold and harsh, had ceased, he broke into a surprised little chirp, and then uttered quick, sharp notes of reproof or remonstrance. Jenny understood either the language of the bird, or what the wild, startled eyes looking into hers said, for the hand that had lain in his was tightly clinched beside her, telling a tale she would not let her face repeat.

When the lamp had been lighted in her cottage that night, she stood irresolute by the window from where she could see the Brodie-Perkins habitation. On her way to the dining-room she had come unawares on Si Perkins instructing a waiter to bring tea to their cottage; and though she had asked no question, her eyes had rested wistfully on the partner's stern face. Now she paced the room, her face flushed, her hands clasped above her aching head, then dropped again idle and nerveless by her side.

"It is too late," she said, at last; "and it can never, never be. Then why make myself wretched over it?" and with a sudden revulsion of feeling she raised the curtain and looked steadily over to the other cottage. "It is only the law of reprisals, after all, Ben Brodie! To be sure *you* did not break my heart — but — that other man — and — you are all men." Her voice had died to a whisper; and, drawing writing material toward her at the table, she was in the midst of her letter before the vengeful light died out of her eyes. Once she laid her head on her arm and sobbed bitterly; but she finished the letter, closed and directed it, and turned down the light so that she could not be seen going from the cottage. The night air was damp and chilly, and before descending the three wooden steps that led from the little stoop to the ground, her unsteady hand sought the dress-pocket to drop her letter in; and then she drew the shawl and hood close about her.

She shuddered the next morning, as she threw a last look back into the room from which her trunk and baggage had already been taken, and she muttered something about the dreariness of an empty room and an empty heart. But when her numerous dear friends came to the stage to bid a last farewell, Jenny's face looked so radiant that many a one turned with secret envy from the woman to whom life must seem like one continuous holiday. Si Perkins, with eyebrows drawn deep down, was attentively studying a newspaper by the open window of the reading-room; and when Jenny threw a look back from the stage, she fancied that a trembling hand was working at the blinds of the two partners' cottage; and the sallow, ghastly face, and wild, startled eyes of yesterday, rose up reproachfully before her.

The day dragged slowly on; "from heat to heat" the sun had kissed the tree-tops with its drowsy warmth, hushing to sleep the countless birds that make the mountain-side their home. With the cool of evening came the low breeze that shook the sleepers from repose, and sighed sadly, sadly through the pines.

"Has the stage come in?" asked Ben Brodie slowly, as he lay with closed eyes and feverish brow on his bed in the cottage.

"Nearly an hour ago," answered Si Perkins, in his growling voice. He had tried hard to maintain his usual key, but his eyes rested with deep concern on his friend's face as he spoke.

"And was there any one in the stage whom you knew?"

"No one."

The sick man opened his eyes, and closed them again wearily. His lips worked spasmodically for an instant; then he asked resolutely, but in an almost inaudible tone, "Did not *she* come back, Si? Are you sure? Did you see all the passengers?"

"It's no use, Ben; she's gone, and she'll never come back."

"But, Si"— the quivering lips could hardly frame the words — "have you been to her cottage? I had not asked you to look, you know; but will you go to her room now, and see if she has not come back?"

Without a word Si took his hat, his lips twitching almost as perceptibly as Ben Brodie's. When he had reached the door the sick man said, "You are not mad, Si, are you? Have patience with me; I shall be better — so much better — soon, and then you will forgive me."

Si turned and held the feverish hand a moment, muttering that he'd go to — a very hot place if his partner bade him, and then left the room.

Though he knew the utter folly of such a proceeding, he went to the vacant cottage, and peered through the open blind into the vacant room. There was something so death-like and still about the place that he turned with heavy heart and eyes bent down to the three steps that led from the stoop to the ground. Something white shimmered up out of the crevice between the stoop and the first step, and he bent down, saying to himself, "If it's only a scrap of paper, Ben is spoony enough to want it, and kiss it mebbee, because it was hers."

The dampness of the past night had saturated the paper, and drying again in the sun, a portion of the letter — for such it proved to be — adhered to the board as Si attempted to draw it out. The letter unfolded itself, and fluttered lightly before Si's face, who bestowed a blessing on the "cobweb" paper, and then doggedly sat down to read what was written on it. His shaggy eyebrows seemed to grow heavier as he read, and his face turned a livid brown and then red again. When he had finished, he threw a hasty look over toward their cottage, and crushing the letter in fierce but silent wrath, he dropped the wad into his pocket and slowly retraced his steps.

"She has n't come?"

If Ben had moved from his bed during Si's absence, the latter did not notice any derangement of furniture or bedclothes, and he now dropped heavily into a chair beside his friend's bed.

"When you get well, old fellow, we must go."

"Where? To San Francisco?"

"San Francisco be ——. No; to Siskiyou."

There was no response. The fever had gone down, and Ben lay pale and still, like a corpse almost, except that his fingers seemed striving to touch something which evaded his grasp. The wind had grown stronger, and on it came borne the notes of the grossbeak, who strays down from the mountaintops in the evening, and makes those who hear him think of home, of absent friends, and of all we hold dearest, and all who have gone from us farthest in this world.

"How mournfully the wind sings!" said Ben, softly. "It seems like her voice calling to me. But I will never see her again —. She could not think of me as I did of her. I would lay down my life for her; but she could only like me a little. She was too good for me."

"Ben, Ben! I can't bear to hear you talk so. Oh! that wicked, wicked woman!"

"Hush, Si; she was an angel; and when I was sick she taught me to pray." The gaunt hand that had been raised as if to ward off the harsh words his partner would say, fell back on his breast, where he laid it across the other. "Our Father who art in heaven—" The fingers stiffened, and the heavy lids sank over the weary eyes.

"Ben, old pard, look at me! Speak to me!" He bent over the motionless form, and laid his hand caressingly on the wiry black hair. "Don't you leave me alone in the world." The trembling hand glided down to his friend's breast and laid itself over the heart. But the heart stood still; and as he drew back his hand, it touched a cold, smooth object that fell to the floor. He stooped, and lifted a small vial to the light, and as he did so a great scalding tear fell on the label, just where the word "Poison" was traced in large letters.

When Si Perkins returned to the Placer Mines, on Yreka Flats, he brought with him only two articles which he seemed to consider of value. They were always kept under lock and key. The one was a small vial, with the word "Poison" on the label, blurred and blotted; the other a letter, carefully smoothed out, after having been, to all appearances, cruelly crushed and crumpled.

The letter ran thus:

"HOT SPRINGS, June 28.

"DEAR JIM: I am coming home, and may be in San Francisco even before this reaches you, unless I should be seized with a notion to remain in San José, or visit the Warm Springs, or the Mission. My wrist is not strong yet; and to tell you the truth, only 'the persecutions of a man' are driving me away from here. I can see you laugh, and hear you saying, 'At your old tricks, Jenny.' But though I shall recount the whole affair to you when we meet, I shall not allow you to laugh at the discomfiture of the gentleman from Siskiyou. He is so terribly in earnest; and—oh! I remember but too well the blow you struck my heart when you first told me that you could never belong to me; that I could never be your lawful wife. But I don't mean to grow sentimental. You may please issue orders to Ah Sing and Chy Lun to 'set my house in order,' and look for me any time between this and the 'glorious Fourth.'   JENNY."

SOMETHING ABOUT MY PETS.

MANY a bitter tear they have cost me — the different pets I have had: not their possession, but their loss, which followed as inevitably as fate, and as surely as day follows night. As far as my recollection goes back, my four-footed friends have occupied prominent places in my affections, and have eventually become the cause of great sorrow. The first doubt I ever felt of the justice and humanity of the world in general, and my kinsfolk in particular, was because of the cruel death of my favorite dog, Arno, who had been given away after my older brother's death, to a family who had more use and room for a large hunting-dog than my widowed mother.

At first, he refused utterly to stay with his new master; but when he found that the doors of his old home were steadfastly closed against him, he would lie in wait for me as I went to school; and on my way home in the afternoon, he would always follow me, drawing back his nose and fore-paws only in time to prevent their being pinched in by the sharp-shutting gate, and looking wistfully through the paling with his big, honest eyes. Perhaps my elders did not understand "dog-language" as I did; but I knew that Arno fully appreciated the feeling which led me to throw my arms around his neck and weep bitter, childish tears on his brown head; and he felt comforted by my sympathy, I am sure, for he would lick my hands, and wag his long-haired tail with a little joyous whine, before trotting back to the broad stone steps in front of his new master's house. But night always found him under my chamber window, which looked out on a narrow lane, used as a thoroughfare; and here I could hear his deep-mouthed bark all night long, as he kept fancied marauders and real dogs from encroaching on our premises and his self-chosen battle-ground. For he met his death here, at last.

He had become quite aged; and the other dogs of the neighborhood had frequently made common cause against him, for blocking up (to them) the passage in the lane, but had never yet been able to rout him. One night, however, they attacked him with overpowering numbers, and punished him so severely that it was found to be necessary, or, at least, merciful, the next morning, to send a bullet through his head and end his misery. To me this all seemed terribly cruel, and I cried wildly, and sobbed out my reproaches against everybody for having left him to lie out in the street at night, instead of allowing him a safe shelter in the house. I refused to be comforted, or adopt any other dog in his place; but bestowed my affection and caresses impartially on all the stray dogs and horses that happened to cross my path.

Some time after I was married, a little spotted dog, of no particular breed, sought shelter from the rain on the basement-steps, one day, and refused to "tramp" when the shower was over. She was a short-legged, smooth-haired little thing, with the brightest eyes I ever saw in a dog's head. Tiny soon became my pet, and amply repaid us for the food and shelter we had given her. She learned everything, and with such ease, that I sometimes suspected I had taken into my family one who had formerly been a public circus performer. She could stand on her hind legs and beg for an apple or a piece of sugar; she could find and fetch a hidden handkerchief, glove, or cap; she could jump through a hoop, and could pick out from among a lot of articles the shawls, comforters, or hats belonging to myself, or any member of the family. On the approach of a buggy to the house, she would rush to the window, and if she recognized it as the captain's, would scratch and whine till I opened the door for her, in sheer self-defence. Dashing up to the buggy, she would wag her tail with such vehemence as threatened to upset her little round body — begging in this way for a glove, or the long buggy-whip, to drag into the house.

Tiny also knew the name of the different members of the family, whether they occupied the same house with us, or only came on visits. If mother came on a visit, for instance, I could send Tiny from the kitchen with a key, a paper, or anything she could carry, and on my order, "Give it to mother," she would carry it to the parlor, or wherever mother might be, and lay it carefully in her lap, or on the sofa beside her. On the order, "Kiss the captain," she would immediately dart at that gentleman, and, if he ever so artfully avoided her little tongue for the time being, she would watch the first opportunity to climb into his lap, or jump on to a piece of furniture, to execute the command.

Soon after Tiny's advent, a young stag-hound was given to the captain, and him she took under her wing, though in size he could boast of three times her own volume. Dick, I am very sorry to own, was not so well treated as Tiny; and I smite my breast even now, and say very penitently, "*mea culpa*," when I think of how I hurt him, one day. I was lying on the sofa, half asleep from the heat and the exertion of cutting the leaves of a new magazine. Presently, Dick approached, and before I could open my eyes, or ward him off, he had jumped on the sofa and settled full on my head and face. Angry and half-stifled, I flung the dog with all my might to the floor, where he set up such a pitiful crying, that I knew he must be seriously hurt. Jumping up, I saw him, quite a distance from the sofa, holding up his foreleg, on which his paw was dangling in a loose, out-of-place manner. Comprehending what I had done, I carried him into the next room, and poured the basin full of water, in which I held his paw; and then bound rags on the dislocated limb, steeping the paw into the water occasionally, to keep down the swelling till the captain should come. Sorry as I felt for having inflicted such pain on the poor animal, it was a perfect farce to watch his proceedings, and I had laughed till my sides ached before the captain got home. It so happened that mother and one or two other near friends came in during the course of the day. As soon as any one entered the room, Dick, who had been allowed to take up his quarters on a blanket in the sitting-room, would hobble up, hold out his rag-wrapped paw, and, elevating his nose, would utter heart-rending cries of pain, thus "passing his hat for a pennyworth of sympathy," as unmistakably as I have known human beings to do many a time before. Then, with cries and grimaces, he would induce the beholder to follow him pityingly into the next room, where he would immerse his foot in the water, as I had made him do, once or twice. During this performance Tiny would keep close behind him, and with little sympathetic whines, would echo all his cries and complainings; and this show was repeated whenever they could get a fresh spectator.

At the same time, we had in our possession a horse, which, for sagacity, kindness, and docility, outshone all the horses I have ever had the fortune to become acquainted with. Not the most partial admiration of Kitty's many virtues could lead me into believing her to be beautiful, though she was by no means an ugly horse. A bright bay, with well-shaped head, she was too short-bodied, though the long legs seemed to lay claim to an admixture of English blood. Kitty was a saddle-nag as well as buggy-horse, and the captain always chose her when he had a fatiguing ride to take; though, for my part, I should have scorned to be seen mounted on an ugly, stump-tailed thing like her.

This is ingratitude, however; I have never had a more devoted friend than Kitty. She was assigned to the duty of taking me out to "mother's house," where she was always well pleased to go, for I used to take her out of the harness and let her run loose under the orchard trees. I have never met with a horse so expert at picking apples as she was; she never injured the trees, and seemed always to know exactly which were the best "eating apples." When the time came to go home, Kitty, like a sensible, grateful horse, was always on hand; the only trouble was to get her back into harness again — it generally being just milking-time then, and I never liked to admit to any of the men that I could not harness a horse as well as saddle it. So, it often happened that, after I got on the road, Kitty would stop short and refuse to go a step farther. Whipping would do no good on such occasions; she would only switch her tail, stamp her foot impatiently, and turn her head around, as if to say: "Don't you know that I have good reasons for acting so?" On throwing down the lines, and examining the harness, I would be sure to find that some buckle had been left unfastened, or some strap was dragging under her feet. One day a soldier came to my assistance, and he said it was the greatest wonder in the world that the horse had not kicked the buggy to pieces, for I had fastened a buckle on the wrong side, and with every step she took the buckle had pressed sorely into poor Kitty's flesh. I could appreciate Kitty's good behavior all the more for having seen her kick dashboard and shafts to splinters, one day, when the captain drove her, and some part of the harness gave way.

The friendship, however, was reciprocal; for many a bucket of cool, fresh water, many a tea-tray full of oats, and many an apple and lump of sugar had Kitty received at my hands, when she stopped at the door, or was taken into the back yard, to await her master's leisure to ride. The saddle she liked best, for under it she could move about in the yard. She would follow me like a dog, and tried to make her way into the basement one day, where I had gone to get some grain for her. I always kept a sack of oats in the house, as we had no stable, and the horses were boarded at a stable down town; but Kitty would have gone without her dinner many a time had it not been for the "private feeds" I gave her, as the captain's opinion was that horses should not be "pampered and spoiled." Kitty knew how much I thought of her, and sometimes presumed on it, too. I have known her — at times, when the captain brought her into the yard late at night, previously to sending her to the stable — to set up such a whinnying, stamping, and snorting, that, to the captain's infinite amusement, I was compelled to leave my bed and take her a handful of oats or a piece of sugar. And on the street, if I met the captain mounted on or riding behind Kitty, she would instantly step on the sidewalk and make a dive for my pocket, to extract the apple she fancied concealed there. Moreover, she would allow Tiny to climb all over her back; but Dick she always greeted with a snort, and occasionally with a kick.

One day the captain furnished a valuable addition to the "happy family," without, in the least, intending to do so. It seems that just as he was leaving the house, he saw an open market-wagon, and on it two forlorn chickens broiling in the July sun. The man offered to sell him the chickens, so he bought them, threw them over the fence, and called to the servant to unfasten the string fettering the feet of the poor animals. His order was not heard; and I knew nothing of the existence of the chickens till Tiny's barking attracted my attention. There lay the two chickens, gasping and panting, and the dogs, like all little natures, exhibited great delight at being able to worry and distress the poor, defenceless creatures. I dragged the poor things into the shade, cut their fetters, and gave them "food and drink." One of the chickens was a gay-feathered rooster, the other, a plain-looking hen, who exhibited, however, by far the best sense, in this, that she did not struggle to get away from me as "fighting Billy" did, but allowed me to pass my hand over her soft dress, accompanying each stroke with a low crooning "craw-craw," as though wishing to express her satisfaction with her present position. When I thought the chickens were both safe and comfortable in the yard, I went back to my favorite resting-place — a soft rug, in front of the sitting-room fireplace. The summer was extraordinarily warm, and I had repeatedly wandered all over the house in search of the "coolest place," but had always returned to this. Not far from me was a window, from which the shutters were thrown back directly after noon, as there was shade then on this side of the house, and nearly opposite was a door leading to the vine-clad porch. Glad enough to pass a part of the hot afternoon in a *siesta*, I was surprised on waking, and stretching out my feet, to push against a soft, round ball; and the slow "craw-craw" I heard, caused me to start to a sitting posture. There, sure enough, was chicky, cuddled up close to my feet, repeating her monotonous song every time I deigned to take notice of her. I had never believed before that chickens had brains enough to feel affection or gratitude towards anybody; but I wish to state as an actual fact that chicky, as long as she was in my possession, never let a day pass that she did not come fluttering up the low steps to the porch and visit me in the sitting-room. During my regular *siesta* she was always beside me; and if I attempted to close the door against her, she would fly up to the window and come in that way. Indeed, she wanted to take up her roost there altogether; and it was only with great difficulty I could persuade her to remove to the back-yard.

Fighting Billy proved by no means so companionable as chicky: within the first week he had fought, single-handed, every rooster in the neighborhood, and the second week he staggered about the yard with his "peepers" closed, and showing general marks of severe punishment, from the effects of which he died, in spite of aught we could do for his relief.

But our "happy family" was broken up, after awhile: the captain was "called to the wars," and, in spite of all I could say, took Kitty with him, as the "most reliable horse." Kitty never returned; and I spent one whole day, during the captain's first visit home, in saying: "I told you so," and crying over Kitty's loss. Next, Tiny was stolen; and Dick went the way of most all "good dogs"—with our servant-girl's butcher-beau—at whose house I saw him, shortly after Babette's marriage, together with sundry lace-collars, table-cloths, and napkin-rings that had mysteriously left the house about the same time with her. Chicky disappeared the night before Thanksgiving day: perhaps they couldn't get any turkey to give thanks for, and contented themselves with a chicken.

When the captain next came home, he found nothing but a squirrel—but this squirrel was the greatest pet I had yet found. I came by it in this way: two small, ragged boys pulled the bell one day, and, seeing a little wooden cage in their hands, I went to the door immediately myself. How the little wretches knew of my silly propensity for collecting all vagabond, half-starved animals, I don't know; but they showed me a scraggy little squirrel in the cage, and said, with the utmost confidence, they wanted to sell it to me.

"How much do you want for it?" I asked.

"Two dollars," said the oldest, at a venture, and then opened his eyes in astonishment, as much at his own audacity as at my silence—which seemed to imply assent to his extortion.

You see, I had opened the cage, and bunny had slipped out, scrambled up on my arm, and lodged himself close around my neck, where he lay with his little head tucked under my chin. How could I let the little thing go? So I gave the boy his two dollars, for which he generously offered to leave the cage, which offer I declined, intending to make a house-dog of bunny. The sagacity, gentleness, and playfulness of little Fritz are beyond all description; though his bump of destructiveness, I must acknowledge, was also very largely developed. He was still young, and I could keep him on a window-sill quite safely, till I felt sure of his attachment to me, and his disinclination to make his escape. The window-sill and the open window remained his favorite post to the end of his life; though when he grew older, he would occasionally jump from my bed-room window, in the second story, to the grass and flower-beds below. He had not been in the house more than a week before he followed me about like a dog, and took his place close by me at the table, eating and drinking anything I had a mind to offer him. He drank coffee out of a cup, and ate the meat I gave him — holding it in his paws, as little children hold a strip of meat in their hands — nibbling and sucking it, with great gusto.

I cannot conceal that the wood work, the furniture, and all the books, throughout the house, soon displayed ragged edges and torn surfaces; and mother (who had taken up her abode with us), who punished Fritz for his depredations sometimes, was held in high disfavor by him, in consequence. When I was not at home, he would hardly allow her to touch him, and would hide under the pillows on my bed, at her approach, barking and scolding with great vehemence. To me he never said an "unkind word;" on the contrary, I could hardly secure myself from his caresses. Sometimes I would place him on the top of a tall cupboard, or high wardrobe, to get him away from under my feet; but the moment I passed anywhere within reaching-distance, he would fly down on me, and, settling on my hand, face, or shoulder, would fall to licking my face, and nibbling at my ears and nose, to assure me of his favor. I fear I have slapped him more than once for marking my face with his little sharp claws, when making one of these sudden descents. At night, he slept under my pillow; and early in the morning he would creep out, nibble at my eyelids, and switch me with his bushy tail. Without opening my eyes, I would reach out for a handful of nuts — opened and placed within reach the night before — and with these he would amuse himself for a long while, always cleaning his face and paws after disposing of his first breakfast. With sundown he went to sleep; but, of warm nights, when I went to bed late, I would carry his little drinking-cup to him, filled with ice-water. Half asleep, sometimes with his eyes closed, he would take a long drink; but never once, of all those nights, did he return to his pillow without first gratefully passing his little tongue over the hand that held him. That he knew it was my hand, I am quite certain; for if the captain ever attempted to touch him, in the middle of the night, when Fritz was ever so sound asleep, he would immediately start up with a snarl, and snap at the captain's fingers; whereas, if I thrust my hand under the pillow, in the dead of night, he would lick it, and rub his nose against it.

With nothing but a little basket to carry him in, I took him with me for a journey, on a Mississippi steamer. I left him in the basket, while looking after my baggage; but when I returned to my state-room, he suddenly jumped on my head from above, having eaten his way out, through the lid of the basket, and climbed to the top-berth. The stewardess on the steamer tried to steal him, when near port, but Fritz had made such good use of his sharp claws and teeth that she was fain to own: "She had on'y wanted to *tech* the lilly bunny — hadn't wanted to hurt 'm, 't all."

It makes me sad, even now, to think of the closing scene of Fritz's short, but, let me hope, happy life. Once a lady, the mother of a terrible little boy, had come to spend the day with us; and I soon discovered that either Fritz or the little boy must be caged "up and away." So, pretending to be afraid that the boy might get hurt, but in reality fearing only for Fritz's welfare, I carried the squirrel up into the lumber-room, where I brought to him nuts without number, apples, sugar, crackers, and water to bathe in and drink from. There was a pane broken out of the window-sash, but this I covered with a piece of paste-board, and then went down to entertain the lady and her detestable little boy. Seated at the window, not long after, I saw an urchin come running around the next corner, and, when barely within speaking distance, he shouted at the top of his voice: "Say, Missis, they's got him, 'round here in the cooper-yard, and he's dead — the squirrel!" he added, in explanation.

Though by no means in a toilet representing a "street-dress"—in fact, with only one slipper on—I started off on a run, and never stopped till my youthful mentor pointed to a circle of men and boys, gathered around an object lying on the ground. It was Fritz, writhing in the last agonies of death, while the boys were calling each other's attention to the contortions of the poor little body. In a moment, I was among them, had lifted Fritz in my arms, and held him to my face.

"Who did that?" I asked, with pain and anger struggling in my heart; "which of you little brutes killed the poor, harmless thing?"

The little ragamuffin who had led me to the spot, pointed to two boys making ineffectual attempts to hide a long stick, they were carrying, behind them.

"They was a-hitting 'm like fury, and then I runned to tell you; please, Missis, gimme a dime."

Poor little Fritz! He knew me, even in the death-struggle; for he passed his tongue over my hand once more, just before the last convulsive shudder ran through his body, and his little limbs grew stiff and cold. I don't feel, in the least, ashamed to own that I cried — cried many tears — cried bitterly; and I felt dreadfully lonesome when I woke up at night, and, from the sheer force of habit, put my hand under my pillow without finding Fritz there. I made a vow then never to have any more pets; but it was a rash one.

Some years later, when the war was over, the "theatre of our life" was to be shifted from the crowded, populous city to the lonely wilds of the frontier country. When we reached Fort Leavenworth, the quarters in the barracks were all occupied, and a number of our officers were assigned quarters in the Attaché Barracks. The captain had decided to purchase a horse from the government stables, and turn him over to me for saddle-use, as I did not want to go to our frontier-post without a horse of my own to depend on. It was in June; and the little square yards in front of the Attaché Barracks were fresh and sweet with grass and blossoming red clover. The door of our quarters stood open; the captain had gone out, and I was startled by a knock on the door-post. Looking up, I saw the head of an orderly appearing at the door; but, poking over his head, I saw that of a horse evidently taking a strict inventory of everything in the room. Of course, I was at the door, and on the horse's neck, in the course of a very few seconds, for, from the orderly, I soon understood that the captain had sent the horse for me to look at. Colonel L——, with his two little girls, came up just then, and, as we were all going in the same command, the acquisition of a horse for the march had an interest for all parties. Together, we surrounded and admired the beautiful white animal; and the two little girls and myself were soon braiding clover-blossoms into Toby's tail, and trimming his head and neck with garlands of butter-cups — operations which did not, in the least, interfere with his good humor, or his appetite for the juicy grass he was cropping. The captain, it seems, had already tried his speed and mettle; he was not appraised at at any unreasonable figure, and so Toby was mine before we took up the line of march for the Plains.

From the wagon-master I heard, later, that Toby had been captured in Texas, during the war. He had been raised and trained by a woman who had followed him around the country for some time, trying to get her pet back again; but Uncle Sam, no doubt, had the best right to him, and he was placed in the stables of the Fitting-out Depot. One thing certainly spoke for the truth of the story: whenever Toby had been let loose and refused to be tied up again, he would always allow me to come up to him, when he would turn and throw up his heels at the approach of a man.

Toby was soon a universal favorite and proved himself worthy of the preference, though he had one or two tricks about him that were by no means commendable. First: he was an inveterate thief; and then — at times when he was not ridden, but led along by the orderly — he had a mean way of lying back and letting the other horse pull him along, that fairly exasperated me. His thefts, however, were always carried out in such a cunning manner that I readily forgave the sin for the sake of the skill. We had not been long on the march when Toby perpetrated his first robbery. The captain rode him, and when the command halted for lunch, he would come up to our ambulance, dismount, and let Toby go perfectly free — for we had soon found that he would not stray from the command. Toby learned to know the contents and appliances of lunch-baskets very soon, particularly as he received his portion from ours regularly every day. One day, after having dispatched his bread-and-butter and lump of sugar in the neighborhood of our ambulance, he walked over to Colonel L——'s, and while Mrs. L—— was leaning out on the other side, speaking to the colonel, Toby quietly lifted the lunch-basket from her lap, deposited it on the grass, overturned it, and helped himself to the contents. Unfortunately for Toby, Mrs. L—— had spread mustard on her ham-sandwiches, and the sneezing and coughing of the erring horse first called her attention to his presence, and the absence of her lunch-basket.

Not long after, we made camp very early in the day, and the major's folks came to fill a long-standing promise to take tea with us, and spend the evening at our tent. The visit passed off very pleasantly, and an engagement was made to return it at an early day. Toby, who was prowling about the tent, no doubt overheard the conversation, and felt it incumbent on him to fill the engagement as soon as possible. Consequently, he stationed himself near the major's tent-fly the very next morning, and paid close attention to the preparations going on for tea; and just as the cook had put the finishing-touch to the table, and had stepped back to call the family and set the tea and the meats on the table, Toby gravely walked up, swallowed the butter with one gulp, upset the sugar-bowl, gobbled up the contents, and proceeded leisurely to investigate the inside of a tin jelly-can. The soldiers, who had watched his manœuvres from a distance, had been too much charmed with the performance to give warning to the cook; but when he made his appearance, meat-dish and tea-pot in hand, they gave such a shout as set the whole camp in an uproar, and Toby was fairly worshipped by the soldiers from that day out.

But the faithfulness and patience of the horse, in time of need, made me forgive him all these tricks. Months later— when still on the march, in the most desolate wilderness, in the midst of the pathless mountains, when other horses "gave up the ghost," and were shot at the rate of a dozen a day— Toby held out, carrying me on his back, day after day, night after night, till his knees trembled with fatigue and faintness, and he turned his head and took my foot between his teeth, at last, to tell me he could carry me no farther! Not once, but a dozen times, has he repeated this manœuvre; once, too, when we were coming down a very steep hill, he planted his forefeet down firmly, turned his head, and softly bit the foot I held in the stirrup, to tell me that I must dismount.

The most singular devotion of one horse to another, I witnessed while out in New Mexico. The captain found it necessary to draw a saddle-horse for his own use, and selected one from a number which the volunteers had left behind. It had been half-starved latterly, and was vicious, more from ill-treatment than by nature. The first evening when it was brought to our stable, it kicked the orderly so that he could not attend to the horses next morning, and the cook had to look after them. I went into the stable to bring Toby a tit-bit of some kind, and here found that Copp (the new horse) was deliberately eating the feed out of Toby's trough. The cook called my attention to it, and explained that the horse had done the same thing last night; and on interfering, the orderly had been viciously kicked by the animal. I reached over to stroke the creature's mane, but the cook called to me to stop, holding up his arm to show where the horse had bitten him. I went quickly back into the tent, got a large piece of bread, and held it out to Copp. In an instant he had swallowed it, and had fallen back on Toby's feed again, without meeting with the least opposition from that side. Toby evidently had better sense, and more charity, than the men had shown; he knew that the horse was half-starved, and wicked only from hunger.

If I had never believed before that horses were capable of reasoning, and remembering kind actions, Copp's behavior toward Toby would have converted me. Often, when out on timber-cutting or road-making excursions, I accompanied the captain, and, mounted on Toby, would hold Copp by the bridle or picket-rope, so as to allow the orderly to participate in the pleasures of the day. The grass was rich up in the mountains, and Toby would give many a tug at the bridle to get his head down where he could crop it; this, however, had been forbidden by the captain, once for all, and Toby was compelled to hold his head up in the proper position. Copp, however, was allowed to crop the grass; but he never ate a mouthful, of which he did not first give Toby half! Sometimes he would go off as far as the bridle would reach, gather up a large bunch in his mouth, and then step back to Toby and let him pull his share of it out from between his teeth. But no other horse dare approach Toby in Copp's sight. I have seen him jump quite across the road for the purpose of biting a horse that was rubbing his nose against Toby's mane in a friendly manner. One day we met a party of disappointed gold-hunters, who were anxious to dispose of a little, light wagon they had. The captain bought it, thinking to break Toby and Copp to harness. Toby took to his new occupation kindly enough, but Copp could only be made to move in his track when I stood at a distance and called to him. He would work his way up to me with a wild, frightened air; but the moment I was out of his sight, neither beating nor coaxing could induce him to move a step.

But — dear me — those horses have taken up my thoughts so completely, that I have almost exhausted this paper without speaking of the other pets I have had. The horned toad could never make its way into my good graces; nor the land-turtle, neither, after it had once "shut down" on my dog Tom's tail. They were both abolished by simply leaving them on the road. The prairie-dog refused to be tamed, but ran away, the ungrateful wretch, with collar, chain, and all; a living wonder, no doubt, to his brethren in the prairie-dog village, through which we were passing at the time.

But my mink, Max, was a dear little pet. He was given me by a soldier at Fort Union, and had been captured on the Pecos River, near Fort Sumner. He was of a solid, dark-brown color, and the texture of his coat made it clear at once why a set of mink-furs is so highly prized by the ladies. His face was anything but intelligent; yet he was as frisky and active as any young mink need be. It was while we were still on the march, that Max took his place in the ambulance by me as regularly as day came. When we made camp in the afternoon, he was allowed to run free, and when it grew dark, I would step to the tent-door, call "Max! Max!" and immediately he would come dashing up, uttering sounds half-chuckle, half-bark, as if he were saying: "Well, well — ain't I coming as fast as I can?"

On long days' marches he would lie so still in the ambulance, that I often put out my hand to feel whether he was beside me; and wherever I happened to thrust my fingers, his mouth would be wide open to receive them, and a sharp bite would instantly apprise me of his whereabouts. He had his faults, too — serious faults — and one of them, I fear, led to his destruction. Travelling over the plains of New Mexico, in the middle of summer, is no joking matter, for man or mink, and a supply of fresh, cool water, after a hot day's march, is not only desirable, but necessary. But it is not always an easy matter to get water; and I have known the men to go two or three miles for a bucketful. Getting back to camp weary and exhausted, they would naturally put the bucket in the only available place — on the ground; and the next moment, Max, who was always on hand for his share of it, would suddenly plunge in and swim "'round and 'round" in pursuit of his tail — choosing to take his drink of water in this manner, to the great disgust of the tired men.

Company "B" was still with us at this time, and the tent of the company commander was pitched not far from ours. Sergeant Brown, of this company, was in possession of a dozen or two of chickens; and these, I suspect, were the cause of the mink's death. Like all animals out in the wilderness, the chickens could be allowed to run free, without ever straying away from their owner: there was thought to be no danger lurking near for them; but suddenly one or two were found with their throats torn open, and the blood sucked from their lifeless bodies. Max was accused, with the greater show of truth, as the cook of the lieutenant had caught him the next day rolling away an egg, which he had purloined from the lieutenant's stock of provisions. The cook, following Max, discovered that he had already three eggs hidden in the neighborhood of our tent. I grew alarmed for the safety of my pet, though I knew that the men of our company would not have harmed a hair of his brown, bear-like head.

One night I stepped to the tent-door to call Max; but no Max answered. The orderly was sent to look through the tents, as Max sometimes stopped with the men who showed any disposition to play with him — but he could not be found. I spent an uneasy night, calling "Max! Max!" whenever I heard the least noise outside the tent. Next morning I got up betimes, and as soon as I had swallowed my breakfast, went down toward the Rio Grande. The ground grew broken and rocky near the banks of the river, and I half thought he might have returned to his native element. I climbed to a point where I could see the river, and called "Max! Max!" but heard nothing in answer, save the rolling of a little stone I had loosened with my foot. "Max! Max!" I called again; but the dull roar of the water, where it surged lazily against the few exceptional rocks on the bank, was all I could hear. Going back to camp, I found the tents struck, the command moving, and the ambulance waiting for me. Wiping the tears from my face, I climbed in — shaking the blankets for the fiftieth time to see if Max had not mischievously hidden among them.

From a conversation I overheard long afterward, I concluded that Max had fallen a victim to Sergeant Brown's revengeful spirit — in fact, had been slaughtered in atonement for those assassinated chickens.

POKER-JIM.

TWO motherless girls, and only a brother a few years older left to protect them.

When the father died, the mother had turned the old homestead — for there *are* houses in San Francisco fifteen and twenty years old — into a source of revenue from which she provided for the children. The father had left nothing save debts—gambling debts—and the fraternity had not called on the widow to settle these. For her own existence she seemed to need nothing — absolutely nothing — but the caresses of her children, and the happiness and contentment mirrored in their eyes. When she died the girls were old enough, and competent, to look after the house, which the mother had made a pleasant home to many a "roomer" who had come a stranger to the city, had been badgered and harassed by flint-eyed, stony-hearted landladies, and had at last, by some good fortune, found his way into the precincts of the widow's cozy, quiet walls. The son had, through the influence of some of the roomers, obtained a position in a wholesale liquor establishment, where the salary was high, and — the temptation great.

That the two young girls should carry on the house just as their dying mother had left it to them, was something no one in San Francisco would think of commenting upon. And as the proverbial chivalry of the Californian would prompt him to suffer inconvenience and loss rather than to deprive women in any way thrown on his care or his protection, they missed only their mother's love and presence in the home, which remained home to them still. After a while the painful truth dawned on them that their brother was being weaned away from it. His evenings were now but seldom spent with them in the little sitting-room whose ivy-mantled bay-window looked out on the garden, where the flower-beds had moved closer up to the house as the lots became more valuable, and the orchard had been cut down to a few trees on the grass-plot.

At first the excuse was, that customers from the country, buying heavily of the firm, had a right to expect attentions not strictly of a business nature from him, its chief representative. Then his absence from home grew more protracted, and often midnight tolled from St. Mary's before his unsteady feet mounted the door-steps. One night, a lady, attracted to the balcony by an unusually brilliant moon, when she awoke from her midnight slumbers, wonderingly saw a carriage drive up to the house where the two sisters lay in peaceful sleep. She was too far off to see whether there was a number on the carriage, or what the number was. Neither could she distinguish the face of the driver, nor that of the gentleman who assisted another, whom she rightly judged to be Edward Ashburne, from the carriage into the house. That the face of the one who supported, or rather carried, young Edward, was deadly white, framed in by a heavy black beard, was all she could tell. "Poor girls!" she soliloquized; "better that the boy was dead than turn drunkard, and gamble, like his father."

The carriage drove off rapidly after the gentleman — who, as she thought, had helped Ned to the door and rang the bell — had re-entered it; and carriage-driver and ghostly-faced gentleman could never be found or heard of afterward.

What the neighbor-lady heard still further that same night was, first, the furious barking, then the doleful howling of the young Newfoundland dog, which the Misses Ashburne had recently "adopted," and, soon after, a wild, heart-rending cry.

"The horrid boy!" she continued, full of sympathy; "is he so beastly drunk? Could he have struck one of his sisters?"

Aye, good woman; struck them both a terrible blow, but not with his hand, for that lay powerless by his side. And the eyes were sightless that stared vacantly into their own, as they bent over him where he lay stretched out on the hall-floor — his coat folded under his head, his latch-key close at hand. Only a painful gasp answered their pitiful entreaties to "speak once more;" and before the sympathizing inmates of the stricken house could remove him to his bed, he had breathed his last.

"Beaten to a jelly," sententiously remarked one of the men, under his breath, to another, as they left the chamber to the sisters and the more intimate friends of the family.

"Some woman scrape — you can bet on that," was the response. And they joined the others in their efforts to discover the perpetrators of the dastard deed.

But no clue was found, and after a while San Francisco forgot the sisters and their sorrow; and one day, when the neighbor-lady told her ever-fresh story to a new-made acquaintance, she added: "And now they have gone, the poor girls, and nobody knows where."

From the balcony of the two-story frame hotel-building a young girl was watching the sunlight sinking behind the dimly-outlined range of the Coast Mountains. Perhaps her eyes roved so far away because the immediate surrounding of the hotel was not attractive; though the streets devoted to private residences of this little city — to which the railroad was fast making its way—were pleasing to the eye, and rather Southern in their features. The orange, ripening in one cluster with the fragrant blossom, as well as the tall-growing oleander, embowering cottage alike with mansion, spoke of oppressive weather in the summer, and promised glorious, balmy days during the short California winter.

Had the girl, at whose feet a large Newfoundland dog lay sleeping, stepped to the end of the balcony which ran along the whole length of the house, she could have followed the course of the Feather River, which but a short distance away mingled its clear waters with the muddy waves of the Yuba. But she was evidently not engaged in a study of the "lay of the land," though her eyes seemed to follow with some interest the direction of a particular road leading to the hotel. Directly she spoke to the dog, touching him lightly with her toe: "Cruiser, old dog, come, wake up, they are coming."

From out of the cloud of dust rolling up to the hotel emerged hacks and stages well filled with passengers, whom the railroad had brought from San Francisco to Yuba City, and who thus continued to this place and onward. Partly sheltered from sight by the boughs of a tree shading the balcony, the young girl leaned forward to scan the faces of the people who left hacks and coaches and hastened into the house to brush and wash off a little of the biting, yellowish dust clinging to them. It seemed to be a sort of pastime with the girl and her four-footed companion, this "seeing the people get in;" for she made remarks and observations on the looks and manners of people which the dog seemed fully to understand, for he would reply, sometimes with a wag of his bushy tail, sometimes with a short, sharp bark, and then again with a long yawn of *ennui*. Almost the last passenger who alighted was a gentleman whose large black eyes and raven hair would have thrilled the bosom of any miss of sixteen—as, indeed, they startled our young friend, although she might have been two or three years above and beyond that interesting age. The bough that she had drawn down to screen herself behind, sprang up with a sudden snap, which caused the upturning of a pale and rather severe face, from which looked those black eyes with a grave, rather than sad, expression. A sudden thought or memory — she did not know which — shot through her brain as her eyes looked down into his; it was only a flash, but it made her think of her childhood, of her mother — she hardly knew of what.

"Cruiser, old dog," she said; but the dog had squeezed his head under the railing as far as he could get it, as if making a desperate attempt to get a nearer look at the stranger. When he drew his head back he raised himself, laid his forepaws on the railing, and looked hard into the girl's face, with a low, questioning whine. "It's nothing, old boy; you don't know him. Come, now, we'll see if we can help Julia about the house."

Down at the bar, mine host of the "Eagle Exchange" was welcoming his guests, nerving himself to this task with frequent libations, offered by the fancy bartender, and paid for by such of his guests as had made the "Exchange" their stopping-place before, and knew of the landlord's weakness. Stepping from the bar-room into the reading-room, to look for any stray guest who might have failed to offer at the shrine, he met the dark-eyed stranger face to face, and recoiled, either from some sudden surprise or the effects of deep potations, steadying himself against the door-frame as he reeled. The stranger, continuing on his way to the staircase, seemed hardly to notice him, involuntarily turning his head away as if unwilling to view so fair-looking a specimen of humanity degrading himself to the level of the brute.

Later at night we find our young friend, together with her older sister, in the family sitting-room of the hotel. Annie, the younger, is softly stroking the sister's hair as though *she* were the elder, endeavoring to comfort a fretting, troubled child. No word was spoken until the husband-landlord entered the room. Julia gave a nervous start, while Annie touched her gently and soothingly on the shoulder. Mr.

Davison was a great deal soberer than could be expected; and his wife gave a sigh of relief when she found that he was only maudlin drunk.

"Ah, there you are, both together again — as affectionate a pair of sisters as ever I see. Well, well, Julia, girl, maybe I ain't made you as good a husband as you deserve to have, but I'll see that our little sister there is well provided for. By-the-by, Annie, when Tom Montrie comes down from the mountains he'll find good sport: one of the nicest fellows you ever saw has come down from San Francisco, and I'll try to get him to spend at least part of the winter with us. Oh, he's on the sport," in answer to an anxious look from Julia, "but he's a mighty clever fellow — genteel, and all that sort of thing. Tom's made a pretty good stake again this summer, I know; and it'll be a good plan to keep him well entertained while Annie is away teaching the ragged young one — for I suppose she'll insist on keeping on in that stupid school, when she might just as well marry Tom at once and set herself and her poor relations up in the world."

The girl had listened in silence to this long tirade, a burning spot on each cheek alone showing that she heard at all what was said. It was Julia's turn to be elder sister now.

"Annie," she said, "I forgot to tell Peter that he had better use more yeast for the muffins he sets to-night; will you please to tell him so as you go up-stairs?" Drawing her fingers through Annie's curly brown hair, and looking affectionately into her deep hazel eyes, she kissed her good-night; and the sister silently departed, followed up-stairs by Cruiser, who kept watch through the night on his rug outside her door.

To discover the cause of Mr. Davison's unusual sobriety we must go back for an hour or two. When night had set in, the stranger from San Francisco, who had registered his name as J. B. Peyton, was promenading on the porch in front of the hotel, quietly smoking his Havana and thoughtfully regarding the stars. Presently the host opened the door of the reading-room, stepped out on the porch, and closed it behind him again, as though to keep the chilly autumn air from striking the inmates of the room. Approaching the stranger, he eyed him as keenly as his somewhat dimmed vision, aided by the sickly light of a pale young moon, would permit, and then exclaimed, in a tone intended to be cordial:

"It's you, by ——, it is! Give us your hand, and tell us how you are and how the rest of them have fared."

The stranger, in a voice which, like his eyes, was grave rather than sad, replied, somewhat stiffly:

"I am quite well, as you see; whom else you are inquiring for, I don't know." Then, warming up suddenly, he went on, in a tone of bitter reproach: "And you have married one of these poor girls? You should not have done it had I known of it, depend on it."

"Well, well, wasn't that the best I could do for them?" In his tone bravado and reason were struggling for the mastery. "To be sure," he continued, quailing before the flashing eye of his companion, "I have not had much luck of late; everything seems going against me — I am almost ruined."

"You have ruined yourself. Why should *you* have luck?" He was silent a moment, busying himself with his cigar; then he continued: "Where is Celeste? What became of her?"

"Curse the ungrateful, perjured wretch!" answered the other, grinding his teeth with sudden rage; "when my luck first turned she went off, mind you, with a ship-captain, to China. She knew she could never live where I was. I'd—"

"Do with her as you did with —"

"Hush!" whispered the shivering host; "don't speak so loud! Wasn't there something stirring in the tree there?" And, like Macbeth seeing Banquo's ghost, he started backward to the well-lit room.

It is generally accepted that life in California, particularly in earlier days, was full of excitement and change, every day bringing with it some horrible occurrence or startling event. Perhaps, at the date of my story — about 1860 — this excitement had somewhat cooled down; or perhaps it was the life of our young friend only that had flowed along so evenly while at this place. The "horrible occurrence" of her day was the ever-recurring period of her brother-in-law's intoxication, sometimes maudlin, sometimes violent, but always fraught with bitterness and sorrow to her on account of her gentle, long-suffering sister. The "startling event" was the coming in of the hacks and coaches from the railroad terminus, which she watched, half-hidden by the tree, and together with her almost inseparable companion, Cruiser, just as she had done that day when Mr. Peyton made his first appearance at this place. Perhaps her interest in the arrivals was even greater now than it had been before. Often, when about to turn from her post of observation, a pair of grave black eyes, upturned from the porch below, seemed asking a question of her that she vainly puzzled her brain to understand. Once or twice she had started to go to her sister's room at such times, trying to frame the question she seemed to read in the stranger's eye. But the question remained unframed and unanswered; and day after day Annie taught her little pupils at school, came home and helped Julia about the house, and in the evening encountered the sphinx that baffled all her dreamy speculations.

It had been a matter of displeasure to her brother-in-law for some time that the arrival of the stage from Laporte was not noticed by Annie with the same degree of interest as the coming-in of the passengers from the opposite direction.

"Tom'll be coming some day," he said, grumblingly, to his wife, "and that fine sister of yours will take no more notice of his arrival than if a Chinaman had come!"

And so it proved. One morning as Annie, followed by

Cruiser with the lunch-basket, was descending the front steps of the hotel porch, Mr. Davison hastened to block up her road with his portly figure.

"Annie," he spoke majestically, "how often must I tell you that I cannot allow my sister-in-law to plod over to that school-house and bother with those dirty urchins any more? Let them find some one else, for you will not teach there much longer. Come, Cruiser, give us the basket! Annie'll stay at home to-day, at least."

"Don't trouble Cruiser unnecessarily," replied Annie, laughing pleasantly; "I have n't fallen heir to any fortune of late, that I am aware of, and until I do, I'm afraid that both I and Cruiser will have to follow our old vocation."

"You know that a fortune awaits you, Annie," was the persuasive response, "if you would only stretch out your hand for it. How will Tom receive the information, when he gets up this morning, that you have not paid him the attention to remain home for one day, at least?"

"I hope you will not conceal from Mr. Montrie that it is a matter of the utmost indifference to me how he receives the information."

"Your sister will talk to you about this matter," blustered the man. "A girl like you to throw away her chances!"

"I will listen patiently to anything my sister may have to say to me." And Annie, turning, was almost confronted by Mr. Peyton, coming in from an early walk. He lifted his hat with something like reverence, and drew aside to let the girl and her four-footed companion pass.

She did listen patiently to what her sister said to her that evening in the little family sitting-room just back of the ladies'-parlor, on the ground floor. One door of this room opened out on a porch, on the other side of which rose the blank wall of another apartment, built of frame, with only one window looking out towards the street, and the door opposite this window. Between this and the bar-room lay dining-room, pantry, and kitchen; so that no one from the bar-room, which lay back of the reading-room, on the other side of the entrance hall, could see this room with the single door and window.

In California parlance, "the tiger" was kept in this room. If we could have looked into this gaily-furnished apartment about the time Annie was on her way to her room, having left her sister's presence with tear-stained eyes, we should have beheld Mr. Peyton's pale, clear-cut face bending over a table, around which a number of men were seated. The various accoutrements of the game spread out before him, denoted that this man, with the well-modulated musical voice, with the soft, grave expression of countenance, with the quiet, gentlemanly bearing, was "the owner of the tiger."

The individual occupying the seat just across from Mr. Peyton was his opposite in every respect. A tall, broad-shouldered mountain-man, whose rusty beard and careless dress showed that, while "making his stake" in the mountains, he had bestowed but little attention on his personal appearance. No one could have disputed his claims to good looks, though his glittering eyes seemed small, and were certainly too deep-set; and when he laughed, the long white teeth gave a kind of hyena-look to the whole face. Large hands, always twitching, and clumsy feet, forever shuffling, gave him the appearance of a bear restlessly walking the length of his chain. Altogether, in looks and bearing, he contrasted unfavorably with Mr. Peyton; the one, smooth and polished as ivory; the other, rough and uncouth as the grizzly of his mountain home.

But Mr. Davison, who had softly opened the door, and stood silently regarding him a moment, seemed fairly in love with Mr. Montrie's broad shoulders and matted hair — so gently did he touch the one, and stroke the other, as he whispered into the ample ear something which caused the small eyes to flicker with satisfaction and delight. Then, moving around the table to where Mr. Peyton sat, he laid his hand on this gentleman's shoulder, but much more timidly, though the faro-dealer looked delicate, almost effeminate, compared to the huge proportions of the man from the mountains.

"Jim—" he said, but corrected himself—"Mr. Peyton!" in an audible whisper, "I don't want you to be hard on that man yonder; he'll soon be one of the family, you know."

The information was given with many winks and nods and leers, such as men in the first stages of intoxication are generally prolific of.

A single keen glance from the eagle-eyes of the gambler was sent across to where the man from the mountains sat; but it sank to the depths of the man's heart, and went searching through every corner. The next moment Mr. Peyton was deeply engrossed in the "lay-out" before him.

It was long after midnight before "the tiger" was left to darkness and solitude in the little room at the rear of the "Eagle Exchange." In the course of the following morning, when Mr. Davison's brain was pretty well cleared of the fumes of last night's potations, and before the early-morning drams had yet materially affected it, he was made uneasy by the approach of Mr. Peyton, of whom he stood in unaccountable dread.

"Have a cigar, Henry?" Mr. Peyton extended one of the choice kind he always smoked himself; and then, by a motion of the hand, commanded the now thoroughly sobered man into a chair beside his own. The reading-room was deserted, and the paper Mr. Peyton had picked up was carelessly held so that the fancy bar-keeper, who was twirling his elegant black moustache, could not see his lips move.

"Henry," Mr. Peyton began, without further preliminaries, "if you allow that man from the mountains to press his attentions on your sister-in-law against her wishes, I'll break every bone in your body."

The threat seemed almost ridiculous from the delicate, white-fingered stranger to this burly, overgrown piece of humanity; yet Mr. Davison did not consider it so, for he answered, with pleading voice and cringing manner:

"But if he is to marry her—"

"Marry her!" repeated the gambler, while a flash, such as the gate of hell might emit were it opened for a moment, shot from his eyes; "I would kill him first; yes, and tell the girl who it was that—"

"And send them both out on the world again, to work hard for their bread, as I found them?"

"Better that a thousand times than that Annie should be made miserable, like her sister, by being tied to a worthless sot, or a heartless desperado."

"You're hard on me, Jim," whined the other. "If the girl marries this man, a part of his money will go towards paying off my debts, and setting me straight again in this house. He'll be good to her; and what's the harm to anybody? You don't want the girl — I know your queer notions of honor."

"Hush!" He sprang to his feet, and for the first time his voice thrilled, and a quick flush darkened his brow. "Not another word; but so sure as you drive the girl to this step, so sure will I tell her sister who you are." His figure appeared tall as he moved away, and his shoulders looked broad and strong as those of the man whom he left cowering in his chair behind him.

This interview over, Mr. Peyton seemed utterly oblivious of the existence of the family at the "Eagle Exchange." Mr. Davison said to himself, with an inward chuckle, that he had "gotten round Jim before, in spite of his keen eyes, and was likely to do so again;" while Annie, still and white, looked like a bird wearied out with being chased, and ready to fall into the snarer's net. Once or twice, in meeting Mr. Peyton, it seemed to him that her hazel eyes were raised to his, with a mute appeal in them; and at such times he lifted his hand hastily to his forehead, where a heavy strand of the raven hair fell rather low into it, near the right temple, as if to assure himself of the perfect arrangement of his hair.

But in spite of all of Mr. Davison's cunning and contriving, Mr. Montrie evidently made slow progress in his suit; for his visits to "the tiger" grew longer and more frequent; and soon it came to be the order of the day that the afternoons, as well as the nights, were spent in the little room across the porch. A number of new arrivals from the various mining-camps in the mountains lent additional interest to the games; and bets were higher, and sittings longer, day after day. It was impossible to tell from Mr. Peyton's unchanging face whether luck had been with him or against him; but Mr. Montrie seemed all of a sudden elated, either with the winnings he had made off "the tiger," or the success he had met with in another quarter. Whichever it might be, Mr. Peyton, coming unexpectedly upon him, as he sat in close consultation with Mr. Davison one morning, could not have heard the mountain-man's invitation to drink to his luck, for he passed straight on without heeding the invitation. Mr. Davison quaked a little before the sharp glance thrown over to him; "but then," he consoled himself, "d— it, Jim is such a curious mortal, and, like as not, he's forgotten all about it; he don't care for the girl, no how."

The afternoon saw them again gathered around "the tiger," the man from the mountains betting with a kind of savage recklessness that boded no good to those who knew him well. He had not forgotten the slight Mr. Peyton had put on him in the morning, according to his code of honor, but was casting about in his mind for some manner in which to express his indignation.

"What do you want to be quarrelling to-day for, Tom?" asked a lately-arrived mountain-friend of him. "I see that gal of your'n this morning; took a good look at her when she went to school; and, bless my stars, if you don't know better than to grumble all the while on the very day when—"

"Your interest in the game seems to be flagging, gentlemen," came Mr. Peyton's voice across the table, with a somewhat hasty utterance; "shall we close?"

An energetic negative from the rest of the company decided the question; but Mr. Montrie, determined to play marplot, said:

"For my part, I'm tired of buckin' agin 'the tiger.' 'Pears to me a game of poker might be healthy for a change."

Without losing a word, Mr. Peyton gathered up the faro-kit before him, and laid cards on the table. Mr. Montrie's friend, a slow-spoken, easy-going man, called Nimble Bill, was seated at the right of this gentleman, across from Mr. Peyton's accustomed seat at the table; while beside Mr. Peyton sat two or three others, who had "come down in the same batch" with Mr. Montrie's friend.

The game progressed quietly for some time, Mr. Montrie alone manifesting uneasiness by frequently consulting his watch and casting longing glances through the window.

"Tom, old fellow, I believe you're regularly 'struck' at last," laughed his friend. "It's mighty nigh time for that school to let out, I know; so we'll let you off easy, and say no more about it; ha, ha, ha!" and he turned for approval to the snickering men at the table.

Just then Mr. Peyton raised his hand quickly to his head, and the light from the diamond on his finger flashed directly into the man's eyes.

"By-the-by, that's a mighty fine diamond you've got; I

should n't mind getting one to present to Tom's wife when he gets married. Now, what mought be about the price of one like that, Mr. — what did you say the gentleman's name was?" and he turned to his friend's working face.

"'Poker-Jim,' I should say," shouted the angered man, "from the way he's been handling them cards this afternoon."

There was a hasty movement among those present; the motion of Mr. Peyton's hand, as he threw it quickly behind him, was but too well understood by all, and hurried steps rushed toward the door. When the smoke had almost cleared away he was almost alone with his victim; only the friend, against whom the dying man had fallen, was in the room beside him. But from the outside approached heavy steps, while a shrill female voice sent shriek after shriek through the house. Mr. Davison's ashy face appeared at the door:

"Oh, Jim! what have you done? Let's lay him down here easy, Bill; and now run for the doctor, quick; and tell the other fellows to keep still, if they can."

"Go to your wife, Henry," ordered Mr. Peyton, with extended hand; "the poor thing is in hysterics."

A look into the gambler's face told the man he must obey; but in his perturbation, he did not see the white figure that glided by him into the room.

"Why did you do it?" asked the girl, wringing her hands, but looking into *his* eyes without a glance at the prostrate body.

"I had to kill the brute to keep him from marrying you, Annie. How could I let you fall into his hands — you, the daughter of the woman who sheltered me and gave me a home, when, a poor deserted boy, I lay bleeding from a brutal blow on the street. Annie, do you not know me?" He raised the strand of hair that always lay low on his forehead, and a deep scar appeared under it.

"Jimmy!" she cried, between surprise and joy. "But, oh!" she continued, sadly, "I have found you but to lose you again. You must go, quick, before they can send the sheriff or the doctor."

"We must part; yes, and perhaps never meet again on earth. But, ere we part, I must give your heart another wound. Your brother — it was I who —"

"Murdered him!" shrieked the girl. "Cruiser!" she called, wildly; and the faithful animal, as if knowing the import of the conversation in the room, threw himself with a fierce, yelping bark against the door.

"Hold!" and he caught the girl as she sprang to open it. "Hear me out, while I have yet time to speak. It was I who brought him home, so that he might sleep quietly in the church-yard, instead of finding a grave at the bottom of the Bay. Ask Henry who killed him; ask him whether 'Celeste' was worth the blood of the poor boy, and he will not refuse to tell the truth."

At the door Cruiser was scratching and whining, accompanying the man's hurried words with a weird, uncanny music; and now he howled again as he had howled on the night of poor Ned's death.

"Farewell, Annie; your sister and that dog will soon be the only friends you have. I can neither claim you nor protect you. Farewell; be happy if you can, and — forget me."

"Never! never!" sobbed the girl.

A hand, softer even than her own, was passed tenderly through her hair and over her brow; a single kiss was breathed on her lips, and the next moment she was alone, the dog, her sole friend, crouching, with every demonstration of devotion and affection, at her feet.

THE TRAGEDY AT MOHAWK STATION.

WE called it our noon-camp, though it was really not after ten o'clock in the morning. Ours was the only ambulance in the "outfit," though there were some three or four officers besides the captain. The captain had been ordered to report at head-quarters in San Francisco before going East, and was travelling through Arizona as fast as Uncle Sam's mules could carry him, in order to catch the steamer that was to leave the Pacific coast at the end of the month. It is just a year ago, and the Pacific Railroad was not yet completed; which accounts for the captain's haste to reach the steamer.

When we made noon-camp at the Government forage-station called Stanwick's Ranch, we had already performed an ordinary day's march; but we were to accomplish twenty-five miles more before pitching our tent (literally) at Mohawk Station for the night. These "stations" are not settlements, but only stopping-places, where Government teamsters draw forage for their mules, and where water is to be had;—the station-keepers sometimes seeing no one the whole year round except the Government and merchant trains passing along *en route* to Tucson or other military posts.

Lunch had been despatched, and I was lounging, with a book in my hand, on the seat of the ambulance,—one of those uncomfortable affairs called "dead-carts," with two seats running the entire length of the vehicle,—when the captain put his head in to say that there was an American woman at the station. White representatives of my sex are " few and far between" in Arizona, and I had made up my mind to go into the house and speak to this one, even before the captain had added:

"It is the woman from Mohawk Station."

The captain assisted me out of the ambulance, and we walked toward the house together. The front room of the flat *adobe* building was bar-room, store, office, parlor; the back room was kitchen, dining-room, bed-room; and here we found "the woman of Mohawk Station." I entered the back room, at the polite invitation of the station-keeper, with whom the captain fell into conversation in the store or bar-room.

The woman was young — not over twenty-five — and had been on the way from Texas to California, with her husband and an ox-team, when Mr. Hendricks, the man who kept the forage-station at Mohawk, found them camped near the house one day, and induced them to stop with him. The woman took charge of the household, and the man worked at cutting firewood on the Gila and hauling it up to the house with the station-keeper's two horses, or at any other job which Mr. Hendricks might require of him. She had been a healthy, hearty woman when they left Texas; but laboring through the hot, sandy deserts, suffering often for water and sometimes for food, had considerably "shaken her," and she was glad and willing to stop here, where both she and her husband could earn money, and they wanted for neither water nor food — such as it is in Arizona. It was hard to believe she had ever been a robust, fearless woman, as she sat there cowering and shivering, and looking up at me with eyes that seemed ready to start from their sockets with terror.

"May I come in?" I asked, uncertain whether to venture closer to the shrinking form.

"Yes, yes," she said, breathing hard, and speaking very slowly. "Come in. It'll do me good. You're the first woman I've seen since — since — "

"Tell me all about it," I said, sitting down on the edge of the bed, as familiarly as though I had been her intimate friend for years; "or will it agitate you and make you sick?"

"No," she made answer; "I am dying now, and I have often and often wished I could see some woman and tell her the whole story before I die. It almost chokes me sometimes because I can't speak about it; and yet I always, always, think about it. I haven't seen any one but my husband and the station-keeper these last three weeks — there is so little travel now.

"You see, one Saturday afternoon there were two Mexicans came up this way from Sonora, and stopped at Mohawk Station to camp for the night. It was a cold, rainy, blustering day, and the men tried to build their fire against the wall of the house. It was the only way they could shelter themselves from the wind and rain, as Mr. Hendricks would not allow them to come into the house. Pretty soon Mr. Hendricks drove them off, though they pleaded hard to stay; and Colonel B., who had arrived in the meantime, on his way to Tucson, told Mr. Hendricks that, if he knew anything about Mexicans, those two would come back to take revenge. Perhaps Mr. Hendricks himself was afraid of it, as he picketed his two horses out between the colonel's tent and the house, for fear the Mexicans might come in the night to drive them off. But they did not return till Sunday afternoon, when, after considerable wrangling, Mr. Hendricks engaged them both to work for him. The colonel had pulled up stakes and had gone on his way to Tucson Sunday morning, so that we were alone with the Mexicans during the night. But they behaved themselves like sober, steady men; and the next morning they and my husband went down to the river, some three miles away, to cut wood, which they were to haul up with the team later in the day. Have you been at Mohawk Station, and do you know how the house is built?" she asked, interrupting herself.

"We camped there on our way out," I said; "and I remember that an open corridor runs through the whole length of the house, and some two or three rooms open into each other on either side."

"Very well; you remember the kitchen is the last room on the left of the corridor, while the store-room and bar is the first room to the right. Back of this is the little room in which Mr. Hendricks's bed stood, just under the window; and opposite to this room, next to the kitchen, is the dining-room.

"It was still early in the day, and I was busy in the kitchen, when I heard a shot fired in the front part of the house; but as it was nothing unusual for Mr. Hendricks to fire at rabbits or *coyotes* from the door of the bar-room, I thought nothing of it, till I saw the two Mexicans, some time after, mounted on Mr. Hendricks's horses, riding off over toward the mountains. When I first saw them, I thought they might be going to take the horses down to the river; but then, I said to myself, the Gila don't run along by the mountains. All at once a dreadful thought flashed through my head, and I began to tremble so that I could hardly stand on my feet. I crept into the corridor on tip-toe, and went into the bar-room from the outside. From the bar-room I could look on Mr. Hendricks's bed. He was lying across the bed, with his head just under the window. I wanted to wake him up, to tell him that the Mexicans were making off with his horses, but somehow I was afraid to call out or to go up to him; so I crept around to the outside of the house till I got to the window, and then looked in. Oh, dear! oh, dear! I can't forget the dreadful, stony eyes that glared at me from the bruised and blood-stained face; and after one look, I turned and ran as fast as I could. Perhaps I ought to have gone into the house, to see if he were really dead, or if I could help him or do anything for him; but I could not. I ran and ran, always in the direction my husband had taken in the morning. At one time I thought I heard some one running behind me, and when I turned to look, the slippery sand under foot gave way, and I fell headlong into a bed of cactus, tearing and scratching my face and hands and arms; and when I got up again I thought some one was jumping out from the verde-bushes, but it was only a rabbit running along. Before I got many steps farther I slipped again, and something rattled and wriggled right close by me. It was a rattlesnake, on which I had stepped in my blindness. I ran on until I could not get my breath any more, and staggered at every step; and just when I thought I must fall down and die, I saw my husband coming toward me. He was coming home to see what was keeping the Mexicans so long in bringing the horses down to the river; and when I could get my breath, I told him what had happened. We went back together, but I would not go into the house with him; so he hid me in a thick verde-bush, behind some prickly-pears, and went in alone. Directly he came back to me. He had found the corpse just as I had described it. To all appearances, Mr. Hendricks had thrown himself on the bed for a short nap, as the morning was very warm. The Mexicans must have crept in on him, shot him with his own revolver, and then beaten him over the head and face with a short heavy club that was found on the bed beside him, all smeared with blood.

"Then my husband said to me: 'Mary, you've got to stay here till I go to Antelope Peak and bring up Johnson, the station-keeper. You can't go with me, because it's full twenty-five miles, if not more, and you can't walk twenty-five steps. But those Mexicans are going to come back while I am gone — I know they are, because they haven't taken any plunder with them yet. They'll hide the horses in the mountains, most likely, and then go down to the river to look for me; and after that they'll come back here, and they'll look for us high and low.'

"I knew that what he said was true, every word of it; and

the only thing he could do was to find me a good hiding-place a good ways off from the house, but still near enough for me to see the house, and the window where the dead man lay. Well, first I watched David till out of sight, and then I watched the window, and then I watched and peered and looked on every side of me, till my eyes grew blind from the glaring sun and the shining sand.

"All at once I heard some voices; and I almost went into a fit when I heard footsteps crunching nearer and nearer in the sand. They were the Mexicans, sure enough, coming up from the river, and passing within a few steps of my hiding-place. Both carried heavy cudgels, which they had brought with them from where they had been cutting wood in the morning. When they got near the house they stopped talking, and I saw them sneak up to it, and then vanish around the corner, as though to visit the kitchen first. A few minutes later I saw them come out of the bar-room, and, oh, heavens! I saw they were trying to follow my husband's footprints, that led directly to the verde-bush behind which I was hiding; but the wind had been blowing, and it seemed hard for them to follow the trail. Still they came nearer; and the terror and suspense, and the sickening fear that came over me, when I saw them brandishing their clubs and bringing them down occasionally on a clump of verde-bushes, wellnigh took what little sense and breath I had left, and I verily believe I should have screamed out in very horror, and so brought their murderous clubs on my head at once, to make an end of my misery, if I had had strength enough left to raise my voice. But I could neither move nor utter a sound; I could only strain my eyes to look. After a while they got tired of searching, and went back to the house, where they stood at the window a moment to look in on the dead man, as though to see if he had stirred; then they went in at the bar-room, and came out directly, loaded with plunder.

"One of the men carried both Mr. Hendricks's and my

husband's rifle, and the other had buckled on Mr. Hendricks's revolver. They had thrown aside their *ponchos*, and one had on my husband's best coat, while the other wore Mr. Hendricks's soldier-overcoat. Even the hat off the dead man's head they had taken, and also, as was afterwards found, the black silk handkerchief he had on his neck when they killed him. Again they took their way over toward the mountains, and then everything around me was deadly still. Oh, how I wished for a living, breathing thing to speak to, then! I should not be the poor, half-demented creature that I am to-day, if only a dog could have looked up at me, with kind, affectionate gaze. But the half-open eyes of the man seemed staring at me from the window, and I kept watching it, half thinking that the dreadful, mangled face would thrust itself out.

"By and by the *coyotes*, scenting the dead body in the house, came stealthily from all sides, surrounding the house, and howling louder and louder when they found that they were not received with their usual greeting — a dose of powder and ball. At last one of them, bolder or hungrier than the rest, made a leap to get up to the window; but just as his fore-paw touched the window-sill something was hurled from the window, which struck the wolf on the head and stampeded the whole yelping pack. This was too much; and I must have fainted dead away, for my husband said that when they found me I was as stiff and cold as the corpse in the house. What I thought had been hurled from the window was only a piece of a cracker-box, used as target, and put out of the way on the broad *adobe* window-sill, where the paw of the *coyote* had touched it and pulled it down over him. I would not go into the house, and as Mr. Johnson thought it best to give information of what had happened at Stanwick's Ranch, we all came down here together, and I have been here ever since. My husband is waiting for a chance to go back to Texas. I wish we could get back; for I don't want to be buried out here in the sand, among the *coyotes* and rattlesnakes, like poor Mr. Hendricks."

The ambulance had been waiting at the door for me quite a while; so I thanked the woman for "telling me all about it," and tried to say something cheering to her. When I turned to leave the room she clutched at my dress.

"Stop," she said, nervously; "don't leave me here in the room alone; — I can't bear to stay alone!"

She followed me slowly into the bar-room, and when the man there went to the ambulance to speak to the captain, she crept out after him and stood in the sun till he returned.

"The poor woman," said I, compassionately; "how I pity her!"

"The poor woman," echoed the station-keeper; "those two Greasers have killed her just as dead as if they had beaten her brains out on the spot."

The shades of night were already falling around Mohawk Station when we reached it. It was quite a pretentious house, built of *adobe*, and boasting of but one story, of course; but it is not every one in Arizona who can build a house with four rooms, — if the doors *do* consist of old blankets, and the floor and ceiling, like the walls, of mud.

A discharged soldier kept the station now — a large yellow dog his sole companion. The man slept on the same bed that had borne Hendricks's corpse, and the cudgel, with the murdered man's blood dried on it, was lying at the foot of it.

"And where is his grave?" I asked.

The man's eye travelled slowly over the desolate landscape before us. There were sand, verde, and cactus, on one side of us, and there were sand, verde, and cactus, on the other.

"Well, really now, I could n't tell. You see, I was n't here when they put him in the ground, and I have n't thought of his grave since I come. Fact is, I've got to keep my eyes open for live Greasers and Pache-Indians, and don't get much time to hunt up dead folks's graves!"

LONE LINDEN.

"IT is just the place for you; Clara will find it sufficiently romantic, Miss Barbara can have Snowball and Kickup both with her, and you, dear friend, will be pleased because the rest of us are."

The letter was signed "Christine Ernst;" and Mrs. Wardor, when she had finished reading, continued in her quiet, even tones:

"What an unaccountable being she is; I thought her cold and unfeeling, because she dismissed that fine young fellow so unceremoniously, when we all thought her heart was bound up in him."

"Ah, me!" sighed Clara, fair of face, blue-eyed, and with feathery curls of the palest yellow. "How little we know of the sorrow that sits silent in our neighbor's breast. The sentiment—"

"Oh, bother sentiment!" broke in Miss Barbara, impetuously, flinging back the heavy braids of unquestionably red hair that had strayed over her shoulder. "Daisy, my snowball, imagine, if you can, a large lot, a meadow, or paddock, or something with grass, for Kickup, you and me! Oh, won't it be jolly, though?" And seizing the sweet Daisy, a squat, broad-faced Indian girl, whom Barbara's father, an army contractor, had picked up somewhere around Fort Yuma, they executed a species of war-dance that sent chairs, crickets, and bouquet-stands flying, and caused Mrs. Wardor and her other companion to exchange significant head-shakings.

Having suddenly loosed her hold of Daisy in the wildest of

the dance, and sent her spinning into the corner where her head struck the whatnot, Miss Barbara approached the elder lady, panting, and with deep contrition.

"Forgive me, Aunt Wardor; I shan't forget my young-lady manners again for a whole week. But it did seem such a relief, just the thought of getting away from this cramped little house, and into the open air again, that I could not help being rude to Lady Clara." She seized the slender fingers of the young lady, in spite of the little spasmodic motion with which they seemed to shrink from the hearty grasp.

"But, Barbara," urged Mrs. Wardor, somewhat mollified by the affectionate "Aunt," "when a girl of your age avers that she is a young lady, how can she constantly forget herself, and act the child and the romp again."

A flush passed over the girl's face, a handsome face, full of life and animation, which a few little freckles seemed really to finish off, as she turned sharply from both, and seated herself in the most stately manner at the grand piano, the recent birthday gift of her father.

Barbara was his only daughter, "and he a widower," who was surprised one day to find that she was receiving the marked attentions of a young gentleman matrimonially inclined, at the springs where she was spending her vacations, with all the assurance and matter-of-course air of a "grown-up lady," when he had never dreamed but that she was only a child. He thought to cut the matter short by returning her instantly to the seminary; but soon learned from the conscientious lady at the head of the establishment that the young gentleman was persistent in his devotions, and Miss Barbara as persistent in breaking the rules of the institution. Then he bethought him of a lady whose calm dignity and quiet self-possession had always somewhat oppressed him when he had occasionally met her in his wife's parlors, during that estimable woman's life time. And recollecting how his wife had honestly lamented that her daughter could not live under the influences of a cultivated mind, and the refined manners which she, herself, did not possess, he went boldly to Mrs. Wardor one day, and proposed that she should take charge of the self-willed girl, who insisted on being treated with the consideration due a young lady owning a declared, though forbidden lover. To Mrs. Wardor the proposition was acceptable; some years before, true to the "gambling instincts" of an old Californian, her husband had staked his all on some favorite mining stock, and, after losing, had taken his chances of striking something better in the next world, by blowing his brains out when he found himself "on bedrock" in this. Like a sensible woman, she had given up her elegant establishment without grieving very much, had secured a smaller house, and thought herself fortunate in finding a class of boarders who shocked neither her sensitive nerves nor her fastidious taste.

Among the very limited number was a young girl who had left the Fatherland when quite young, and had been educated by an older brother, since dead. Her love and talent for music, together with what she called her Deutsche Geduld, had stood her in good stead, and Miss Ernst was now considered one of the best music teachers on the Coast.

When Barbara Farnsworth was placed in her charge, Mrs. Wardor felt justified in restricting the number of her boarders to two, outside of this young lady — so liberal were the terms Mr. Farnsworth urged upon her. The one other boarder besides Miss Ernst, was the fair lady with the golden curls, who had lost mother and husband within the year, but found an ample fortune at her disposal on the death of the latter. The mother had been Mrs. Wardor's most cherished friend, and the fittest place for Lady Clare, as Miss Barbara called her, seemed Mrs. Wardor's house. Here she had found already domiciled Miss Ernst, who, a few months later, to the astonishment of everybody, left her home and the city, in consequence of a quarrel with her betrothed, as he was supposed to be by people who knew other people's business better than their own. A close friendship had sprung up between the two young women, and Clara, it was surmised, was the only one who knew of Miss Ernst's reasons for the unlooked for departure, just as Miss Ernst was the only one who knew much, or anything, of Clara Hildreth's "heart-sorrows."

That she had had such sorrows, no one could doubt who looked into the large blue eyes, with their melancholy expression, or noticed the droop of the small, gracefully-poised head. It was not surprising that this tender, clinging creature should miss the prop and staff afforded by the resolute yet sympathetic nature of her friend; and when the letter came suggesting that Mrs. Wardor spend the summer in San Jose, where Christine could be one of her family again, the idea was seized upon with avidity by all, and in three days' time, Miss Barbara had convinced her father, Clara, and Mrs. Wardor, that the place Christine Ernst had described was just the place for them.

"Let's go at once," said Miss Barbara, late in the evening, with her usual precipitation; but Mrs. Wardor quieted her by enumerating the thousand and one things to be done before the removal could be effected — first and foremost among which was the task of securing the house before it could be moved into.

It was decided that Mrs. Wardor and Clara should go to San Jose on the next morning's train and return at night, leaving Miss Barbara to the care of her "Indian maid" and the servants in the house.

Arrived at the depot in San Jose, they found Christine, whose dark hair, olive skin, and Roman features utterly belied her purely German descent. She embraced Clara with the protecting air of an older sister; and pressing Mrs. Wardor's hand, led them to the carriage awaiting them.

"You have worked too hard, I fear, Christine," said Mrs. Wardor. "You look tired and thin."

"Not tired," was the answer, "but I am among strangers, and have so missed my home. You know how we Germans cling to people we love."

"Yes?" Perhaps Mrs. Wardor was thinking of the lover, discarded, among strangers in a strange land. Clara held her friend's hand, and asked how far they would have to go — she felt that Christine was pained.

"Only a short way; but the owner of the place is a queer genius, a German, like myself, with whom no one can live in peace, they say. But I know we can, though he insists on occupying a little hut in one corner of the grounds. Fifty people have wanted the place, but he has never been in a humor to let it since the last occupant moved out. I mean to bring the charms of his mother-tongue to bear upon him, though I know it will make me hoarse for a week, more especially as he is slightly deaf."

The carriage had stopped at the gate, and the three women made their way through a well-kept garden to a little shanty they espied at the farthest end of it. The dwelling-house itself consisted of a one-story *adobe*, to which had been added, much later, a frame building of two stories. The *adobe* part of the building contained kitchen, breakfast and sitting-room, from which a low bay-window reached out into the garden, where flowers stole up almost to within the room, and the ivy, mingling with the bright green of the climbing rose, reached upward to soften the abrupt joining of the gray *adobe* with the glaring white of the frame portion. This, though the more stately part of the building, had not the home-look of the *adobe*, around the flat roof of which ran a low railing, making a balcony of it for the service of the new wing.

"How happy we shall be here," exclaimed Clara, with genuine delight. At this moment a strange figure, clad in loose garments, and with flowing gray beard, deep-set eyes, and holding a long pipe in his mouth, came into sight. Depositing the pipe carefully behind a garden vase, the man advanced with dignified yet courteous bearing. He looked with the questioning scrutiny peculiar to people hard of hearing, from one to the other; but when Christine's words reached his dull ears at last, it was to fair-faced Clara he turned inquiringly.

"Wie sagten Sie, Fräulein? Sprechen Sie Deutsch?"

Christine repeated her question, and he turned slowly toward her. "I thought it was she who spoke the German," motioning toward Clara; "but I like your looks, too," he continued, taking Christine's hand into his with a sudden, fatherly impulse. "And you would come and live in my house, lady," he said, addressing Mrs. Wardor in his German-English. "Take care — I say it to you — take care. It is a lonely place, and makes to be alone in the world every one who lives in it. See me, an old man, alone — alone. It is a bad spell on the place; it will make you alone, too."

The three women exchanged glances. Alone? Whom had they belonging to them? It was only their friendship for each other that made their "alone" different from that of the old man before them.

"And these flowers, so beautiful," he continued, "will you love them, too? I will nurse them for you; but don't be afraid — the old man will not be troublesome to you." He had misunderstood the movement among them; they were only congratulating each other on having accomplished so easily what Christine had been taught to look upon as a difficult task. They hastened to assure him how glad they would always be to have him with them; and he looked wistfully at Clara again, muttering, "Ah, I thought she was the German."

"There it is again," said Christine, turning to her; "I

never try for a beau but you coax him away from me with your blue eyes and yellow curls. I shall act out my character of a dark Spanish beauty some day, and leave you with a jewel-hilted dagger in your heart for luring my own true love from his faith to me."

They followed their guide to the other side of the house, where, near his own cabin, arose a little knoll or mound, evidently artificial, though not smoothly finished. A sparse growth of grass covered it, and on one side there was a ragged depression, as though a tree might have been torn from the soil at some past time. Just above this stood a linden tree, lonely enough. There were no other trees on this side of the house, though pepper, poplar, and cypress trees were distributed with a good deal of taste through the rest of the grounds.

"Lone linden," mused Clara; and though the words were spoken low, the old man seemed to have read it from her lips.

"The other people have called it so, and it seems right. The only one left," he said, softly passing his hand over the bark of the tree. "You would not think how many they were at one time; but they are all dead and gone. My dear ones all lie buried here."

"Here?" echoed Clara, touching the mound.

"No, not the bodies, you know; es ist nur die Erinnerung," he turned to Christine. She bowed her head silently, and with the deep "verstandnissvolle" look of her honest eyes she had won the old man's confidence forever.

They turned back to the more cheerful part of the garden, trying to shake off the gloom the linden with its deep shadow had thrown on them, and Clara railed at her friend for looking solemn as an owl. "Not a line of poetry have you quoted to-day — not a note have you sung."

At the same time the old man was saying to Mrs. Wardor, "See, lady, all these lilies, white as snow. At home, in Germany, they were my mother's pet flowers, and I am keeping these to be planted on my grave." And Christine, stooping to break three of them, chanted dolefully —

>"'Drei Lilien, drei Lilien —
>Die pflanzt mir auf mein Grab.'"

"There" — she turned to Clara — "that's music for you."

Right here, let me confide to the reader Christine's great failing — the weak point in this strong nature. She had a queer habit of keeping up a sort of running comment on any conversation that took place in her presence — any occurrence that came under her observation; comment in the shape of bits of poetry or song, that she sang softly to herself. But she *could* not sing — and that was the great failing. Think of a music-teacher who could not, if life depended on it, sing a dozen notes in the same key, but would drop lower and lower, "till her voice fell clear into the cellar" — according to the girl's own statement.

Mr. Muldweber seemed loath to part with his prospective tenants, but was assured that the close of the week would find them at Lone Linden. When they reached the depot, the train that was to take Mrs. Wardor and Clara back to the city was ready, and Christine had only just time to apostrophize Clara's eyes —

>"Lebt wohl ihr Augen, ihr schönen blauen,"

before it started.

On reaching home, Miss Barbara met them at the threshold, with flaming cheeks and sparkling eyes. "Such a romp as I have had with Snowball," she explained; and the Indian girl laughed like an imp of the devil. Mrs. Wardor chided the young lady for romping, but Clara drew back from the girl with an uncomfortable feeling. Clara's cheeks boasted but a delicate pink tinge at best, and to-night, in the glare of the gas, after the day's fatigue, she looked almost haggard beside the robust, health-glowing girl.

"How old are you, Lady Clare?" she asked in the course of the evening.

"Twenty-two. Why?"

"Oh, nothing; only when I get to be as old as you are I shall wear black constantly, just as you do, particularly if I have lost all my color, too."

"A wise resolution. I never had your color, though. Neither my face nor my hair was ever red — nor my mother's, before me. Perhaps she did not stand over the hot fire as much as your mother did."

"Yes — I know they say mother 'lived out' as cook when she first came to California; but then — *she* did n't have to marry to get a home."

It was all out now; though the girl sent the shaft almost at random, it had struck the sore spot. Clara had married for a home. Her mother had expended her meagre fortune on Clara's education, never doubting that the girl's loveliness would attract a goodly number of suitors, from whom the most suitable, that is, the wealthiest, could be chosen. Whether Clara was less worldly or more romantic—at any rate she lost her heart to a young man in society, who was considered an ornament of that society — though it would have puzzled a common mortal to discover why. His upper lip boasted a full, silken moustache, and he could turn over the music sheets, standing beside the young lady performing on the piano, with unequalled grace; he sang a languid tenor, and could fasten his eyes on a lady with a melting, melancholy look, as if sighing in his heart, "could I but die for thee."

It was what he spoke out aloud to Clara, when, after months of intimate acquaintance, he understood that Clara's mother wanted to see her daughter "settled." But he did n't die; he only bewailed his fate, his inability to make her his cherished wife, and lay all the treasures of the Golden State at her feet. To quote Christine's hard, unsympathetic opinion, he was "a graceless monkey, a fortune hunter, without ambition enough to try for a living for himself, let alone for the woman he professed to adore." Amid tears and protestations of breaking hearts and darkened lives they parted: Clara to give her hand, at her mother's entreaties, to a man of great wealth and corresponding age and respectability — her lover to continue his search for a wife who could boast of money besides beauty and amiability.

Miss Barbara's heart was good in the main, and she would not have hurt Clara as she did had she not been wild with an excitement for which there seemed no cause. She was heedless, to be sure; and her temper — well, she had red hair.

Only three days later, early in the morning, we see them all at the depot, and comfortably seated in the cars — Mrs. Wardor, Clara, Barbara, and Daisy — with Kickup aboard the train, but in a different car — Kickup being only an Indian pony, and the shaggiest kind of one at that. Miss Barbara and "her maid," as she grandly styled the moon-faced Indian sometimes, sat behind Mrs. Wardor and Clara — Clara and Barbara each sitting nearest the window. Clara in deepest black, with the delicate flush on her face, looked the most interesting of young widows, and whenever she raised her dove-like eyes, was sure to encounter the gaze of the many who stood outside. Just as the sharp click of the starting-bell rang through the cars, Clara, looking up, caught sight of a figure that caused her heart to beat full and fast. Yet her face grew pale as she noted the form of which the words "an elegantly attired gentleman" would, perhaps, give the best idea.

He leaned against one of the wooden pillars supporting the depot roof, with a dejected, melancholy air. Almost involuntarily Clara leaned forward, but sank back the next moment, her face ablaze, her lips trembling. The impish laugh of the

Indian girl that had struck her so unpleasantly on the night of her return from San Jose, again fell on her ear, and Miss Barbara's irrepressible "te-he" mingled with it. Had she then betrayed her heart's secret to these two foolish, giggling things? Her cheeks burned with mortification, but in her heart there was a strange gleam of happiness. He knew, then, that she was free; he had heard of her leaving the city, and chose this delicate way of intimating to her that —. Ah! well; she was still in deepest mourning, and must not think — anything — for a while yet, at least.

Mrs. Wardor, her mind filled with doubts and misgivings as to whether she had brought just the things she wanted for the summer in San Jose, had noticed nothing of the little episode, but catching sight of Clara's face as they left the cars, she exclaimed, with genuine gladness in her tone, "Why, Clara, I know this summer in the country will do you good; your eyes are bright with anticipation!"

Christine met them at the depot, and as the carriage rolled smoothly toward their new home, she told them of what other arrangements she had made with old Mr. Muldweber. He owned a horse of venerable age, which could be driven by the most timid lady, and the old gentleman was willing that they should use the horse, but, as of the garden, so he wanted to take care of the animal, too. This was cheerfully agreed to, and when she went on to say that she had hired a phæton — really quite a stylish affair — Miss Barbara almost smothered her with kisses, which would not have happened, by the by, if there had been any place for Christine to hide in.

At the gate stood Mr. Muldweber. "What a funny old man," laughed Miss Barbara. "A patriarch," said Clara; but Christine declared, with more than her usual energy, that no one should say anything disrespectful of or to Mr. Muldweber in her presence.

With chivalrous bearing he welcomed Mrs. Wardor to her

new home, and his address, delivered with true German earnestness, would have checked Miss Barbara's mirth, even without Christine's warning; and Christine herself could only repeat, as she kissed Clara's fair head, "Der Herr segne Deinen Einzug."

Then she led her up-stairs, where she had two rooms, opening into each other, fitted up for Clara and herself, with windows reaching to the floor leading to the balcony. The other window in Christine's room looked toward the Coyote Hills, the corresponding window in Clara's room disclosing a view of the Santa Cruz Mountains.

"Now tell me what you have on your mind, little one," she said, drawing Clara down by the window, and looking off toward the cool, deep shadows of the redwoods on the mountain, she listened to blushing Clara's recital of the morning's occurrence, while she hummed softly (ending full three notes lower than she had commenced):

> "I have gazed into the darkness —
> Seeking in the busy crowd
> For a form once —"

"Perhaps I have done him wrong after all," she interrupted herself; and aloud she said, cheerfully: "The name of this place will be changed before we leave it, I know. But down there is Mr. Muldweber; I mean to ask him about Lone Linden, and his singular fancy for that tree." She knew Clara would be happier left alone to dream over the vision of the morning, and her heart really went out in sympathy to this lonely old man, who had such a longing, hungry look in his eyes as he stood with his arm thrown around the lone linden, his other hand shading his eyes while he peered down the road toward the town.

> "No one hastens home at twilight,
> Waiting for my hand to wave."

Christine's dreary singing would hardly have enlivened Mr. Muldweber's spirits if he had heard it; but it ceased ere she came close up to him. With his usual gallantry the old man spread his handkerchief on the grass covering the broken mound for Christine to rest on, and before darkness had spread over the plain and crept up to the mountain-tops, she knew more of the old man's history—which was the history of the linden tree — than she had ever expected to learn. He had learned to love the girl during the few days that the fitting-up of the house had thrown them together; and he could speak his mother tongue to her — he never would have said so much in English.

. When he had left the mining-school at Freiberg in the Fatherland to come to the great America, he had brought with him from the old *Edelhof*, where he was born and raised, a handful of seed from the linden trees that formed his favorite avenue. He meant to build up just such a place in America, and he carried the linden seed with him through the United States and then into Mexico, where his knowledge of scientific mining was of more use at that time. Into Mexico he carried his bride, a young German girl, whose parents had died on their way out from the Fatherland, and who died herself of *Heimweh*, in the strange, wild land to which her husband brought her. But she left him a son, to whom he gave a new mother, a dark-eyed señorita from Durango. Then he drifted on toward California, before it was California to us, and settled finally in the Pueblo of San Jose, near the mission of Santa Clara, after it had ceased to be a mission. Here he built the old *adobe* — a house quite pretentious for those times, and he threw up the mound, smooth and round, and discernible at some distance, and planted the linden seed he had so carefully hoarded. But he did not sow the seed broadcast; it was a tree for every member of the family — no more. As the señorita from Durango had presented him with quite a little herd of Muldwebers, however, he had begun to entertain hopes of growing something of a forest in the valley, when the dark eyes of the señorita were closed one dread night, and never opened again to the light of this world.

The wealth she had brought him had weighed but little in her husband's estimation; he had learned to admire her goodness of heart and nobility of character. It was a heavy blow; but, strange to say, his heart almost turned from her children at that time and clung again to the child of his first love, the German girl who had died of being homesick. He grew intolerant of Spanish, would not even speak English, but shut himself up with his oldest son to teach him the language he had neglected for so long. Then died the two sons of his Spanish wife, and, though he mourned their loss, he drew still closer to his first-born.

But he had conceived the singular fancy that the spirit of his dead could not rest while their trees lived; and he cut them down, one by one, with his own trembling hands, and, weeping, made a fire of their straight trunks and graceful branches, and buried the ashes deep in the earth. It was about this time that his German friends, of whom there were now quite a number in San Jose, began to whisper among themselves that Mr. Muldweber was getting very queer — eccentric, in fact — if not worse than eccentric. His son, among the first pupils of Santa Clara College, was brought home, and pursued his studies as mining engineer under the guidance of his father, whose intellect and mental equilibrium seemed perfectly restored, if they had ever been wavering.

Then death ruthlessly deprived him of the last remaining child of the Spanish woman — a daughter with eyes as dark as her mother's, and cherry lips and dimpled cheeks; and he turned from his first-born and only child now, shunning and avoiding him, as he had neglected all his other children at one time. The boy, or rather young man — for he had passed the age of twenty-one — bore his father's whim like the sensible fellow he was, understanding well the grief, perhaps self-reproach, that was preying on his parent's heart; and they lived on, apart, though under the same roof. When he could no longer bear his father's coldness, amounting almost to aversion, he left home, hoping that absence would work a change. No letter was ever returned for the kindly-meant missives sent by him, and when the thought of his father's growing age and loneliness overcame his pride, and he returned, he found the homestead let to strangers, and his father established in his little hut, more unreasonable than ever.

He tried by kindness to conquer the old man's injustice; but one day he spoke such hard, cruel words to his son, that pride and manhood rebelled against the indignity, and he left the old homestead forever, he said, vowing to live, under a strange name, "where his father should never hear of him again, living or dead."

A shiver ran through the old man's frame; the day had gone to rest, and the wind blew coldly through the branches of the lone tree above them; but he would not listen to the girl's suggestion, of coming into the house with her.

"No!" he said, "I must speak of the wrong I did to the boy right here, under his tree; he is not dead, I know — the spirit of his mother comes here sometimes and tells me so. She had such blue eyes — like her that is with you; but her heart was not strong like yours, either. You see," he continued, "I was crazy then with grief and loneliness, and self-reproaches, and I said to him, when he spoke kindly and cheerfully, that he was the 'laughing heir,' waiting only for me to follow his brothers, in order to lay claim to the riches that I hoped would be a curse to him. Ah! I see his white face before me every night, and hear his last words ringing through my head: 'So shall they be a curse to me if ever thou seest me again. Leave thy wealth to strangers, old man, thou hast no longer a son.'"

He had arisen and stood erect, unconsciously giving a dramatic representation. The hand he extended had grown firm, but his face gleamed white and ghastly, through the falling gloom. Then the hand sank powerless as he complained, "And he will keep his word — though he was so good — my Rudolph."

He looked up in sudden astonishment; Christine had laid her hand on his shoulder and gazed eagerly into his face. "Rudolph," she repeated, and her hands wrung wildly a moment, dropped by her side in a kind of quiet despair. But the old man hardly noticed her. He stood on the mound again, his form bent forward, as if to catch the first glimpse of any who might be coming up the road, and he shook his head slowly as he muttered to himself, "Er kommt nicht, er kommt noch immer nicht." Christine held out her hand to him. "Come, let me lead you," she said; but the old man did not understand all the words meant.

Late at night, sitting by the open window, from where she could see his domicile, she caught herself humming,

"'T is said that absence conquers love,
But, oh! believe it not."

And she stopped. She *was* thinking of Rudolph. Yes, but she had fancied at first that she was "singing out of his father's heart," not her own. Poor Rudolph! Now she knew what had exiled him from his father's home, and she, alas! had driven him from the new home he had meant to build for himself. And she had thought herself right. A bankrupt suicide's daughter, how could she, a German, with all the deep religious prejudices of that people burnt into her soul, dream of becoming anything more than a friend to the man she honored above all others?

People said she had led him on, had jilted him, and he had left the country. Could she recall him? And how? Yet she could not leave this lonely old man to die, as he was surely dying, of the remorse in his heart and the bitter regrets for his injustice to his son.

No one, coming upon the family at the Lone Linden the very day after their advent to the place, would have suspected them of being strangers there. It was home to them at once. The garden, with its "two ornamental palms," as Christine called them, its wealth of flowers and sparkling fountain, lay all day in the laughing sunshine, and the beams that crept in through the bay-window of the sitting-room played hide-and-seek amid the ivy trailing its glossy leaves across the opposite wall. It was here that Christine's piano stood, and as Miss Barbara always sought the more gayly-furnished parlor as soon as her music-lesson was ended, so Clara learned to despise that apartment, and spend much of her time in this room.

Toward sunset, when shadows grew heavier, and the evening breeze shook the foliage, the broken mound with its single tree had always a dreary look about it, and even Clara was moved into saying, "If Mr. Muldweber should die, I would not dare come to this tree in the evening sun — it would be haunted, I know. I should see the old gentleman or his wraith standing there with his arm around the tree, and his other hand shading his eye. How lonely he looks; is he waiting for any one, I wonder?"

"Poor old man," said Christine, evasively, and she repeated,

"No one hastens home at twilight,
    Waiting for my hand to wave."

"Stop, or I shall get the blues, too." Clara raised her hands to her ears in comical despair, and Christine laughed good-naturedly at the effect of her singing.

So the pleasant, sunshiny days passed on, with no event more stirring than an occasional letter from Miss Barbara's father to break the monotony of life.

M

It was Mr. Farnsworth's desire that Miss Barbara should be treated and looked upon as a child, and it would have gladdened his heart could he have seen her, in the cool of the morning or late in the afternoon, with Snowball and Kickup in the enclosed lot called the Meadow, behind the house. Whether it had ever been the intention of Mr. Farnsworth to have Miss Barbara use the four-footed thing called Kickup as a saddle-horse is not known; it is a matter of doubt, however, whether any one had ever been on its back long enough to discover what was its best gait. To be sure, Miss Barbara made it a point to require her "maid" to "ride around the ring;" and she would urge the pony close up to the fence for this purpose, assist Daisy to mount, and then give a jump to get out of reach of Kickup's heels, for he had never been known to have more than two feet on the ground when any one was on his back; indeed, as a general thing, he never touched the ground again till his burden lay there too. There was no more danger of injuring Snowball's limbs than the pony's, and as they were taken both from the same tribe, back in Arizona somewhere, it is to be presumed that they knew each other. But Miss Barbara was neither cruel nor a coward. She never failed to reach Kickup's back, and from there the ground again, sometime during the day's performance, to Snowball's unbounded delight; and at night she always complained to Mrs. Wardor that "her pony wasn't fairly broken yet," "Which is not so surprising as that your bones are unbroken yet," Christine would say sometimes; for which Miss Barbara would give her a supercilious look out of her wide-open eyes, as though to say: "What do you know about it? Your father was never an army contractor."

About this time Mr. Farnsworth, in his letter to Mrs. Wardor, commenced to promise a visit he intended making them before the summer was over; and Mrs. Wardor commenced saying to Barbara, when she proved particularly unmanageable, "Do try to behave like a lady, so that your father may see you are no longer a child." And the suggestion always had the desired effect for the time being; but the sight of Snowball driving Kickup into the meadow would as regularly upset all her good intentions.

One day Christine came into Clara's room, with a troubled look on her face. "What is it?" asked Clara; "is your aged *protégé* more depressed than usual this morning? Has he refused to enjoy his long pipe, or has he regaled you with a longer account than usual of his son — Hans, I think, you said his name was?"

Christine laughed in spite of herself. Clara had heard something of Mr. Muldweber's trouble with his son, and took it for granted that Christine knew all about it, though she had not the remotest idea of how deeply she was interested; and one of Clara's fancies was that Mr. Muldweber's son was a tow-headed youth, and his name was Hans.

"Mrs. Wardor has had another letter from Mr. Farnsworth," said Christine.

"Again threatening a visit? But why should that make you look so serious? Are you thinking of his displeasure at not finding his Barbara an Arabella Goddard?"

"Thank God, I never held out that prospect to him. No—" she continued, absently; "I don't like his letters, and I fear Mrs. Wardor misunderstands him — misunderstands him entirely. He inquires very particularly for Lady Clare in his letters, too."

"And not for you? Ah! then the cat's out of the bag," she laughed; "you are jealous of me again."

"The vanity of some people—" Christine joined in the laugh; but the troubled look returned to her face as she went on. "That poor old man troubles me too; he is failing fast, and his son must come soon, or I fear he will never see him again."

"Then why not send for him?" asked Clara, innocently; "or does he not know where to find him?"

"No," answered Christine, savagely, after a moment's hesitation.

"Poor old man," sighed Clara; and she was careful after this to meet the forlorn figure wandering restlessly through the grounds with all the sweet consideration it was her nature to show those who were in pain or trouble.

Still the old man never spoke to her of his Rudolph as he did to Christine; it was to the brave-hearted German girl he poured out his long pent-up complaints and lamentations; it was only to her he revealed how the yearning for his first-born was eating his heart away. Often she was on the point of telling him all; he would say then, she thought, that she had acted quite correctly; would commend her for not having fastened herself with her accursed name upon a blameless man, with fame and fortune before him. But he would still demand at her hands his son — his son whom she, more than himself, had made an exile and a wanderer.

So the day passed on, and the cloud on the horizon of Lone Linden grew darker and heavier; but no one saw it gathering save Christine. Instinctively she felt that their fair Paradise would be destroyed when the storm should burst, but she knew not how to divert the threatened deluge.

When Clara rushed into her arms one day, flushed and breathless, crying, "Oh, I knew he loved me — I felt that he had never forgotten me," her heart misgave her — the first harbinger of threatened desolation had come. With difficulty she prevailed on Clara to tell her calmly what had occurred, and, triumphant and happy, she explained that Mrs. Wardor had received a letter from Mr. Farnsworth, to say that at the end of the week he should visit Lone Linden, bringing with him young Mr. Heraclit Gupton, nephew of General Gupton, commanding the Department of the Pacific.

"Poor, blind Mrs. Wardor," Clara went on to say, "saw nothing in this but Mr. Farnsworth's desire to entertain a young gentleman whose uncle had it in his power to award heavy army contracts; indeed, how could she know that Heraclit Gupton was — was — "

> "I have lived and loved — but that was to-day;
> Go bring me my grave clothes to-morrow."

Christine filled up the pause, her voice more dreary and inclined to "drop into the cellar" than ever.

Clara looked sobered and disappointed at this unexpected comment, but attributed it to a sudden recollection of Christine's own "what might have been."

"What makes you so sad, Christine? Is Mr. Muldweber really sinking as fast as Mrs. Wardor thinks?"

"Sinking fast, child; only the promise that his son shall be brought here, if among the living, before the moon fades, has kept the old man alive."

"Oh! Christine, stay and be glad with me now," pleaded Clara, "the time for mourning will come soon enough."

But Christine could not be made to rejoice, and all the comment she made on the other's enthusiasm was,

> "Oh! Lady Clara Vere de Vere,
> You put strange memories in my head."

And Clara flew up-stairs to dream over this broadening flood of sunshine as she had dreamed over the first faint glinting.

Had not Miss Barbara been strangely absent-minded about this time, she must have observed how the color in Clara's cheek grew brighter, and her eyes held a deeper, richer light. And if any expression so soft as a "dreamy look" could ever have stolen into this positive young lady's face, one would certainly have said it was there now, though it vanished like a dream, too, whenever the Indian girl's impish laugh fell on her ears. The Indian girl herself seemed to be the only member of the family that was not more or less *distrait* after the arrival of Mr. Farnsworth's last letter, for even Kickup showed resentment at Miss Barbara's sudden neglect of her "saddle horse." It was only natural that Mrs. Wardor's mind should be on hospitable cares intent, which accounted for her being oblivious to a good many things going on around her.

Saturday had been named by Mr. Farnsworth as the day on which he was to be expected, and as the members of the family arose from the breakfast-table that morning, Miss Barbara astonished Mrs. Wardor by a demand for her mother's diamonds, to wear in honor of her father's coming.

"Nonsense, child," said Mrs. Wardor; "what would the young gentleman coming with your father think, to see a school-girl loaded down with diamonds? Leave them in my trunk; they are better there. You might take a notion to have a romp with Kickup before taking them off, and they would be scattered in the meadow."

But Miss Barbara was determined to carry her point, and broke out at last, the rebellious blood rising to her head, "I think I should be allowed to have them, at any rate; they are *my* diamonds, and father promised mother that they should never go to the second wife if he did marry again."

Mrs. Wardor's face flushed as red as Barbara's, but Christine's remained unmoved, calmly marking the notes on a sheet of music, while Clara gave one startled look, as though she had just made a discovery.

Early in the afternoon Miss Barbara appeared in the garden, where the hot sun blazed down on the fiery hair, the burning cheeks, and the flashing jewels. Her eyes were hardly less sparkling than her diamonds, and as she threw a searching look down the road and across the plain, toward the town, they seemed to glitter and glint in all the colors of the rainbow, just like the stones in her ears and at her throat. Later,

Clara came to the hall-door, but drew back when Barbara came to join her; the girl's appearance gave her a "scorched" sensation, she said to Christine, who seemed blind to the shadows that coming events were casting before them. At least there was neither glad anticipation nor nervous haste noticeable in her as in the rest, but her heart was very heavy within her. Nevertheless she chided Clara for having dressed in black after all, when she had firmly decided to wear white; and she urged her back into the garden, for she knew her soul was flying across the road to the city, to meet the form she had dreamed of day and night since Mr. Farnsworth's announcement.

The afternoon breeze was gently stirring the fragrant flower heads when she entered the garden again and approached Miss Barbara, who had taken up her station by the low picket fence where the ground rose above the level of the road. Clara, too, sent out a wistful look across the plain. Perhaps she had sighed, for she felt the girl's eyes on her, and as she looked up, it came back to her painfully what Barbara had once said about her lack of color. Could her heart be growing envious of the girl? She did not ask herself the question, but she felt the impulse to turn and leave her, and would have done so had not a start and flutter on the girl's part told her that a vehicle was in sight.

She did not look down the road; she would not betray her feelings to the merciless eyes of this red-headed girl; but her own heart beat so that Barbara's agitation entirely escaped her. She turned toward the house. She *must* press her hand to her heart to still the tumultuous beating. On the balcony stood Christine, an affectionate smile lighting up the dark features as she threw kisses to her and pointed to the light carriage now quite near the gate. Then the color came back into Clara's face, and, with a sudden joyous impulse, she fluttered her handkerchief in the breeze, and laughed like a glad child reaching out its hand for a long-coveted toy. Mrs. Wardor came to the door; the carriage stopped at the gate that minute, and two gentlemen sprang to the ground.

Just how it all took place, perhaps none of them ever knew — not even Christine, who had remained on the balcony, a deeply-interested, though not indelicate, spectator. They lingered in the garden a little while, and before they entered the house Mr. Farnsworth had pompously announced to Mrs. Wardor that this was the young gentleman who had so faithfully and persistently paid court and attention to his daughter Barbara; that he had at last been touched by his unwavering devotion, and had decided to make his only child happy — as happy as he himself hoped to be some day in the not distant future.

"Bless your soul," he added, in an undertone, to Mrs. Wardor, who had just had an unaccountable attack of heart-beating, "if I had known that Barbara's 'young man' was General Gupton's nephew, she should have had him six months ago, and welcome." He was interrupted by Barbara's asking permission to go driving with her "young man," and, the father consenting, they were soon speeding over the road in the light carriage that had brought the gentlemen.

At her window up-stairs sat Christine, her hands folded idly in her lap, her eyes absently following the couple in the carriage. But on the bed, in her own room, lay Clara, her head buried deep in the pillows, her slender hands covering the white face, sobbing as if her heart would break. And through the half-open door came the saddening chant of Christine:

> "I have just been learning the lesson of life,
> The sad, sad lesson of loving."

Could the words but have penetrated to the room below, they might have been echoed there by another. Mr. Farnsworth was again making an announcement to Mrs. Wardor — though in a manner not quite so pompous — indeed, almost hesitating.

"Yes," he was saying, "my daughter cannot blame me, since I have made her happy, that I too should look for a suitable companion. When I say suitable, I mean one better fitted than the first Mrs. Farnsworth to my — ahem ! — to my — more advanced mental attainments. I have for some time past observed the — ahem ! — sweet disposition and — ahem ! — amiable character of your friend and *protégé* — Clara. Good gracious, madam, are you sick? Can I do anything for you?"

"No, thanks; only a sudden dizziness that sometimes seizes me in warm weather;" and, thanks to Mrs. Wardor's self-possession, it was over directly. As Mr. Farnsworth took it for granted that it was quite essential for a fine lady to have nerves, and even fainting-fits, he saw nothing remarkable in Mrs. Wardor's sudden dizziness and pallor. Then she said Clara was one of the sweetest-tempered women she had ever met with, but she knew nothing of the state of her heart or affections; he must lay the case before the lady herself. And here she suddenly remembered not to have given full directions for supper to the Chinaman in the kitchen, and left Mr. Farnsworth to his own meditations in the parlor. Then the sun went down, and Christine, paying no heed to the sound of carriage-wheels approaching — thinking the happy lovers had returned—was startled by the sharp ring of the door-bell. She sprang to her feet; she felt that the bell called to her, and she was at the door before the servant could reach it. A tall, bearded man stood before her, who, taking advantage of the girl's being utterly disconcerted, drew her quickly to his breast. She rested there only a moment.

"Oh, Rudolph! your father," she said, with a tone of reproach in her voice.

"Take me to him, Christine," and Mrs. Wardor, who had drawn her head back discreetly a moment before, now came fully out of her sitting-room to welcome Rudolph to his home.

"All the afternoon you left me by myself," said Mr. Muldweber, querulously, as Christine softly entered his room. "Ah! if my boy would only come, he would never let his old father lie here alone," and he turned his head to the wall so as not to look at Christine.

"Forgive me," she said; "but poor Clara so needed me. And I have brought news from your son — from Rudolph. He is coming soon — he will be here —"

"He is here now!" cried the old man, opening his arms, but turning his eyes to the ceiling, as though he expected his Rudolph to flutter down from there in the shape of a seraph or an angel.

A few hours later Mr. Muldweber's room, which had seemed so lonesome in the afternoon, was filled to its full capacity. The old man sat in his easy-chair, holding one hand each of Rudolph and Christine in his own, and near them were Mrs. Wardor and Clara. Her friend's happiness was a consolation to her, so much so that she could think, without breaking into tears, of the trio in the parlor of the other house, talking over their plans for the future, just as our friends were doing here.

Mr. Farnsworth intended going back to the city on the morrow, heavily laden with "The Basket" (the German term for the mitten or the sack), which Clara had given him.

In Mr. Muldweber's shanty reigned a soft, subdued happiness, like the half-sad light of the moon flooding in through the window.

"It will be Lone Linden no longer," the old man said, "since I have so large a family. See, I will not crowd you in the big house; I will stop in my dear little hut. There will be only room enough in the other house for Rudolph and his wife and her two sisters" (the old man was naturally gallant), "whose knight I will be till some one worthier and better shall fill my place. And the red-headed one will go next month?" he asked, turning to Mrs. Wardor. With a sigh of relief he continued, "And the black Kobold will go with her I hope, and the four-footed one too. How they used to break my beautiful white lilies and throw them to that animal. Ah! you cannot make me believe anything — if that horse were not possessed by the evil one he never could have eaten those flowers—stem and all." They could not help laughing, and parted almost merrily.

But out in the garden, in the tender white moonlight, Rudolph drew Christine close to his heart and looked searchingly into her eyes.

"Are you at peace with yourself now, Christine, and satisfied to be mine — satisfied and happy? Then why are those tears in your eyes?"

She struggled out of his arms, and passing her hand over her eyes, she fell irresistibly into her old habit, and sang, soft and low,

> "Mag auch im Aug' die Thräne stehn —
> Das macht das frohe Wiedersehn."

MANUELA.

"POOR Mrs. Kennerly" was more lachrymose than usual to-day; her eyes paler, her hair more faded. Paul Kennerly, the keen-eyed, robust counterpart and husband of the lady, was measuring the room with impatient steps. When her pale-blue eyes shed tears and grew paler, his flashed fire and grew deeper blue; when her light-yellow hair hung limp and loose about her eyes, his darker, heavier locks rose obstinately from his forehead, and were shaken back, now and again, as a lion shakes his mane. While the profuse tears coursing over his wife's cheeks seemed to bleach their original pink into vapid whiteness, his own flushed hot and red with the quick blood mounting into them.

Yet, Mrs. Kennerly, of whom her friends spoke only with the adjective "poor" prefixed, was not a martyr; on the contrary, to the unprejudiced observer, the great tall man, in spite of flashing eye and reddened cheek, appeared much more in that light and character.

"Laura, *will* you stop crying just for two seconds, and listen to what I have to say?"

"Oh, my poor sister! my poor sister! Coming home, and unwelcome in her own dead father's house! unwelcome to her own brother-in-law, at the house of her poor dead father —oh!"

Before she had finished her lamentation, Mr. Kennerly had left the room, shutting the door behind him with a crash, and crossing the corridor with long, heavy strides. Then his steps resounded on the veranda, where the June sun threw deepening shadows of the old locusts that stood sentinel in a half circle on the lawn. Pacing back and forth, with knit brows and downcast eyes, the wooing beauties of the summer day were lost on him, as they were without charm or joy to the weak-minded woman fretting and complaining in her darkened room up-stairs.

Unnoticed by him was the short sweet grass on the lawn, and the rows of blossoming lilacs and budding roses that hedged it in on either side, down to the road; unheeded on his ear fell the gentle murmuring of the wind in the cluster of poplar, beech, and elm that stood bowing and swaying by the large old gate. Was it possible that he had ever pushed through its portals (a wanderer returned to his early home), an expectant bridegroom, to meet the meek-eyed bride whose phantom only seemed now to haunt the old-fashioned, hospitable house? Again Paul Kennerly threw back the hair from his forehead with the lion-like motion that had grown more abrupt and hasty year after year. Then the footsteps on the veranda ceased, and soon soft, full chords, such as a master-hand only could strike on the piano, sounded through the wide corridor, and floated up to the ears of the self-willed invalid. Louder and stronger grew the strains; and the woman, in her feebleness, cowered on her lounge up-stairs, and complained fretfully, "Now he storms again!" while the man below seemed to have forgotten everything; his own existence, perhaps — the existence of the woman, surely.

Yet she was present to the waking dreams he dreamed of his early youth — they could not be dreamed without her. She had been his playmate, his *protégé;* as her younger, stronger sister had been his natural antagonist and aversion. The father had been his guardian. And when Paul went as sutler and trader to New Mexico, just as Laura was budding into girlhood, it was tacitly understood that on his return he would claim her as his betrothed. Years passed, and when old Mr. Taylor felt his end approaching, he begged Paul to return, and be to his two daughters the protector that he had been to Paul's helpless childhood. Soon after Laura's marriage, Mr. Taylor died, firm in the belief that he had made a happy man of his favorite, Paul.

Before the mourning year was over, a schoolmate of Paul's, an army officer, some years his senior, came to spend a month's furlough at the old Taylor mansion. When he left, he was the willing slave and avowed suitor of Regina, the queenly younger sister of Laura. If there were no hearty congratulations from Paul's side, I doubt that either Colonel Douglass, in his happiness, or Laura, in her self-absorption, felt the withholding of his kind wishes; and Regina cared very little either for his favor or his disapproval.

Even before they were married, Regina knew that after a few short weeks spent in the home-like, elegant quarters at the arsenal, they must leave the ease and luxuries of civilization for the wilds of some frontier country. But Regina was content to reign over the limited number of hearts to be found in a frontier's camp, as she had reigned over her train of admirers in the ball-room and at the watering-places; and, to the delight of her husband, she uttered no word of complaint when an order from the War Department sent them to an adobe-built fort on the Rio Pecos, in the most desolate part of all New Mexico.

"Now, I should like to go with you, Hal," had said his brother-in-law, when he read him the order; and he raised his head and flung back his hair, as though he felt the wild, free wind of the Plains tossing it.

Paul rode back from the arsenal slowly that evening; and the nearer home he came, the lower drooped his head, the darker grew his brow. At home he paced the floor uneasily, paying little heed to the feeble whimpering of his wife, who had been frittering her life away between camphor-bottles and sentimental novels since Regina had left the house.

The drawing-room, where the piano stood, and where the windows opened out on the veranda and the lawn, was his harbor this night, as often when either his own thoughts or the selfish complainings of his wife drove him distractedly about the house. But this night there sounded a single soft strain through his "storming,"—as his wife called it,—and the strain grew wilder and sweeter, till suddenly lost, as the note of some clear-voiced, frightened bird is lost in the howling of the midnight storm.

Then had come days of calm, during which the piano remained closed, and he sat meekly under the drivelling talk of his wife, and in the close, dark atmosphere which alone, she insisted, suited the delicate complexion of her face and of her mind.

After that, an occasional letter from his brother-in-law, now at his station on the Rio Pecos, or an extra twist of the cord matrimonial, which, since the day of his marriage, seemed literally to encircle his neck, would set the lion to fuming in his cage; and, with the toss of his hair from the forehead, would commence the wandering through the house which always ended with "storming" the piano.

But the days are passing while we travel back into the past; and one, not far distant, brings Regina, the unwelcome. Before she had been in the house many days, she knew from her sister's rambling talk what Paul had said of her coming before she came — knew that he did not believe what the colonel had written about the disastrous effects of the New Mexican climate on his wife's health; but believed, rather, the rumors that had come to him from all sides, each varying a little from the rest in detail, but all agreeing in the main. Regina's marble face, and nervous, transparent fingers, might have confirmed the theory of failing health; but there was something in the momentary flash of her dark eyes, as she listened to her sister's quavering voice, that told of energy or despair, such as woman gains and gathers only from a sudden calling forth of all her passions and powers for the defence of her life, her honor, or position, as the case may be. It may have been only once, in the long past, that this power was called out; but, like the heat-lightning at the close of a hot, murky day, it throws baleful gleams on the cloud-darkened horizon of her life forever after.

"My sternly-virtuous moral brother-in-law," Regina said softly to herself, seated on a low stool in the room where her cradle had stood, "would fain drive me from my own father's house, for a fancied injury to the fair name of the Kennerly-Taylor family. Ah, well! the end of all days has not come yet."

Her head sank on her bosom, as she sat watching the shadows of the tree-clump by the gate, growing longer and deeper in the fading light of the western sun; and a tear stole into her eye and trickled slowly down her pure white cheek. Her sister, creeping up to her, and looking into her face with what affection she was capable of, shed more of her easy-coming tears.

"I told him they were slandering you. Papa always said you were too proud to do a wrong and not acknowledge it. And Paul was always hard on you, I know; and it's all a lie and slander; for even if you were not my sister, I could tell, as any one could, from your face, that you are good and without sin. I know from the stories I have read — they all have just such pale, faultless faces when they're persecuted; and afterwards the misunderstanding is cleared up, and they get married. But then, you *are* married." She had gotten into deep water now; and thinking, probably, that her younger, cleverer sister would solve this problem as she had so many others, Laura picked up her camphor-bottle and returned to her own room. Regina remained, her "pale, faultless face" turned to the dying light, a pensive, half-pained, half-sad expression on her lips and in her eye, looking almost like a saint striving to forgive and bless her traducers.

Yet the woman was not without sin; though how much was to be laid at her door none could tell.

Out in New Mexico, the rumor ran, at the lonely adobe-built post on the Rio Pecos, where her husband, the colonel, was stationed, there was also a post surgeon, a young, handsome man, of fascinating manners, of unquestioned skill and bravery, and born of an Italian mother, from whom he had inherited passion, temper, and disposition, together with Southern eyes and curly, silken hair. His courage had probably come from his American father; none but such could have a son who, in his dare-devil bravery, would go so far as to capture and tame a young panther, and chain him outside his door, to act as watch-dog and protector. And so great was the love of this animal for his master, that he was known to leap and roar for joy when seeing him approach after an absence from home.

Of course, Regina was expected to visit and admire the panther as a "natural curiosity;" and her hand, too, it was said, the beast would lick with every sign of affection and submission. Rumor said, that in the dead of night, when no one else could approach the doctor's quarters within a hundred yards, she could pass by and into the doctor's rooms without hindrance or opposition from Royal, the panther. And, moreover, rumor went on to say, that whenever the colonel was away on duty, looking after those troublesome Navajoes and uncertain Apaches, Regina's white robe was frequently seen flitting past the uncanny keeper of the doctor's door.

But there came a day — a night, rather — when Royal, after a short but terrible conflict with a midnight invader, lay dead on his master's doorsteps, and over the body strode the invader into the presence of the young doctor, who, with an almost superhuman effort, tried to shield the queenly, white-robed form that fell prone to the floor. To be sure, he received a bullet in his temple; and the dark, silken curls were dank and stiff with gore when the sun lighted up the low adobe room next morning. However, he had saved *her* life; for the colonel became cool when he saw the destroyer of his peace and honor lying dead at his feet.

There was no public trial — not even a court-martial. The colonel had killed the doctor in a duel; but nobody demanded a record of the event, and the reprimand he received was not by sentence. But he was ordered to Fort Marcy, near Santa Fé. The colonel had borne off a cut across the forehead, extending upward till under the hair, in one of the pitched battles with the Indians; and he was known to suffer from headache and irritation of the wound to such a degree, at times, that over-excitement, from anger or other cause, made him almost crazy. He was an old, valiant, and valued officer; and the War Department, not supposed to know any uninvestigated matter, would excuse many things in such a one, even though it could not approve them.

Then it was that the colonel's wife had returned to the States "for her health," — as her husband was particular to write to his brother officers stationed at the barracks and arsenal near to the western city where his wife's home was.

Who can tell how rumor travels? When Regina made her appearance at the arsenal, the very women who had once been proud of her notice seemed hardly to remember a passing acquaintance with her; and, stung to the quick, she had barely strength to control her face and hold high her head till the door of her carriage had closed on her. She laid back her head, throbbing and aching, yet filled with a thousand plans for regaining her position and punishing those who had so humbled her.

It was one of Paul's restless days; and she heard him "storming" on the piano as her carriage entered the gateway. With sudden interest she raised her head, while her face grew animated with some struggling thought.

When night had set in, and the broad hall-door was thrown open to admit the soft breeze and the tender moonlight, Regina, for the first time since her return to the home of her childhood, approached the piano in the drawing-room and ran her fingers over the keys. The door stood open, and from her seat she could see into the hall, and catch a glimpse of Paul's shadow every time he passed the hall-door in his walk on the moonlit veranda. Not a muscle of her face moved as she continued in her play, striking chords and running *roulades*, without any apparent purpose save that of touching once more the old familiar key-board. Paul's shadow flitted by, regularly and restlessly, never varying an inch in his distance from the door as he passed it. Suddenly the chords melted into a melody low and sweet, yet swelling almost into wildness in its yearning, longing tenderness.

Regina listened intently, and — surely Paul could not have paused suddenly in his walk on the veranda! Directly his footsteps came again, halting and uncertain, and Regina repeated the air, throwing into it more intensity, even, than at first. She seemed absorbed in her playing, though she knew full well when Paul's hesitating footsteps crossed the threshold, and moved nearer the drawing-room entrance. When he stood in the door, she looked up, as though unwilling to be disturbed in her musical meditations. One look at the deathly-pale face, above which the dark blonde hair rose like a lion's mane, assured her that she would gain — *had* gained — her end; and she played on, as though forgetting his presence in an instant. Presently, a hoarse, unsteady voice reached her ear:

"Where did you learn that air? Who taught you the song?"

She looked up unconcernedly.

"That air? Do you like it?"

He nodded his head impatiently.

"Where did you learn it? Who taught you?"

"That song? Oh, I learned that in New Mexico."

He looked at her wildly for a moment, but her gaze was so steady that he dropped his eyes and moved slowly away.

Late in the night, when Regina awoke from a sleep sweeter and sounder than any she had yet enjoyed, she heard Paul's steps in the hall-way, on his way to bed.

"You have left me alone all night again," complained his wife, when he entered the room; "and I have had one of my nervous spells."

"You keep the room so confoundedly hot and full of camphor that it smothers me to stay here," was the crusty reply.

"Would you want me to keep the windows and shutters open, so as to let the mosquitoes come in and devour us?"

"Why do you keep the light burning till twelve in the night, then?"

"But, Paul, I can't read in the dark, can I? And I want some pastime, I am sure, so sick and feeble as I am," weeping for very pity of herself.

"Throw those foolish books out of the window; the camphor-bottle, too; let air and daylight into your room, and you'll soon get well and strong," he answered, willing to be kind and anxious to hush her distracting sobs.

Regina, in her room, breathed a little sigh of satisfaction; for though she could not hear the conversation, she could guess very nearly what Paul's reception had been: "Ah! my clever brother-in-law, yours is not a bed of roses, either;" and with this comforting reflection she dropped off to sleep.

Next morning, at the breakfast-table, Regina watched with

placid interest the haggard face of Paul, and the furtive looks he threw over to where she sat. During the morning his wife was attacked with sick headache, "from reading those trashy novels," he said; and by night he was wandering through the house again, groaning in very anguish of spirit, and flying, at last, to his only refuge, the piano. Through the loud clanging of the chords there breathed a strain, now and then, of the song Regina had played; but in a moment it was drowned by the louder crashes, which almost shook the house, and seemed the outpouring of some wild spirit in its abject misery. Day followed day, and as the season advanced, and autumn set in, with stormy days and long, moonless nights, Paul grew more restless; and one night, when he had wandered through the house all day — "as though driven by the Fury of Remorse," Regina said — she went, unobserved, into the drawing-room, from where soon came the strains of the song that had so agitated Paul. Again his heavy steps approached the door, and, as he entered the room, Regina said to herself, "He has grown ten years older since that evening last summer, and he is ripe for my purpose now."

"You learned that song in New Mexico?" he asked, trying to speak in his usual quiet tones. "I suppose it is a popular air among the Mexicans?"

"Not a common one, though it is a Spanish song;" and she softly sang the refrain, "*Ela—Manuela!*"

Had she stabbed him to the heart he could not have turned paler, or sprung forward quicker, than at the uttering of the words.

"She taught it you! Tell me quick, for God's sake!"

. He had clutched her arm, and was shaking her without knowing it.

"Gently, my dear brother-in-law," she said, sneeringly; and he shook the hair back from his forehead, and regained his self-possession by a strong effort.

"You wanted to know who taught me the song? My information has a price."

She had folded her hands in her lap, and was looking quietly into his face.

"Name it!" he burst out impatiently.

"It is a high price; but I can give you *all* the information you may want in return. Here is a sample."

She had turned the music-stool on which she was seated, and while he paced up and down the room to hide his agitation, she continued in the tone of one holding easy converse with a good friend:

"I learned this little Spanish song from a very pretty girl in New Mexico. She said she had once taught it to an American, a tall, handsome man, with blue eyes and fair face, who must have been in love with her, I think, for he had always substituted her name, in the refrain, for the name which the author of the song had put into it. She, too, must have been fond of this American with blue eyes and dark blonde hair; for, though not in the least conceited, or aware of her own attractions, she always sang the refrain with her own name, Manuela, instead of the original name, Juanita, simply because this American had wished her so to do. The air is beautiful, I think; and the words are very pretty too." She turned to the keys again, as though to repeat the air.

"Stop!" he said hoarsely, arresting her hand; "you will kill me. What is the price you ask?"

"The price is high," he groaned, when she had coolly and in unfaltering tones stated her conditions to him. "But if you promise to keep to your word, I will do my best."

"You will succeed, then," she said, holding out her hand, and speaking almost cordially as they parted for the night.

When she reached her room she seemed for once to have fallen into Paul's *rôle* of Wandering Jew; but her steps were noiseless, though the thoughts that danced and chased through her brain *would* come to her tongue, in quick, triumphant words.

"My upright, truthful judge and brother-in-law — to bring about a reconciliation between his best friend, my husband, and his 'erring but loving wife.'" A haughty look flashed in her eyes: "Regina — and pleading for forgiveness! Ah, well — even a queen must sometimes stoop to conquer!"

The weeks passed slowly on; and, absorbed though Laura was in her camphor-bottle and her novels, she could not but notice that Paul had altogether changed in his behavior toward her sister; and she rejoiced over this in her own fashion:

"I always told Regina that her innocence would come to light, and she would triumph over the machinations of her enemies, and get married to a — But she *is* married—I forget. Well, it will all come right, and she'll be ever so happy, I know."

Poor thing! She could not live to see her so. The camphor-bottle, the close, dark room, and the Frenchy novels were too much for her; and before the spring had brought any flowers to strew on her grave, they had laid her in a darker, closer room than she had yet been in. Her husband and Regina followed the coffin, dressed in deep mourning; and Regina's face, as well as Paul's, was paler and sadder by a good many shades than usual.

Meanwhile, letters passed frequently between Paul and his friend and brother-in-law; and one day, when the roses and lilacs that bordered the lawn were shedding fragrance and beauty together over the old homestead-grounds, Paul announced to his sister-in-law that he would accompany her on her journey to New Mexico.

How the wind of the plains through Paul's hair made it look more than ever like a lion's mane! and how like the Paul of long ago he looked, mounted on his fiery black horse! Something like pity for him sometimes stole into Regina's heart; but she would sneer at herself for the feeling. "Did he pity me when I came home broken-hearted — repentant?"

The long hours of their rest — for the colonel had seen to it that his wife had not to travel in the plebeian stage, but was furnished train and escort at Fort Leavenworth — she beguiled with telling, bit by bit, the story of her acquaintance with Manuela, who had found her way to the fort on the Rio Pecos, one day, where they had been stationed. Regina had been captivated at once by the girl's gentle face and soft black eyes; and when, after an acquaintance of some weeks, she surmised that the girl was looking for the man who had once loved and then, unaccountably, deserted her, she felt only pity for one who could so unselfishly and devotedly love any man as to give up home and friends, and wander through what must seem the wide world to this poor girl, in search of him. That the man was Paul, she felt quite sure; though she had never expressed the least suspicion of this to the colonel.

This much only could Paul learn from his sister-in-law; and that she knew, even now, where the girl could be found; further than this she would not say; would not tell him that Manuela had lived in her own household, half as domestic, half as companion; that she had been induced to this by the vague hope that while with Americans she might more easily learn of those who arrived, or returned, from the States to the Territories; that on leaving Santa Fé she had exacted a promise from the girl to remain in the colonel's quarters and employ until she should send her permission to leave her post.

And so they reached Santa Fé — Paul hopeful and expectant as a young bridegroom; Regina·calm and thoughtful, but trying to look cheerful when she knew of Paul's eyes resting on her; when unobserved, the dreary, despairing look crept back into her eyes, and her face, white as marble, grew rigid as the face of a statue. When the cluster of square, low-built adobe houses, called Santa Fé, rose up before them, Paul could hardly restrain his impatience; but he had promised to be guided in all things by his sister-in-law, and he had now to abide by her decisions. "It would be painful and embarrassing to have any one, even her own brother-in-law, present at her first meeting with the colonel," she said, and therefore requested Paul to remain over night in Santa Fé, and ride over in the morning to where Fort Marcy lay, on the low rise of the hills bordering the plain.

Since Regina so wished it, let the meeting between herself and husband be entirely private. We will not draw aside the veil till the next morning, which came up with a blaze of broad, staring sunshine, promising an unpleasantly hot day. The commanding officer's quarters, though surrounded by a neat paling-fence, was as bare and innocent of the least attempt at a garden as all the rest of the quarters were. The red, hard earth alone stared up at the hard blue sky; outside the fortress walls, ungainly cactus and stunted mesquit bushes made the plain look only the more inhospitable and barren.

The quarters were low, but cool; and as the doorways were only hung with curtains, the breeze that swept over the plain had free access to every room in the house. The large sitting-room at the colonel's quarters had been darkened since early morning, and the heat excluded as much as possible, for the colonel was threatened with a severe attack of the torturing headache that sprang from the badly-healed wound in his forehead. As the sun rose higher, he succumbed to the pain; and as he threw himself on the wide, low lounge, in intolerable suffering, Regina stepped lightly to his side, to supply the usual remedies. But a cold look and colder words drove her back from his couch; and as he called to Manuela to bathe his head, in gentle, almost tender tones, she for the first time felt a deadly hatred toward this girl, whom she knew still to be an angel in virtue and purity.

Struck to the heart, she left the room, only to throw herself on the hard floor of the next apartment, where she grovelled in an agony of anger and pain. Suddenly the sound of horses' hoofs fell on her ear, and she sprang up with one wild bound, and flew to the door, just in time to motion Paul, who had already dismounted, into her presence.

"Now has my time come!" She could hardly restrain herself from crying it out aloud to the frowning mountain and the arid plain. "Ricardo, thou shalt be avenged! avenged thou, my poor heart, for the tears and the blood wrung from thee for many, many bitter days!"

The light of the sun shining into Paul's eyes, blinded him; and though he saw the finger laid on her lips, he could not see the dishevelled hair and bloodshot eyes, and approached her, looking for some glad surprise. He had donned a Mexican costume, and the little silver bells on the outside seam of his pantaloons jingled musically at every step; while the short jacket, showing the pistol-belt under the red sash, set his figure off to full advantage.

He spoke laughingly: "You see I have turned Mexican, every inch of me!" then he caught the wild eyes, with their frenzied look, and he grasped her hand, exclaiming, "Good God! what has happened?"

"Happened?" she echoed with a demoniac laugh; "we have been deceived — outraged — cheated out of our life's happiness — both you and I! Behold the traitor and the serpent!"

Drawing aside the curtain that hung in the door-arch between the two rooms, she beckoned him to approach, and pointed silently to the group in the next room. Bending over the reclining form of the man on the lounge stood a girl, whose face, of angel goodness, was turned in profile to the two intruders at the doorway. The man's eyes were closed; and as the girl stooped lower, his hand stole softly around her form, and nestled there, lovingly, tenderly, as though it had found a long-sought resting-place. Pliant braids of glossy black hair fell far below the girl's waist; and her eyes were of the almond shape, that we find in the faces of those descended from the people of Castile.

In a moment Paul's burning eyes had taken in the picture, and an inarticulate sound came over his lips. The woman beside him watched him with the eyes of a tigress; and he never knew — was it *her* touch that guided him, or did his own evil passions move his hand from his reeking brow to the pistol in his belt? There was a sharp report, a shriek and a groan, and the next minute Paul Kennerly was dashing over the plain, mounted on his fleet black horse, the wind tossing through his hair, and raising it from his bare brow, where it reared itself proudly, like the mane of a lion when he flies from captivity and death.

THE ROMANCE OF GILA BEND.

TRAVELLING from Los Angeles to Tucson, you can, if you choose, sleep under a roof almost every night, providing you have good teams. There are Government forage stations along the whole route, where travellers are "taken in" by the station-keepers, though not on Government account. I do not say that it is pleasant at all these stations, particularly for a woman, as she will seldom or never meet one of her own sex on the way. When we left Fort Yuma, Sam, the driver, assured me that I would not see a white woman's face between there and Tucson. He was mistaken. I met not only one, but a whole family of them, one after another.

The day that brought us to Oatman's Flat was murky, dark, and gloomy — a day in full harmony with the character of the country we were travelling through. We descended into the Flat by an abrupt fall in the road that landed us at once among a clump of scraggy, darkling willows, drooping wearily over a sluggish little creek. In the distance we could see the white sand of the bed of the Gila, and half-buried in it the ghastly, water-bleached limbs of the trees that the river had uprooted year after year in its annual frenzy. We could not go the upper road, on account of the Gila's having washed out a portion of it, and the lower road seemed to be regarded by Sam with all the disfavor it deserved. Verde or greasewood, as ragged and scraggy as the willows, covered the whole Flat, except where, towards the centre, a dilapidated shanty stood on a sandy, cheerless open space. Not far from it were the remains of a fence, enclosing some six paces of uneven ground, and on the only upper rail left of the inclosure sat a dismal-looking, solitary crow.

There was something so repulsively dreary about the whole place that it made me shudder, and when Sam, pointing to it with his whip, said it was the spot where. the Oatman family had been murdered and lay buried, I was not in the least surprised. Only one of the whole family had escaped — a little chap who had crawled away after he had been left for dead, and brought the white people from the next settlement to the scene of the massacre. There was nothing to be done but to bury the mutilated corpses; after this, the place had been deserted and shunned by the few who lived here, though there had been no more Indian depredations committed for years past.

I was glad that the road did not take us very near the shanty, though I watched it with a strange fascination. Sam, too, had his eyes fixed on something that might have been the shadow of one of the victims, flitting by the black gap which had once been the door. The place was so weird that the ghostly shadow seemed to belong there; it chimed in so well with the rest, that I accepted it as a part of the uncanny whole. We had been going along at the usual leisurely gait, but Sam whipped up the mules all at once, and leaned out of the ambulance to speak to Phil, who drove the army wagon containing our baggage. The road was good and solid, so I took no alarm at first; but when the speed was continued, and the baggage-wagon kept thundering close behind us, I ventured to ask, "Is there danger from Indians here?"

"There hain't no Indians been seen around here for more'n three years," was the answer, which satisfied me at the time.

When we came to Burke's Station, where we were to pass the night, a surprise awaited us. The house, a squalid *adobe*, was built in the style common along the route — an open passage-way with rooms on either side. The principal room to the left was bar-room and store-room; the room to the right was reception-room, sitting-room, bed-room, and behind it was the kitchen. The passage-way was dining-hall. When the tall young Missourian, mine host, had ushered me into the room, he stepped to the opening leading to the kitchen and called out:

"Here, Sis, come and speak to the lady."

Obedient to the call, a bashful, half-grown girl appeared, wiping her hands on her apron, and looking up timidly from under her long eyelashes. I took her by the hand. "How do you, child? How in the world did you get here, and where is your mother?" I asked.

Sam and Phil stood in the hall-door nudging each other, until Sam could restrain himself no longer.

"Why, that's his wife," pointing to the young Goliah from Missouri, "and her dad and mam's living in the old shanty down on the Flat. I'll be derned if they didn't give me the worst scare I had yet — thought they was Indians, shore!"

I looked from one to the other. "And how old are you?" I asked the girl.

"Almost fifteen!" was the answer; and when the men withdrew she told me about the rest of her family, whom I would probably find along the road.

Sis was badly dressed; a coarse cotton gown, made with a yoke about an inch and a half in depth, was drawn up close around her neck, and hung loosely about her slender, immature form; her naked feet were thrust into coarse boots, and a large check apron completed her costume. But there was a shy, daisy-like grace about her that made one forget the dress and see only the dove-like eyes and half-pensive smile on her face. Her husband treated her in all things like a child, and she obeyed him without a murmur or a question. When we left he told us that we would find Sis's aunt at Kenyon's Station, and charged us to say that Sis was well, and not the least bit homesick.

We made Kenyon's Station early in the day, Sam and Phil greatly enjoying the prospect of seeing another white woman here. She appeared on the threshold, a brawny, coarse-handed woman of about forty, tidy-looking, in spite of her bare feet and the short pipe in her mouth. By her side appeared a shock-headed girl of twelve, with eyes agog and mouth open at the strange apparition of a civilized-looking white woman. The husband stood beside the ambulance — six feet and a half in his cowhide boots — a good-humored smile on his leathery face, and lifted me to the ground as though I had been a feather. Though the house, like that at Burke's Station, was only *adobe*, there was an air of homely comfort about it, inside and out, that made it much more cheerful than the other place.

Aunt Polly was an excellent housekeeper — as viewed from a Texan standpoint — and after she had in the most *naïve* manner satisfied her curiosity in regard to my looks and general make-up, she commenced preparations for dinner. Sarah Eliza Jane, sole daughter of the house and race, stayed by me in the room. Sitting in a low, home-made chair, she stared steadily at me, sitting on a taller home-made chair, till she had comprehended that the bits of braid and lace in my lap were to be manufactured into a collar similar to the one I wore in my dress. When she learned that the collar was to be for her, she ran out to the kitchen, shouting for her mother to come and see what I was doing. The mother's delight was as frank and hearty as the daughter's, and all at once the secret leaked out that the family was in possession of a fine American cow. Never speak disparagingly to me of Pikes and Texans. The least kindness shown to them is returned tenfold, and the smallest advance of friendliness is met by them half-way. When dinner (or supper) was placed on the table, there came with it the most delicious butter I had eaten for many a long day, to say nothing of a glass of buttermilk, the sweetest I ever tasted. But I must tell you how Aunt Polly made the butter, in case you should emigrate to Arizona without a patent diamond churn. The cream was put into a high tin quart cup, and beaten with a spoon till the butter came — which it did in about fifteen minutes.

By the time dinner was over we had become quite intimate, and Aunt Polly having resumed her pipe, gave me a short account of her history since emigrating from Texas. The two most striking incidents were the loss of her former husband by a stroke of lightning, about ten months ago, and the acquisition of her present husband by a stroke of policy, about three months ago. Though she did not show me the weeds she had worn on becoming a widow, she exhibited the gorgeous "good clothes" she wore on again becoming a wife. She stood at a little distance from me and spread out the second-day dress, so that I could see the whole of the pattern, consisting of detached bouquets — brilliantly variegated in color and gigantic in size — scattered over a plain of light sky-blue. The dress worn for "the occasion" was a gauzy white muslin, which must have had a delicate effect — if she wore bare feet and a pipe in her mouth with it. Her husband had proved kind and indulgent. Since their marriage he had been at Maricopa Wells, and had bought at the store there another beautiful dress of many colors—which, alas! had run out of his saddle-bags, after a two hours' hard rain, on his way home. I saw the dress pattern, and — oh, it was pitiful.

After this display of good-will and fine clothes on her part, she said she had a favor to ask of me, too. She pointed to my trunk, and said her husband was crazy to know whether there was a waterfall in it? He had read so much about waterfalls in the stray papers that fell into his hands that he had the greatest curiosity in the world to know what it was, and to see one with his own eyes. He imagined it to be a kind of box or bag that ladies wore on their heads to carry their hair in, and, seeing no foreign matter on my head, he "reckoned that I packed it with me in my trunk." Aunt Polly had shrewdly guessed it to be a new fashion of "putting up" the hair; but they both had about as correct an idea of it as a blind man has of colors. With deep regret I owned that there was no waterfall in my trunk; but seeing their disappointment, I succeeded, with the aid of a pair of stockings and a pin-cushion, in putting up my hair into quite a little Niagara, to the great delight of these fashion-worshipping people.

How charming the grove of trees looks, when you draw up under their shadow at Gila Bend, after days of travel over tedious sand-plains or through wildernesses of grease-wood and cactus. The whisper of the wind in the trees, the bark of the dog that ran out to meet us, and the cackle of the busy hens around the doorway, told us that we should find good and happy people here. There was the solitary house as usual, but it seemed more pretentious than those at the other stations. The passage-way was higher and wider, the rooms more numerous, and finished with whitewash and good glass windows. At the windows curtains; a gay-colored counterpane on the bed, and wolf-skins in front of it and the lounge.

The station-keeper was a black-bearded, good-looking man, and his name was George Washington — (I won't give the rest of his name — it's too long). I knew I should find Sis's elder sister here as Mrs. George W. ——, for she had been married on the same day with her Aunt Polly. The blue eyes, under long, silken lashes, that met my gaze on the threshold at Gila Bend were like Sis's, only these were the eyes of a woman; there were the same pretty movements, too, only there was more of self-assertion in them. She might have been eighteen; from out of the muslin dress she wore shone the whitest shoulders that belle ever exhibited in a ball-room. Her hands and feet were small, and her rich brown hair, oddly, though not unbecomingly dressed, lay on a forehead white and pure as that of a child.

No wonder George W. was proud of his wife, and had tried hard to win as such the barefooted girl whom he found one day, with her family and some sorry ox-teams, camped near his house, on their way from Texas to California. It was quite a large family. There was the girl's mother, her stepfather, her sister, her brother, the aunt, and the aunt's little girl. Aunt Polly seemed to be the leading man, for to her belonged the two best ox-teams, one of which was driven by herself, the other by the girl, Dorinda. She had hired or bought her niece from the step-father for this purpose, after she had lost her husband by lightning, and Dora had been faithful to her task, although pretty nearly worn out crossing the Desert from Maricopa Wells to Gila Bend, where George W. first found them. After he had taken a deep look into the girl's eyes, he very disinterestedly invited the whole family to come into his house — as far as they would go in — to rest there from the long, hard journey. The family was treated to the best the house afforded, and the oxen were fed on such hay as they had perhaps never dreamed of before.

The Texans were in no hurry to move on, and George W. was in no hurry to have them go; being a bachelor, he was naturally fond of ladies' society. Dora, Sis, and the ten-year-old brother soon became warmly attached to him, and they, with the big dog, Bose, would daily wander off to the Gila to catch fish. When they got there the two barefooted girls and the brother would wade into the stream with ever fresh zest, as they recalled that dreadful drag across the waterless desert. Bose always went into the water with them, George W. alone remaining on the bank, fishing-line in hand.

One day, when Dora had watched the cool, clear water gliding swiftly over her sun-browned feet in silence, she raised her eyes suddenly from under the long, shading lashes:

"Why do you never come into the water? Don't you like to stand in it?" she asked of George.

"Come and sit beside me here, and I will tell you!"

She nestled down beside him, and he called to Bose, who laid his head on his master's knee and looked knowingly from one to the other.

"About three years ago, before I had built this house of mine, I lived in a little shanty, about a mile from the river— just back here. The summer was very hot. I had suffered much from the sun and the want of water in crossing the country, and after the man who came out here with me had gone on to Fort Yuma, I was left entirely alone. When I see you over your ankles in the water now, I am often tempted to call you back, only I know that you are young and strong, and I remember but too well what pleasure there is in it. Besides, you do not remain in it as I did, for long weary hours every day, standing in the shade of a willow catching fish for my dinner. There was little else here to eat then, and I never left off fishing till I was taken with rheumatism, from which I had suffered years before. I was all alone and could not move, and had nearly perished for want of water, because I could not walk down to the river to get it. Nor could I cook anything, because beans require a great deal of water, and I would have died alone in my shanty, if it had not been for this dog." (Bose wagged his tail to indicate that he understood what was being said.) "A dozen times a day Bose would trot down to the river, dip up a small tin pailful of water, and bring it to me where I stood or lay. Otherwise the faithful old fellow never left my side, day or night, and though he would, no doubt, nurse me through another spell of rheumatism, it would be dreadful to be sick and alone here after you and your people have left me."

Dora was stroking the dog's rough coat. "It would be dreadful," she repeated, absently, a tear rolling from her lashes to her cheek. Her words and the look in her eyes thrilled the man to his inmost soul.

"Dora," he said, and arrested the hand travelling over Bose's head; "Dora, I am old enough to be your father—"

"Yes," she replied, looking up artlessly—but there was something in his face that made her eyes drop and the warm blood flush her cheeks.

When he spoke again it was of something quite different, and after awhile the conversation turned to her family. Her stepfather did not always treat her well; he had struck her cruelly once, and her mother dared not interfere, she knowing his temper but too well. George could hardly keep from putting his arms about her to shield her from the man's rough ways, and in his heart he vowed that it should be different if Dora did but will it so. The stepfather and aunt had spoken of pulling up stakes soon, but what wonder that Dora was averse to going?

In the evening George W. proposed to the stepfather that he remain at the station and "farm it" near the river, while the mother kept house for them all and served meals to the travelling public of Arizona. From sheer perverseness the stepfather refused, saying that he wanted to go on to California, and George W. determined to hasten matters in another direction. He hovered as much as possible about Dora, who, since the day by the riverside, had taken Bose into her confidence and affection. Wherever she went the dog went, too, and his master augured well for himself from this, though Dora was shy and more distant than when she first came to Gila Bend.

One day the Texans commenced gathering up their "tricks" and making ready to go. Dora's eyes were red, and George W., to cheer her, perhaps, proposed that she should go with him to where he suspected one of the hens had made a nest in the bushes by the river bank. When they came back she seemed even more shy, though she stole up to him in the twilight, where he stood by the big mesquite tree, and hastily put her hands into his. He drew her to him quickly, pressed her head to his breast, and murmured: "Thanks, my little girl!" as he touched her hair with his lips. An hour later there was clamor and confusion at Gila Bend. George W. seemed to have caused it all, for to him the aunt vehemently declared that she *would* have the girl to drive her ox-team into California — she had hired her and paid for her; and the stepfather shouted that he had control of the child, and go she should, whether or no.

Poor George passed a sleepless night. The picture of Dora, barefooted and weary, toiling hopelessly through the sand on the desert, was always before him, and he swore to himself that she should not go from him; that he would shelter her henceforth from the cruel, burning sun, and the sharp words and sharper blows of her stepfather. In the morning, after exacting a promise from the aunt and the stepfather to remain until he returned, he started out alone on his trusty horse, Bose running close by his side. When he had left the shelter of the trees, he halted and looked keenly about him in every direction. A sharp bark from Bose made him turn toward the river. Swift of foot as the antelope of the plains, Dora was crossing the stretch of land between the road and the river, and when she reached the lone horseman waiting for her, a light bound brought her foot into the stirrup and her flushed face on a level with his.

"Thanks, my little girl, I knew you would come," he said, as on the night before; but this time he held her face between his hands and looked searchingly into her eyes. "What if they should try to take my little girl away before I come back — would she go off and leave me?"

She met his look fearlessly and confidingly. "Tell me what direction you are going, and I will run away and follow you, if they break up before your return."

"Toward Fort Yuma. I shall ride day and night, and return to you in ten days. Good-bye; keep faith and keep courage."

"Good-bye!" for the first time the soft, bare arms were laid around his neck, and the blushing, child-like face half-buried in his full black beard. "Let me keep Bose here," she called after him, and at a word from his master, the dog sped after her over the cactus-covered ground.

At Gila Bend, preparations for departure on George's return were kept on foot — purposely, it seemed, to keep before Dora's eyes the fact that she was expected to go with her people when they went. The days passed, one like the other; there was no event to break the monotony of this desert-life. Yes, there was a change; but none knew of it nor perceived it, except, perhaps, Dora's mother. From a thoughtless, easily-guided girl, Dora was changing into a self-reliant, strong-spirited woman. Her mother knew of her resolve as well as though she had heard her utter it; she looked upon her eldest-born with all the greater pride when she discovered that "the gal had a heap of her dad's grit," as well as his mild blue eyes.

When the morning of the tenth day dawned, Dora was up betimes, mending, with deft fingers, all the little rents she could find, in her thin, well-worn dress. Never before had she felt that she was poor, or that she wanted more than the simple gown and the limp sun-bonnet making up her attire.

"Moving" had been their permanent state and normal condition as long as she could think back; and she had known mostly only those who lived in the same condition. She had never seen town or city; yet, in the settlements through which they had passed, she had seen enough of backwoods finery to know that her wardrobe was scantily furnished. At last, one by one, the tears gathered slowly in her eyes, and she leaned her head on the edge of the bed where her sister lay still asleep, and sobbed till Sis woke up and looked at her with wondering eyes.

In the course of the day, Dora went to the river two or three times, Bose always close at her heels. Whatever may have been the character of the mysterious consultations they held, in the afternoon the dog was missing until near sundown, when he dashed into the station, panting and with protruding tongue, his tail wagging excitedly while lapping up the water Dora had filled his basin with. Unobserved she stole away, and when quite a distance from the house, Bose came tearing through the cactus after her, "pointing" in the direction from where a light dust arose. The little cloud came nearer, and soon a horseman could be discovered in it. A race began between Dora and the dog, and when the different parties met, Bose was fain to leap up and salute the horse's face, because the rider was otherwise engaged. When Dora was perched in front of him, the horse continued the journey in a slow walk, while the girl looked the question she was too timid to ask. George answered her look: "Yes, darling, I think your aunt will be satisfied."

"Then you have brought a man?" Her curiosity had conquered, for she could see no human being beside themselves.

"I have." His laugh made her shrink a little — like the *mimosa sensitiva*, when touched by ever so dainty a finger — and, he added, soberly, "Two of them. One is the station-keeper at Kenyon's Station. Their wagon will come into sight directly; but I don't want them to see my little girl out here with me."

An hour afterward a heavily laden wagon, drawn by two stout horses, was rolling into Gila Bend, followed by Mr. George W., mounted on Bess. A pleasant welcome was extended by all to the new arrivals; even Bose, the hypocrite, barked and capered and flounced his tail as though he had n't greeted his master, two miles down the road, a little while ago.

Supper was served by the mother and aunt — this latter lady being narrowly but furtively watched by the station-keeper of Kenyon's Station. All thoughts of business or departure seemed banished for that night. The aunt and the newly-come station-keeper enjoying their pipe in quiet harmony, a little apart from the rest, so much taken up with each other that the second man was left entirely to the family. The next morning this second man was offered to the aunt by George W. as a substitute for Dora; but, as the Kenyon's station-keeper had offered himself to her as a husband, earlier in the day, the substitute was declined. Neither George nor the second man, however, seemed put out about it. Indeed, there was something suspicious about the readiness with which he went to work on the half-finished corral building at the station. The aunt and the stepfather did not seem to notice this. Only the mother thought her own thoughts about it.

Later in the day, when the father and the brother were with the man at the corral, the aunt with her station-keeper, and Sis thoughtfully kept employed by her mother, Dora found a chance to steal out to the wagon, where George was waiting for her. From under the wagon sheet he drew two or three bundles, which, on being opened, contained what Dora thought the finest display of dry-goods she had ever seen. Lost in admiration, her face suddenly fell, and a queer, unexplained sense of something painful or humiliating jarred on her feelings when several pairs of ladies' shoes and numerous pairs of stockings made their appearance from out of one of the bundles. She drew back, hurt and abashed, and when George asked —

"But, Dora, don't you like your finery? I thought you liked pink. Isn't this dress pretty?"

She answered confusedly, "I — I didn't know they were for me — and besides — I can't take them. I know I am a poor — ignorant girl — but —" a sob finished the sentence as she turned to go to the house.

But she did not go. I don't know what George W. said to her while he held her close to him. It was something about his right to buy finery for his little wife, and the like nonsense, which Dora did not repeat to Sis when she presented to her a dress of the brightest possible scarlet.

That night they all sat out under the trees together. There was no more reserve or secrecy maintained. A dozen papers of the choicest brands of tobacco and half a dozen bottles of "Colorado river water," from Fort Yuma, had wonderfully mollified the stepfather. The mother would have been happy, even without the indigo-blue dress that fell to her share, and Buddy was radiant in new suspenders and a white store shirt. As soon as possible a Justice of the Peace was imported from Arizona City, to which place he was faithfully returned, after having made two happy couples at Gila Bend.

Many months after, on my way back from Tucson, we came quite unexpectedly, between the latter place and Sacaton, on a new shanty. It was built of unhewn logs of cottonwood and mesquite trees, the branches, with their withered foliage, furnishing the roof. A certain cheerful, home-like air about the place made me surmise the presence of a woman.

I was not mistaken; for though the only door of the hut was closed, and I could see no window, a loud but pleasant treble voice rang out directly: "Dad! Bud! come right h'yere to me. I know that's her comin' thar — I jist know it is," and a little lithe body rushed out of the door and up to the ambulance, as though she meant to take wagon, mules, and all by storm. A rough-looking man came slowly from behind the house, and Bud, with a selection of dogs at his heels, clambered over a piece of fence — merely for the sake of climbing, as there was plenty of open space to cross.

The delegation insisted on my alighting, which I did in consideration of Dora's mother being at the head of it. The family had moved back here from Oatman's Flat, where they had given Sam his Indian scare on our way out. Once in the house I no longer wondered how she had discovered the ambulance, with the door closed and no windows in the house. The walls had not been "chinked," so that between the logs was admitted as much light and air as the most fastidious could desire. All around were the signs of busy preparation. It was near Christmas, and they were expecting company for the holidays — a family moving from Texas to California had sent word by some vehicle swifter than their ox-teams that they would be with them by Christmas-day.

Though the house contained but this one airy room, it was neat and well kept. Just outside the door there were two Dutch ovens, and this was the kitchen. Beyond the half-fenced clearing the willows and cottonwoods grew close by the river, and the mild December sun of Arizona lying on the rude homestead seemed to give promise of future peace and well-doing to these who had planted their roof-tree on the banks of the Gila.

The mother sent her love and a fresh-baked cake by us to her daughter. A loaf of the same cake was given to me, and I can say that it tasted better than what I have often eaten at well-set tables, though there was no cow to furnish milk or butter, and only a few chickens to lay eggs. At Gila Bend, you remember, they had chickens, too; and when I got out of the ambulance there some days later, I stopped to admire a brood of little chicks just out of the shell.

"How pretty they are," said I, looking up into George W.'s honest face.

"Ah!" he exclaimed, his eyes lighting up, "but go inside, to Dora."

He led the way to the room, and there, in a little cradle, lay a sweet, pretty girl-baby — the first white child, so far as history records, that was ever born at Gila Bend.

A LADY IN CAMP.

CAMP "Andrew Jackson," in the southern part of Arizona, had not always been without that brightest star on the horizon of an army officer's outpost life, "A lady in camp." If you happened to be of sufficiently good social standing, and clever fellow enough to be received and entertained by the officers of the One Hundred and First Cavalry — which had long garrisoned Camp Andrew Jackson — one or the other of them might tell you, confidentially, lounging in a quartermaster-made chair under the *ramáda* of the sutler-store, as far as he knew it, the story of this lady.

Camp Andrew Jackson was a two-company post; and the officers of both companies, or the number remaining — after a liberal deduction by detached service, furlough, and sick-list — had congregated one day, years ago, to discuss the chances of the major's arrival in the course of the night or the following day. The place of congregating was the sutler-store, or the *ramáda* in front of it; time, between "stables" and "retreat."

"Don't I tell you," asserted young Grumpet, in his most emphatic manner, "don't I tell you that when I was in Tucson, the general told me that he should not be able to let the major have more than five men and a corporal for escort from Tucson out here; and do you think that Major Stanford, with that young wife of his — a shining mark for Apache arrows — would venture on the road, in broad daylight, with this small number? No, indeed. I tell you he'll start out from Tucson about this time, reach Davidson's Springs at midnight, and get in here toward morning in good order and condition."

"Seems to me I should n't be afraid to start out from Tucson, and go anywhere in broad daylight, with *my* wife," said old Captain Manson, the post-commander, grimly.

An amused expression passed over the faces of the younger officers; everybody in camp knew, from hearsay, if not from personal observation, that the captain and his wife lived like "cats and dogs" when they were together, and that he would probably have let *her* go out from Tucson anywhere, in broad daylight and all alone, without the slightest fear or compunction, had she been in Arizona.

"For my part," continued Mr. Grumpet, who had been assigned to the One Hundred and First, and ordered to Arizona immediately after graduating from West Point, one year ago, "I shall be rejoiced to welcome a lady to the camp. One grows rusty at these outposts in the course of years, without the refining influence of ladies' society—without opportunities of any kind for cultivating and improving one's intellect and manners."

"The One Hundred and First has always had an excellent library, embracing books suited to a wide range of capacities and intellect, from a 'First Reader' to 'Corinne' and the 'Cosmos.' And, as far as *tournure* and manners are concerned," continued the gruff captain in a lower tone, and turning to the post-adjutant beside him, "why, I'm sure the doctor and I have made Chesterfieldian prodigies of Tom, the pup; Bruin, the grizzly; and Chatter, the parrot!"

From the laugh that followed, the junior lieutenant of Company "F" knew that something had been said to create this merriment at his expense; but he consoled himself with the thought that "old Manson" felt sore because Major Stanford would relieve him in the command of the post, and probably make him (Grumpet) post-adjutant, as he belonged to the major's company. Left in command of Company "F" by the senior lieutenant's absence, and officer of the day at the same time, Mr. Grumpet felt that he had no more time to devote to this class of mortals; so, bidding them a disdainful "*Adieu*," he proceeded to his own quarters, where he arranged sash, sabre, and belt to the greatest advantage on his sprightly person, and then awaited the summons to the parade-ground.

Whatever his meditations might have been, as his eyes wandered over the interminable sand-waste before him, they were interrupted by the spectacle of a cloud of dust arising in the distance. Quickly returning to his brother officers, he called their attention to this phenomenon.

"If it is not a smoke that the Indians are raising for a signal, it must be the major with his party," was Captain Manson's opinion.

To Mr. Grumpet's infinite disgust he could not find time to argue this question with his superior officer, for the arbitrary tones of the bugle called him to the parade-ground, and when he next found time to contemplate the landscape, the major's outfit was already in sight and slowly nearing the camp.

There is nothing martial in the appearance and progress of a military "outfit," unless accompanied by a command: the rough, gaunt mules drawing the dust-covered ambulance or carriage, followed, as the case may be, by one, two, or three heavy army-wagons; the jaded, worn horses of the escort, and the tired-looking, travel-stained men forming the escort, make a decidedly demoralized and demoralizing impression toward the close of a long journey.

The two occupants of the elegant travelling-carriage accompanying this train were in a state of involuntary *déshabillé*, owing to the sand-storm through which they had passed early that morning, during which the major's hat and a number of

Mrs. Stanford's veils and wraps had taken to flight. Marcelita alone, seated beside the driver in the front of the carriage, had sustained no losses; as her *rebozo*, the only outside garment she possessed, had been so tightly wrapped around her that the storm had vented its fury in vain on her belongings.

Marcelita was one of those moon-faced, good-natured Mexican women we meet with in New Mexico and Arizona. She had probably decided in her own mind — though it was not very deep — that it was just as easy to smoke her *cigarritos* lounging on the floor of the *adobe* quarters of Camp Andrew Jackson, earning thereby *dos reales* per day, and a never-failing supply of *frijoles con carne*, as it was to perform the same amount of labor in Tucson, where nothing could be earned by it, and the supplies of the dainties just mentioned were by no means certain or unfailing. So Marcelita became Mrs. Stanford's maid. "Tiring-maid," I should have said; only I am very certain Marcelita would have drawn Mrs. Stanford's stockings on her arms, and one of the richly embroidered petticoats *over* the plainer-made dresses, had the attiring been left to the taste and judgment of this dusky child of the soil.

Captain Manson alone greeted the major and his wife when the train drew up at the commanding officer's quarters, the younger officers discreetly awaiting the morrow to pay their respects. In accordance with true "army spirit," Major Stanford's quarters had been furnished with the best Camp Andrew Jackson could boast of, in the way of household goods and furniture, when it had become known that he was to bring a young wife to camp. Not the officers of the army alone possess this knightly spirit; every soldier in the command is always ready and willing to part with the best and dearest in his possession, to contribute to the comfort or pleasure of "the lady in camp." Major Stanford had not been with his company since the close of the war; still, when the captain courteously inquired whether there was any particular individual in the company whom he would prefer to take into his personal service, the major requested that Holly — who had already been an old soldier, while the major was cadet at West Point — might be sent him.

Holly demonstrated his joy at being thus distinguished by his "old lieutenant;" and on returning to the men's quarters had so much to say about the beauty, grace, and goodness of the major's wife, that the men immediately grew enthusiastic, and before tattoo obtained the sergeant-major's permission to serenade this first lady in Camp Andrew Jackson, providing a sufficient number of instruments could be found. And Mrs. Stanford was awakened from her early slumbers by "music," the first night she spent in this camp.

There are always a number of tolerable musicians to be found among almost any body of soldiers. The One Hundred and First had always been celebrated for the musical talent in the rank and file of its members; and though the Graces and the Muses had been somewhat neglected of late years, they threatened now to take possession of every individual man, with truly alarming fervor. Indeed, Mrs. Stanford's life was made very pleasant at this dreaded outpost in Arizona — albeit in a little, cheerless room, with mud walls and mud floor, carpeted half with soldier blankets half with old tent-cloth. A washstand of painted pine-wood, and a table of the same material in its native color; a bench to match; one or two camp-chairs, and a camp-cot with red blanket — representing a sofa — made up and completed the *ameublement* of Mrs. Stanford's best room. But there were red calico curtains at the little windows, and a bright rug upon the table; and books, and the thousand little *souvenirs* and pretty trifles always to be found in a lady's possession, were drawn out of trunks and boxes, and other hiding-places, to give the room a civilized aspect.

Still, it was not pleasant in this close-built room, with the door shut; and open, the sand and reptiles drifted in promiscuously. It became one of Marcelita's chief duties, in time, to examine the nooks and corners of the apartment before closing the door for the night, to make sure that no intrusive rattlesnake had sought admittance, and to shake up pillows and blankets before her mistress retired, to see that neither centipede nor tarantula shared her couch. Otherwise it was tolerable; even young Grumpet was agreeable, though he had not been made post-adjutant, but he was Mrs. Stanford's most favored escort in her rides, and that made up for all other losses and disappointments.

The country was not altogether a howling wilderness, either; though the road that passed close by the major's quarters led into the most desolate, the most Indian-ridden part of all Arizona, still, at a point where the road made a sudden fall, a narrow path branched off, and ran immediately into a little valley, where grass and wild flowers were kept fresh and blooming, by the spring at the foot of the hill. It was an oasis such as is frequently found in Arizona, more particularly at the foot of the mountain ranges; and to this spot Mrs. Stanford, accompanied by the major, Marcelita, or some one of the gentlemen, often bent her steps, at times when no Indians were apprehended in the vicinity of the post. The evenings at the garrison were dedicated to quiet games of whist, or interchange of the various news of the day. On Tuesdays, these conversations were liveliest; for the mail came in from Tucson on that day, and letters from the different outposts and the East were received and discussed.

One Tuesday there was, among the official papers laid on the post-commander's desk, an order from Department Headquarters directing that provision be made for furnishing quarters to a company of infantry. Camp Andrew Jackson was to be made a three-company post, on account of the growing depredations of the hostile tribes of Indians. It was not until weeks afterward that any speculations were indulged as to what company, of what regiment, had been assigned to the post; but at the hospitable board of the major's one evening, after a late tea, it was the irrepressible Grumpet who proclaimed that he knew to a certainty all about the matter in question. Company "H" of the Forty-third Infantry was coming, and had already reached Fort Yuma, *en route* to Camp Lowell (Tucson).

"Then Crabtree is in command of the company; or has Captain Howell been relieved? ·He was on detached service in Washington, the last I heard from him," remarked Major Stanford. But Mr. Grumpet interrupted:

"There you are wrong, again; Crabtree is not with them at all."

"Why, how's that?" was asked from all sides; even Mrs. Stanford had looked up.

Whenever Grumpet had a good thing he always made the most of it; and it was irresistibly charming to let Mrs. Stanford see that he knew more than all the rest put together.

"Ahem! Mr. Crabtree, senior lieutenant of Company 'H,' Forty-third Infantry, has exchanged, with the sanction of the War Department, with Mr. Addison — Charlie Addison, you know — of Company 'D,' Sixty-fifth Infantry."

In an "aside" to himself, he continued: "Well, I declare! I've astonished Mrs. Stanford by my superior knowledge. Why, she's actually staring at me."

So she was; or, at least, her eyes were wide open, and her face was pale as death.

"Are you sick, Eva, my child?" asked the major; "or do you see anything that frightens you?"

"Neither," she answered, passing her hand over her face; "only tired a little."

"There," put in the doctor, "I *thought* Mrs. Stanford had

P

baked those tarts and prepared the salad, with her own hands, to-day, and now I am certain of it; and I prescribe that the gentlemen immediately depart from here, and leave Mrs. Stanford to rest, and her own reflections."

Her own reflections! They crowded on her fast and unbidden, when left alone by her husband and the rest of the officers. Marcelita, after having repeatedly assured her mistress that the house was free from invading vermin, had settled down on the floor, with her back against the wall, when she found that Eva paid no heed to what she said. After awhile she grew bolder, and lighted and smoked *cigarritos*, enjoying them to her heart's content, while Eva was enjoying "her own reflections."

"My dear child, did I stay out late? We all went into the sutler's a little while, after taps. Did you sit up to wait for me?" asked the major, kindly, breaking in on Eva's reflections.

Marcelita had started up out of a sound sleep when the major had first entered the room, and she rolled into her own little tent now, into her bed, and back into the arms of the drowsy god, without once thinking of scorpion or tarantula.

Weeks passed before any more tidings of the Forty-third were heard; then they entered Camp Andrew Jackson one day — not with fife and drum, and colors flying, but silently, quietly; with shoulders stooping under the load of knapsack and musket — packed all day long through scorching sun and ankle-deep sand. It was not till Eva saw the line of tents newly pitched, on the following day, that she knew of the arrival.

"Yes," said the major, "they have come; but both Captain Howland and Lieutenant Addison appear very reserved. I don't think either of them will call till a formal invitation has been extended them. Perhaps we had better invite them all to dinner some day — that will place them at their ease to visit here, later."

Invitations, accordingly, were issued for a certain day; but the Fates so willed it that the horses of Company "F" were stampeded from the picket-line by a band of Apaches, during the night preceding; and Arroyos, the guide, expressed his conviction that he could lead the troops to the *rancheria* of these Indians, and recover the horses taken. Although Major Stanford's position as post-commander would have justified him in sending some subaltern officer, he preferred to take charge of the expedition in person, leaving the post in Captain Manson's hands.

"You look pale, child," said Major Stanford, bidding Eva farewell, while the orderly was holding his horse outside. "I am almost glad, on your account, that the dinner-party could be put off. Your color has been fading for weeks, and if you do not brighten up soon, I shall have to send you back home, to your aunt." And tenderly smoothing the glossy hair back from her face, he kissed it again and again, before vaulting into the saddle.

Accompanied by Marcelita alone, Eva, toward evening, set out on her usual ramble, following the road from which the path branched off, leading into the valley. At the point where the road falls off toward Tucson, she stopped before taking the path that led to the spring, and cast a long, shivering look around her. Wearily her eyes roamed over the desolate land; wearily they followed the road, with its countless windings, far into the level country; wearily they watched the flight of a solitary crow, flapping its wings as it hovered, with a doleful cry, over the one, single tree on the plain, that held its ragged branches up to the sky, as though pleading for the dews of heaven to nurture and expand its stunted growth. An endless, dreary waste — an infinitude of hopeless, changeless desert — a hard, yellow crust, where the wind had left it bare from sand, above which the air was still vibrating from the heat of the day, though the breeze that came with the sunset had already sprung up; the only verdure an occasional bush of grease-wood, or mesquite, with never a blade of grass, nor a bunch of weeds, in the wide spaces between.

Farther on to her right, she could see the rough, frowning rocks in the mountain yonder, looking as though evil spirits had piled them there, in well-arranged confusion, to prevent the children of earth from taking possession of its steep heights, and its jealously-hidden treasures.

Grand, and lonely, and desolate looked the mountain, and lonely and desolate looked the plain, as Eva stood there, her hands folded and drooping, the light wind tossing her hair, and fluttering and playing in the folds of her dress. It was the picture of her own life unfolding before her: lone, and drear, and barren; without change or relief, without verdure, or blossom, or goodly springs of crystal water; the arid desert — her life, dragging its slow length along; the frowning mountain — her duties, and the unavoidable tasks that life imposed on her.

With a sigh she turned from both. Before her lay the cool valley, sheltered from careless eyes, and from the sand and dust of the road and the country beyond. Very small was the valley of the spring, with its laughing flowers and shady trees — like the one leaf from the volume of her memory that was tinted with the color of the rose and the sunbeam.

"And up the valley came the swell of music on the wind" — bringing back scenes on which the sun had thrown its glorious parting rays in times past, when life had seemed bright, and full of promise and inexhaustible joy. But she brought her face resolutely back to the desert and the mountain.

She walked on rapidly toward the spring where Marcelita had spread her *rebozo* on the trunk of a fallen tree, before starting out to gather the flowers that grew in the valley.

Almost exhausted, Eva had seated herself on the improvised

couch, but was startled by a step beside her. Was it a spirit conjured up by the flood of memories surging through her breast that stood before her?

"Eva!"

"Charlie, oh, Charlie! have you come at last?" But already the spell was broken.

"I cannot think why Lieutenant Addison should wish to surprise me here. Would it not be more fitting to visit our quarters, if he felt constrained to comply with the etiquette of the garrison?"

"For God's sake, Eva," he cried, passionately, "listen to me one moment; grant that I may speak to you once more as Eva — not as the wife of Major Stanford. Let me hear the truth from your own lips. Eva, I have come here, to this horrible, horrible country, because I knew you were here. I came here to see you — to learn from you why you were false to me; why you spurned my love — the deepest and truest man ever felt for woman—and then to die"

He had thrown his cap, marked with the insignia of his rank and calling, into the grass at his feet; and the last rays of the sun, falling aslant on his rich, brown hair, made it bright and golden again, as Eva so well remembered it.

"False!" she repeated, slowly, as though her tongue refused to frame the accusation against him; "*you* were false — not I. Or was it not deceiving me — to tell me of your love; to promise faith and constancy to me while carrying on a flirtation — a correspondence with another woman?"

"You cannot believe that, Eva, any more than I could believe what Abby Hamilton told me — that you had left your aunt's house without telling me of it, purposely to avoid me and break every tie between us — till a package, containing all my letters to you, was handed me the day we marched from Fort Leavenworth."

"Those letters had been taken from my desk in my absence.

But I had intrusted Abby with a note for you, when I was called to my sister's bedside. And, was it not Abby with whom you were seen riding?"

"Yes — to meet you at Mr. Redpath's farm; and I afterward sent you a note, through her, to which there came no answer save that package of my own letters."

"Why, then, did you go from me? Had you so little faith in me, so little love for me, that you could make no effort to see me? Was it so great a task to write me a few, short lines!"

"Then none of my letters have ever reached you? Oh, Eva, my darling — my lost one — can you not feel how my heart was wrung, how every drop of blood was turned into a scorching tear, searing my brain and eating my life away, when day after day passed, and no tidings came from you? I was on the point of deserting the command, of bringing ruin and disgrace on myself, when a brain fever put an end to my misery for the time, and I was carried to Fort Lyons, as they thought, only to be buried there. When I returned to Leavenworth on sick-leave, I was told you were gone, and your aunt took good care not to let me know where to find you. She had never liked me; but I could forgive her cruelty to me, did not your wan face and weary eyes tell me that my darling girl has not found the happiness I should have sacrificed my own to have purchased for her."

Eva bowed her face in her hands, and deep sobs seemed to rend her very soul, but no word passed her lips.

"Then your life has been made a wreck, as well as my own, Eva?" he continued, wildly, almost fiercely. "Is it right that it should be so: that we should be robbed of all that makes life sweet and desirable, by the wicked acts of others? Must we submit? Is it too late —"

"Too late," echoed Eva; "you forget that I am the wife of another. We must submit. Do not make the task harder for me than it is, Charlie; promise never, never to come to me again."

"I promise," he said, kneeling beside her, and bending over her hand. "Here at your feet ends my wasted life; for I swear to you that I will never go back into the world that lies beyond this camp. But if you believe now that I have been true to you and to my faith, then lay your hand on my head once again, as you did years ago, before we part forever."

"Forever." For an instant the hand he had reverently kissed was laid lovingly on his soft, wavy hair; then Eva arose, leaving him with his face buried in the damp grass, and the shades of night fast gathering around him.

An orderly with a letter for Mrs. Stanford had been waiting for some time at the quarters. It was from Major Stanford.

"You went out with the major this morning, did you not, Tarleton?" she asked of the man.

"Yes, madame; and the major sent me back with dispatches for Captain Manson, and this letter for you."

The major wrote: "Arroyos' opinion, after closely examining the tracks of the absconding Indians, is, that we had better wait for reinforcements before attacking their *rancheria*. Keep Marcelita in your room. I know how timid you are. If you prefer to have a guard nearer to your quarters, send your compliments to Captain Manson — he has my instructions. We shall probably return to-morrow, by sundown. Till then, 'be of good cheer.'"

"There are more men to be sent out to-night?" asked Eva of the gray-headed soldier. She had always shown particular regard for this man; so he answered more at length than he would have ventured to do under other circumstances.

"Yes, madame; and I heard the men say down at the quarters, that the new lieutenant who came with the infantry was to take charge of the scout."

"Very well; tell Holly to give you a cup of tea and something to eat. Say to the major that I shall not be afraid to-night."

"Thank you, madame." And with a military salute, he retired.

Her husband's letter lay unheeded on the table, and Eva was still in the dark when Captain Manson entered the room, some time later. Marcelita brought candles; and the captain, pointing to the letter, said:

"The major is very anxious that you should not feel the slightest fear to-night. I hope you have worded your answer so that he will not have any uneasiness on your account."

"I sent word that I should not be afraid."

"Nevertheless, I shall place a sentinel near your quarters, if I possibly can. To tell the truth, Major Stanford has ordered out more men than *I* should ever have sent away from the post. If Arroyos was not so confident that *all* the red devils are engaged in that one direction, I should have advised the major to leave more men here. But you need have no fears."

The sound of the bugle and the tramp of horses interrupted him.

"The command is going out; they will reach the major some time during the night. Can't think what on earth brought that youngster — Addison — out here. Been anxious to go on an Indian scout, too, ever since he came: he'll cry 'enough' before he gets back, this time, I'll warrant you. The clang of those cavalry trumpets is horrible, isn't it; cuts right through your head, don't it?"

Eva had dropped her hands almost as quickly as she had raised them to her temples; and with her face shaded from the light, she silently looked on the cavalcade that passed along under the mellow light of the new moon.

She sat there long after the captain had left her; she sat

there still when the early moon had gone down, and Marcelita had closed the door before resorting to her favorite seat on the floor, with her back against the wall, from where she watched her mistress with eyes growing smaller and smaller, till they closed at last. The wind had risen again, and was blowing fitfully around the corners of the *adobe* buildings, causing the sentinel on his lonely beat to draw his cap firmer down on his head. It was just such a gusty, blustering wind as would make the cry of the watchful guard appear to come from all sorts of impossible directions, when "ten o'clock and all is well" was sung out. A dismal howl, as though hundreds of *coyotes* were taking up the refrain, answered the cry; and then the clamoring and yelping always following the first howl was carried farther and farther away till it died in the distance.

Marcelita shook herself in her sleep. "Holy Virgin protect us, they are the Indians," she muttered, with her eyes closed.

Eva had drawn her shawl closer around her; but neither the wild night nor the doleful music had any terror for her; she only felt "her life was dreary," while listening to "the shrill winds that were up and away."

Silence and darkness had once more settled on the camp; but the silence was suddenly rent by fierce, unearthly sounds: yells and shrieks, such as only hell, or its legitimate child, the savage Indian, could give utterance to; shouts of triumph and exultation that made Eva's blood run cold with horror. Marcelita had started to her feet at the first sound, and was tearing her hair wildly, as she repeated, in a paroxysm of terror, "The Indians, the Indians! Oh, saints of heaven, protect us?" The darkness was broken by little flashes of light, where the sentinels, some of them already in the death-struggle, were firing their muskets in warning or in self-defence. A sharp knocking on the door, and voices outside, brought Eva there.

"Open, madame, quick: there is no time to be lost"— it was Holly's voice—"they have attacked the men's quarters first, and we can reach head-quarters and the adjutant's office from this side. It is the only safe place; but quick, quick." And between them—the man who had been on guard near the house and the faithful Holly—they almost dragged Eva from the room, and hurried her into the darkness outside.

The elevation to which exalted rank of any kind raises us, is always more or less isolation from our fellow-beings. Major Stanford's, as commanding officer's quarters, were some distance from those of the other officers, and the space that lay between them proved fatal to Eva's safety.

Every single verde-bush seemed suddenly alive with yelling demons, when the little party had fairly left the shelter of the house behind them.

Holly had no arms, and the other soldier had been lanced through the body; still Eva pursued her way, and could already distinguish Mr. Grumpet's voice cheering the small number of men on to resistance, when a whizzing sound passed close by her ear, and the next moment she found her arms pinioned to her body by the lariat thrown over her head, and felt herself dragged rapidly over the ground, till dexter hands caught and lifted her on the back of a horse. Here she was held as in a vice, and carried away so swiftly that Marcelita's screams and Holly's curses—heard for a moment above all the din and confusion of the impromptu battle-field—soon died away in the distance, as her captor urged his animal to its utmost speed.

On dashed the horse; the angry winds tore her hair, and the spiteful thorns of the mesquite caught her flowing robes, and rudely tore her flesh till she bled from a thousand little wounds, but not a moan or murmur escaped her lips. A merciful fit of unconsciousness at last overtook her; and, when she awoke, she found herself on the ground, her wrists fettered by sharp thongs, that were cutting deep into the tender, white flesh. The first faint glimmer of light was breaking in the East; and Eva could see that quite a number of Indians had met here, and were evidently in deep consultation on some subject of vast importance; for even the savage who was cowering close beside her, as though to watch her, was leaning forward to catch the conversation, with an intent and absorbed air.

They had made their way into the mountains, as the Apaches always do after a successful raid; for the less agile horses of our cavalry cannot follow their goat-like ponies on paths and trails known only to the Indians.

Perhaps Eva was even now lying among the rocks and bowlders that had looked down on her so frowningly yesterday at sunset; perhaps, even then had the foe into whose hands she had fallen marked her for his prey, as he watched and counted — unobserved by the less keen eyes of his "white brethren"— all the chances for and against the success of a sudden onslaught.

From the little flat where they were halting, Eva could catch just one glimpse of the country at the foot of the mountain; and from it she could see — though the mist had not yet cleared away — that they must have ascended to a considerable height. Broken, jagged rocks inclosed them on all sides; a stunted tree or overgrown cactus, here and there, springing into sight as the light grew in the east. A heavy dew had fallen, and Eva was so chilled that she could not have made use of her hands, had they been unfettered. The watchful Indian had noticed the shiver that ran through her frame, and his eyes were fixed on her face, to discover if consciousness had returned. But his eyes wandered from Eva's face directly, and travelled in the direction of the narrow trail by which they had come, winding around the wall of rock, behind which the deliberating savages were seated in a circle, Indian fashion, their legs crossed. At a little distance could be seen their horses, nibbling the scant grass the mountain afforded — and one of these, perhaps, had loosened the little stone that rolled down the side of the mountain.

So the Indian mounting guard over Eva appeared to think at least, for he again turned his attention to the proceedings of the council, when suddenly there came the warning of their sentinel on the rock above them, and simultaneously the shout of "On them, my men! down with them! She is here! she is safe!"

Eva's guard uttered one yell before Lieutenant Addison's ball laid him in the dust; but a dozen arrows were already aimed at Charlie's heart.

"Eva!" he cried, "Eva, have courage; I am coming, I am near you!"

So near that she could see where the arrow had struck his side, and the blue coat was fast growing purple from the blood that followed where the arrow in its flight had made that ugly gash. So near that she could realize how desperate was the struggle between him and the half-naked, light-footed horde that disputed every step to Eva's side, literally at the point of the lance.

But the soldiers were not far behind; and with the strength that comes only of love or despair, the young man reached Eva's side at last. She had not fainted — much as my lady readers may upbraid her for this omission of the proprieties — but held up her poor, fettered hands to him with a look for which he would have laid down his life a thousand times over.

"You are free!" he cried, loosening her fetters with trembling hands; "you are free! And if I have broken my promise — if I have come to you again — I have come only to die at your feet."

THE GOLDEN LAMB.

"OH, dear! this is one of her tantrums again!"

"Well, she *is* the funniest girl I ever *did* see."

"And it is only because I laughed at the way the forlorn old maid, whom she calls her dressmaker, had hunched that lovely lavender till it looks like a fright."

"See how she's jerking it, to make it fit."

"Hush, girls," broke in the mother; "that is not the way to improve her disposition. Don't be watching her; look out here at the window; see the number of sails coming in through the Golden Gate this morning."

The view from the bay-window in the second story front, which was used as a sitting-room for the ladies of the family, was certainly very grand this bright December morning, when the sun, shining from an unclouded sky, kissed the waters of the bay till they looked as clear as the heavens above, with millions of little golden stars rippling and flashing on the blue surface. But far more attractive to the two young ladies, who pretended to be counting the vessels in sight, was the view in the back-ground of the room, where a slender, *petite* figure, with head half-defiantly thrown back, was noting in the tall pier-glass the effects of the changes her quick fingers made in the lavender robe, whose silken folds were sweeping the carpet. The head was crowned with a glory of the brightest, lightest golden hair, while the eyes, flashing proudly from under the long silken lashes, were darker than midnight. Yet the sparkle and the laughter of the noonday sun were in them, when the cloud, just now resting on the child-like brow, was dispelled by a kind word or a sympathetic touch.

"There, Lola — it is perfect now," said Mrs. Wheaton, turning to her youngest daughter, and thus breaking the seal laid on the lips of her two older ones.

Matilda, good-hearted, and really loving her sister, in spite of her greater beauty and her "strange ways," meant to improve the opportunity.

"Yes, indeed, Lola; and I've a good mind to let Miss Myrick make up my olive-green after New-Year's. I really think that if I take as much pains as you do, and go there twice a day to show her, she will be able to fit me splendidly. Don't you think so?"

Lola gave her sister a curious look while she spoke, her face flushed, and after a disturbed expression had flitted over it the hardly banished frown seemed ready to come back. "I don't know what Miss Myrick would want with you twice a day; I don't go there twice a day, I'm sure."

"Oh, I was only thinking — well, you *are* the strangest girl." Miss Matilda would have been offended, probably, had her sister given her time; but Lola's hands were already gliding over her hair, removing hair-pins, switches, and other appendages from the elder young lady's head.

"Let me show you how I mean to dress your hair on New-Year's eve," said Lola, and peace was made. To have her hair done up by Lola was always an object worth attaining — no one else could make Miss Matilda's angular head appear so well-shaped as she.

Miss Fanny meanwhile had picked up a book and thrown herself on the lounge to read, but combs and combing material having been brought in from an adjoining room she soon became interested in the braids and twists with which her sister's head was being adorned. During the progress of the work, she, as well as the mother, threw in suggestions, or made criticisms with a freedom which sometimes caused the short upper lip of the fair hair-dresser to be drawn up until the milk-white teeth shone out from under it, though she responded with the utmost amiability to the hints thrown out and the advice so lavishly given. The mother had never allowed an opportunity like this to pass without "improving her daughters' disposition," as she termed it — striving honestly so to do by trying the somewhat quick temper of the impulsive, affectionate child. Because the girl's eyes flashed fire and her lips curled haughtily when any fancied slight was put upon her, as she thought her shy but loving advances were repulsed, the family had come to look upon the youngest born as having a bad disposition, when really a more amiable child than little Lola had never grown into womanhood.

"She's an odd one, and always has been ever since they gave her that outlandish name," the father would say, stroking his slender stock of reddish-white hair from his forehead till it stood straight up like a sentinel guarding the bald pate just back of it; "she don't look like the rest, and don't act like 'em, either, though I spent more money on her education than both her sisters put together ever cost me."

What he said about Lola's looks was true; the other two daughters had inherited from him their water-blue eyes and florid complexions, while Lola had the eyes of her mother — so far as the color went. But could the pale, quiet woman ever have known the deep, intense feeling, or the heartfelt, open joyousness that spoke from her daughter's eyes? Who could tell? She had come to California in early days a sad-eyed, lonely woman, and — she had not married her first love.

Her name Lola owed to the only romantic notion her mother ever had, as her father said. When the child had grown to be two or three years old, and Mrs. Wheaton had noted but too often the dreary look that would creep into her eyes, even at this tender age, she kissed the little one tenderly one day and murmured, her sad eyes raised to heaven, "Dolores, he called me, and if he be dead, it will seem like an atonement to give the name to my pet child." Her husband, blustering and pompous in his ways — meaning to be commanding and dignified — seldom opposed a wish his wife decidedly expressed, never stopping to ask reason or motive; and the Spanish children with whom Lola's nurse came in contact calling her by this diminutive, the child had grown up rejoicing in her outlandish name, and an unusually large allowance of good looks.

In the meantime Matilda's hair has been "done up" and duly admired, and Miss Fanny, loath to abandon her comfortable position on the lounge, has just requested Lola to bring for her inspection the list of invitations made out for the New-Year ball to be given by Mr. and Mrs. Wheaton.

"Wonder what Angelina Stubbs will wear?" soliloquized Miss Fanny. "And how she'll make that diamond glitter! Wonder if papa will ever give me the solitaire he promised me?" — turning to her mother.

"No doubt of it, if he has promised it," was the quiet reply.

"Swampoodle was up to three hundred this morning. I should think he could afford it." Then glancing at the list again, she continued: "Here's young Somervale's name. I suppose Angelina will be hanging on his arm all the evening."

"Charles Somervale?" asked Matilda. "Papa said we ought not to have him come; he says his salary will no more than pay for the kid gloves and cravats he's got to buy when he attends gatherings like these, and papa thinks it is wrong to encourage a poor young man in acquiring a taste for fashionable society."

"Poor or not," persisted Miss Fanny, "he's got to come, because he's a splendid figure in a ball-room, and such a dancer! Poor, indeed! Why, Angelina Stubbs would take him this moment, and her father would jump at the chance."

"I should think he would — to get rid of her domineering," laughed Miss Matilda. "But our papa isn't a widower, and I doubt that he would give any man a fortune to have him marry one of his daughters."

Miss Fanny's face grew crimson with vexation. "You are very disagreeable sometimes, Matilda. But I don't wonder at your fearing my getting married before you, seeing that you are the oldest of the family."

It was now Matilda's turn to get angry, but the mother's quiet, even voice broke in and calmed the rising storm before the oldest of the family could frame an answer. The leading question — the dresses to be worn the night of the ball — was brought up; and when the mother turned to consult her youngest daughter on some point, she found her no longer in the room.

"Where is Lola?" she wondered.

"Gone to the matinee, probably," yawned Fanny, composing herself for the further perusal of her novel, "and I should have gone too, if it was not too much trouble to dress so early in the day. Dear me, don't I pity Tilly, though!"

"Why?" asked Mrs. Wheaton, regarding her eldest daughter.

"She will have to sit up straight all day long with that bunch of hair on her head. She thinks old Toots is coming to-night, and she wouldn't for the world lose her elegant *coiffure* and the chance of looking pretty in his eyes."

Before she had finished speaking her eyes were fastened on the book again, and whatever Tilly replied about not wishing to receive a solitaire as gift from her father fell unheeded, apparently, on the fair Fanny's ears.

It was a mistake about Lola's having gone to the matinee. If we follow her we shall see her ascending one of the streets in the same quarter of the city in which the paternal mansion — as the novel-writers have it — stood, though in a far less fashionable part. Indeed, there was no fashion about; for a corner-grocery, or a retail fruit-shop occasionally made its appearance among the ranks of the generally neat houses, each of which was provided with a flower-covered veranda, or a trim front yard. One of them boasted of a garden and veranda both — the former set out with well-tended flowers, the latter almost hidden under creeping roses and trailing fuchsias. Everything about the place looked prim and neat; even the China boy, who opened the door for Lola, seemed to have been infected by the spirit prevailing, and his snowy apron fairly blinked in the rays of the sun falling through the curtain of the foliage, thinned by the cold nights of the winter season.

Miss Myrick was in, sewing by the window, seated in her own chair, so low that she could not see out into the garden, for fear of being tempted to waste her time. The parlor was comfortably furnished, homelike and tidy, though Miss Myrick occupied it most of the time with her work. She did not often sit in the little room at the back of the house, which really had a better light — the windows opening to the ground — because there was another garden there, and Miss Myrick was so passionately fond of her bright-hued pets that it once happened that the sewing which had been entrusted to her by a cloaking establishment in the city was found unfinished and she in the garden when the porter came to take the garments home. Since that time she had been a great deal stricter with herself — she never had been strict with anybody else, not even with Charlie Somervale, when he had been left to her a romping, frolicking boy of thirteen by his dying mother.

She was an old maid even then, dreadfully set in her ways, as people said, and the twelve years which had passed since then had made her no younger. Her ways, however set, must have been gentle and good, for they had won the boy back from the almost hopeless despondency into which his mother's death had thrown him, and she had made of him a man such as few are met with in our time. His mother had left him nothing, his father having died in the mines years before, poor and away from his friends.

Dying his mother had said to her friend, "Find my brother; he will provide for the boy for my sake." This, however, Miss Myrick had failed to do for two reasons: she knew of the whereabouts of the brother only that he was in the Indies; and had she known more she would not have prosecuted the search, because — well, Charlie "did n't know exactly, but he guessed that her mother had intended Miss Myrick for her brother's wife, but the brother had declined taking stock in that mine." Charlie was clerk in the bank, and we must forgive him some of his peculiar expressions on the ground that " he heard nothing but stocks talked from morning till night."

As we are aware that the banks close at twelve o'clock on Saturdays, we neet not be surprised to see Charlie coming down the street, on the way to Aunt Myrick's house, his home. Lola seemed very much surprised, so much so that her face flushed when he came in at the door, just as she was about to leave the house. After a few moments' conversation about "the delightful weather — and this time of the year, too — nearly Christmas —" Charlie asked permission to escort Miss Wheaton down the street, which permission was graciously given.

Though we should like much to remain with Miss Myrick in her cozy little home, where nothing indicated that the mistress was compelled to earn her bread with her needle, we have more interest in going with the handsome young couple, moving along in front of us as if they were treading on air. Though there is no lack of deference or respect in the manner with which the young man leans over to whisper something into the ear of the younger Miss Wheaton, he has yet dropped the formal address and speech of which he made use at Miss Myrick's gate.

"Lola," and the little hand on his coat-sleeve is surreptitiously pressed as they turn the corner of a quiet street *not* leading to the paternal mansion, "how can I thank my angel for the unspeakable happiness of this meeting? The bright sun would have been shrouded in darkness to me if you had broken my heart by disappointing me. A thousand, thousand thanks for your visit to — my Aunt Myrick's."

She caught the roguish twinkle in his merry blue eye, and the joyous laugh that rang out on the air could not have offended Miss Myrick herself, had she heard the conversation.

"What pretty speeches," Lola tossed her head mockingly; "did you learn them from Miss Angelina Stubbs?" and another laugh spoke of the lightness of heart which finds food for laughter and gladness in all harmless things.

"I told her the other day when she joked me about my advancing bachelorhood" (they were slowly ascending one of the hills overlooking the bay, and it is impossible to talk fast at such a time, even for a young man six feet tall, with black moustache and corresponding hair, and a beautiful young lady leaning on his arm) "that I should have to wait — till my uncle from the Indies came home; and what do you think she said?"

They had come to a little nook high up, where the great bustling city was almost hidden from sight, and the bay seemed stretching out at their very feet; the houses below them concealed by the brow of the hill. To the right, afar off, were peaceful homesteads and gardens filled with shrubs and trees; and whatever might have been harsh or unromantic in the view, was toned down by the distance and the softening lights of the mild winter's sun.

"Well," asked Lola, seating herself on a little ledge of rock where Charlie had spread his handkerchief.

"She intimated, with becomingly downcast eyes, that I might find a fortune within my grasp any time I chose it.

'Oh, yes,' said I, 'Miss Angelina, but then, you know, it's always a venture. And besides, I have made a vow never to dabble in stocks.' She gave me rather a blank look at first, but thought she would n't stop to explain."

Lola could only reach him with her parasol, and the blow she struck him could not have been very severe, for they both laughed heartily the next moment.

"But I have really heard from my uncle in India — it was a letter sent to my poor mother — only I did not want to tell Aunt Myrick; she never likes to hear the name mentioned."

"Tell me about that story," said Lola, her woman's interest in a woman's heart-story aroused; "you once said that she had been disappointed."

"Not she so much as this uncle whom my mother wanted to marry Miss Myrick. It seems that he was engaged to some other young lady — some lovely maid — but a hard-hearted wretch of a brother, or cruel, unfeeling parent interfered —"

"Don't speak so lightly, Charlie," pleaded Lola, her eyes filling with tears; "it *is* bad to have brother or parent come between yourself and the one you love, is it not?"

"Why, Lola darling, what has happened? Does your heart fail? Do you already doubt your love for me, or the strength to assert it?"

"No, no, Charlie — never fear. It is you or death; you know what I have said," and her tiny fingers clasped his strong hand. "But you know as well as I that papa will interfere when he discovers —"

"That you intend to become a poor man's wife. Lola, you know the law I have made for you — the only command I would ever lay on you," and his voice, though tender, was firm, "when you marry me you will be a poor man's wife, not a rich man's daughter. Not a cent of your father's money, good and kind man though he be, will ever be brought across my threshold, even should he be willing to give you the fortune he holds in store for some wealthy son-in-law. There, my angel, let us have done with tragedy and care." It was easy to make an excuse for stooping, so as to touch her fingers with his lips. "Who knows but I shall be a rich man yet before I claim you? I have been sorely tempted to try my luck in something new they have just struck."

"What? After you told Miss Angelina about your vow?"

"But it is something truly wonderful; I have it from old Bingham himself. He cannot go into it — at least not under his own name — and there are only two or three others to be initiated." He was gazing meditatively at the roof of a house that peeped out from among a clump of trees below and far to the right of him. "There's the money I laid by for paying on the house, and Aunt Myrick, I know, has five hundred in the bank; if I knew I could only double it within the year —"

"Don't touch anything belonging to Aunt Myrick, or she will instantly conceive it to be her duty to work still harder, because you might be unfortunate — and then what would become of the old blind woman and the paralyzed man, and the sick family back of the grocery, and her old gouty cat, and the boy with fits —"

"Hush, hush — I'll not touch a cent belonging to her," vowed Charlie, with his hands to his ears.

The sun was sinking low, and after it had been agreed between them just how many dances Lola was to give to strange gentlemen at the coming ball, and how many Charlie was to claim, and how often Charlie in turn was to dance with Miss Angelina, and how often with Fanny and Tilly, the lovers descended the hill more slowly, if possible, than they had climbed it, and finally parted within sight of Lola's home.

There was to be no New Year's party at the Wheaton mansion this year. "No!" sneered Miss Angelina, "for they disposed of the oldest old maid at the last, and probably expect to get rid of the second at somebody else's ball this year."

I am sure Miss Angelina need not have sneered so, because she tried hard enough to get old Toots herself. But that is neither here nor there; Miss Tilly had received a proposal at that New Year's ball, and Miss Fanny her solitaire — from her father, to be sure; but then that was better than not to receive any. Old Toots, proud husband of the peerless Tilly now for many months, was not old at all, and his name wasn't Toots either. His name was Jacob Udderstrome; and in early days he had been the proprietor of a milk ranch, and having used a tin trumpet for the purpose of making known his coming to the more tardy of his customers, he had been honored with the unromantic appellation without his particular wish or consent. When the country had become more settled Jacob sold out, and being possessed of a great deal of natural shrewdness and a native talent for keeping his mouth shut, he had doubled and trebled his money by simply buying up real estate and selling at the right time.

Fanny was still languishing for the right one; she could never think of entertaining less than a hundred thousand, when Tilly had gotten at least three times that amount. Father and mother seldom interfered with any of their daughters' plans or pleasures, and only once in the course of the past year had Papa Wheaton been seriously displeased. On this occasion he had Lola called into the room, and demanded sternly of her why she had refused the hand and fortune of Hiram Watson? He looked quite fierce and kept brushing up the ridge of hair on his head stiffer and stiffer, till at last it stood alone. Then Lola ventured to ask, "Are you speaking of Mr. Watson the tobacconist?"

"Tobacconist? To be sure I am; a tobacconist is n't to be sneezed at when he 's got a cool half million to back him."

"It was not that I spoke of; I have only to say that I could feel nothing more than respect for him; and I will never marry where I cannot give my heart with my hand."

"That 's your notion of what 's right, is it? What, do you tell me, when I 've spent more money on your education than both your sisters together ever cost me, that you can't marry a worthy, solid man because he won't write sentimental love-letters? I tell you—"

He was talking himself into a rage and turning purple in the face, when his wife entered, and, like the good, quiet angel she always was, put an end to the interview and the father's anger with her favorite child.

Lola told Charlie of the interview, and he thanked her for her devotion, and strengthened her resolution by such words as only Charlie could utter—so full of the heart's deep love and the warmth of a rich chivalrous nature. "On Christmas day, my love," he said, "I shall be able to step boldly before your father and claim you for my wife. I am all but a rich man now, thanks to old Bingham's prompting and the secrecy observed, which has left this thing entirely in our own hands. I have the field almost to myself, and shall realize within the next three months such a fortune as I had never dreamed of possessing."

"Not even if that mythical uncle in the Indies had come home?"

"Hang the uncle—no—I mean, I believe he is dead, poor fellow. I answered his letter last year, but never heard from him again, though he expressed the greatest longing to hear from or see some one who had ever belonged to him. It was hard to tell him that even mother, his only sister, was dead."

"Poor fellow!"

"Yes, mother used to say that he was heart-broken. Having come into the world myself after he left it, for the Indies, I can't well remember him; but I can feel for him now, because I know what I should do if you could not be mine. I should break into your room at night, steal you, and take you to the bottom of the sea with me."

Like a romantic young lady, Lola expressed her entire willingness to visit such a place with him; and she said it so quietly that Charlie, at least, believed what she said.

"Let us talk of life now, not of death," Charles went on. "If I obtain your father's consent to our union at Christmas, will you become mine on New-Year's day? I have a queer notion of wanting to celebrate my marriage — to make it a feast or hold it on a feast day. I believe that people who have determined to pass their days together should begin their new married life with the beginning of the year. Will you assist me in carrying out this romantic idea?"

She called him an enthusiast, a philosopher, and a thousand other contradictory names, but the pressure of her hand gave him assurance of her consent to his wish.

Christmas brought with it skies as blue and days as radiant as those for which we sing songs of glory to Italy. The rains of the season so far had fallen mostly at night, leaving the sun day by day to kiss the brown hills into fresher green, after he had freed himself from the heavy fogs of early morning.

The Wheatons were not a church-going people, though the costliest pew at one of the largest churches was theirs; and while Mr. Wheaton was never known to refuse heading a subscription list for any undertaking, the benevolence of which had been duly proclaimed in the newspapers, Mrs. Wheaton had taught her daughters to delight in unostentatious charity. Presuming on her father's fondness for a late dressing-gown and slippers, on days when the observance of a religious feast or popular holiday required that he should not be seen on

California street, Lola had intimated to Charlie her opinion as to the time the old gentleman would probably be in the most "malleable" humor. It was with some trepidation, nevertheless, that Charlie ascended the steps leading up to the wide hall-door of the Wheaton mansion, after having spent the morning in his own room, shutting out Aunt Myrick, Orlando, the cat, the morning papers, in fact the whole world from his sight.

It was probably owing to the unusually good humor in which Mr. Wheaton found himself this morning, that Charlie was requested to walk into the breakfast-room, where the flying robes adorning Miss Fanny's person were seen whisking out at the other door, as the young man entered the pleasant, sun-lighted room. The last glowing coals were falling to ashes, in a grate, which at this hour of the day seemed an unnecessary ornament for a California house.

"Come in, come in, young man. But where are the girls? Tom, go call Miss Fanny and Miss Lola."

There was no necessity for calling Miss Lola — she was close at hand, though becoming suddenly invisible; and as for Miss Fanny, she remained invisible. She had no notion of taking her hair out of crimps just for Charlie Somervale, when she expected to meet a far more interesting person — Crown Point, Gould & Curry, Eureka Con., report said five hundred thousand dollars — at the Wadsworth reception that night. Had Mr. Wheaton not taken off his glasses when Charlie came in he might have noticed an unusual flush on the young man's face; as it was he shook hands with him so cordially that Charlie's color subsided somewhat, and his heart beat less loud for a minute.

I doubt that either the old gentleman or the young one remember just how the conversation was opened; but in less than fifteen minutes Mr. Wheaton, with motiocs something like those of an enraged turkey-gobbler, and a color darkening face and neck fully equal to the intensest shade that bird can boast of on its gills, flew to the door, and called on Lola to make her appearance, in no pleasant tones. Together with Lola, as though divining the trouble drawing near, came Mrs. Wheaton, though so noiselessly, through a side-door, that no one observed her at first.

"Lola," sputtered Mr. Wheaton, "I have spent more money on your education than both your other sisters together ever cost me; and now here comes this young fellow and tells me, as coolly as you please, that you are engaged to him, and the like nonsense. Engaged, indeed; you are not eighteen yet, and he hasn't got a cent to his name. I thought I had brought up my children to love me at least, if I cannot compel them to obedience; and if you, Lola, go off and leave me in my old age — go away from my house with a beggar — you who have been petted and spoiled; you on whom I had built the hopes of my declining years, you will never darken my doors again, but live a beggar and an outcast forever away from your parents' home."

Mrs. Wheaton had approached the group, and Charlie turned to her.

"It is not as a poor man that I claim your daughter for my bride; see, I am rich — worth a hundred thousand this moment," he drew a package of papers from his pocket; "and I have the ambition and the power to amass a fortune, and place your daughter where she will never miss the comforts and luxuries of her childhood's home."

He stepped over to where Mr. Wheaton stood listening in incredulous silence to what the young man said.

"And may I ask from where this fabulous wealth springs so suddenly?" he asked, breaking the silence.

"I own to having tried my luck, against the strict advice and wish of my employers, in mining speculations. The venture has proved successful. I say nothing in extenuation of the fault — if fault I have committed — save that I wanted to offer to Lola a home which should not be too great a contrast to her father's house. Old Bingham —''

"Old Bingham," interrupted Mr. Wheaton, purple in the face; "and the name of the mine?"

"The Golden Lamp," answered Charlie, proudly, holding up for Mr. Wheaton's inspection the papers he had drawn from his pocket.

"Lola!" shouted Mr. Wheaton in his shrillest tones, seizing the girl by the arm and dragging her away from Charlie's side, as if the young man had been afflicted with a sudden leprosy, "come to me, my child. He's a beggar, I tell you — a beggar and worse; for all his friends will turn from him for his indiscretion. The whole thing is a gull; there isn't gold enough in the mine to show the color. Here's the paper. Where did you have your eyes this morning?"

Charlie stood like one paralyzed; his fingers clutched tighter the roll of papers in his hand, and he gazed with a strange, bewildered stare into Lola's eyes, as though trying hard to understand what the dreadful things he heard meant. Lola seemed to comprehend quicker, and the look she bent on Charlie was full of tender pity, as she watched the lines that black, hopeless despair was writing on his face. Mrs. Wheaton had snatched the paper from her husband's hand and was reading:

"The chosen few who thought that for once they could fleece the golden lamb driven quietly into a little corner for their own benefit, have come out leaving their own wool behind. We are speaking of the Golden Lamb Mine, which was to have been paraded in the market about the first of January, to lead astray with its deceptive glitter all who were foolish enough to believe without seeing. The few shares that had already been disposed of 'to strictly confidential friends,' by the shrewd managers of the concern, have gone down from five hundred dollars to five dollars, at which figure they went begging late in the afternoon yesterday, no one having confidence in a swindle so promptly and completely exposed."

"Lola," it was Charles's voice, but so changed and broken that Mrs. Wheaton dropped the paper to look into his face.

Lola sprang to his side, and he groped for her hand as though its slender strength could uphold the man who but an hour before looked able to move mountains from their place. Blindness seemed to have fallen on his eyes, for he repeated the call when the girl stood close beside him.

"My darling," she murmured, seizing the hand that was still seeking hers, and, heedless of her mother's presence or her father's wild gestures, she pressed the icy fingers to her lips, breathing broken words of love and comfort into Charlie's ear.

"Lola!" the name again rang through the room; it was her mother's cry, and the sharp terror in it struck like a knife to the girl's heart, "your father — quick! Would you kill him? Do you not see — he is dying! Oh, my child, my child, cast off everything, but do not load your soul with his death! God help me to guide you." There was something in the woman's eye that spoke of more than alarm at the symptoms of an approaching attack, such as she had always feared for the father of her children.

She had never loved this man with the absorbing passion of which her heart was capable; but as she knelt by his side, giving him every aid in her power in a frenzied, hurried manner, so different from her usual placid ways, her wide-opened eyes seemed to look back through the shadows and mists of long, dreary years, and she spoke wildly and rapidly to her child.

"Oh, Lola! don't blacken your soul with this crime — I too loaded the curse on me; I have borne it for years — and all the useless remorse, the vain, bitter regrets. Give up all you hold dear in life, but do not, do not try to find your way to happiness over the stricken form of your father!"

Lola shook like a reed in the storm, and breaking away from Charlie she knelt by her mother's side.

"Father!" she pleaded, "father, speak to me — call me your pet again — your dearest child; see me — I will never, never leave you, father, only speak to me once again."

No one heeded Charlie, and he staggered from the house, muttering between his clinched teeth:

"So they will all turn from me — and she was the first."

Hours passed ere the old man found speech and consciousness again; and the physician who had been summoned shook his head warningly. "It was a narrow escape," he said; "careful, old man, careful. What is it the Bible, or some other good book says — 'let not your angry passions rise?' Who's been vexing you?"

Lola, his special favorite, whose eyes he had seen opening on the light of this world, was not present, or her ghastly face might have prevented him from asking the question.

Mrs. Wheaton was again the quiet, sad-faced woman, solicitous only for the comfort and well-doing of the man who had been to her the most indulgent of husbands. It was hard to say what was passing in her heart; perhaps the crater had long since burned out, and the silver threads running through her raven hair was the snow that had gathered on the cold ashes. For Lola there was neither rest nor sleep, and she insisted on watching through the night by her father's bedside, though assured that there was no necessity for keeping watch.

Early the next morning she went out, not clandestinely, but with a determined step and an expression in her eye than which nothing could be more sad and hopeless. She returned after many hours, and though her eyes had lost none of their dreary expression, there seemed to be some purpose written in them that could also be traced in the lines drawn since yesterday about the firmly closed mouth. Her mother, concealed by the heavy curtains drawn back from the window, watched her gloomily as she passed through the room gathering up some music that lay scattered on the piano, as though she meant never to touch its ivory keys again.

"Ah, me!" she sighed, "she is young to learn the bitter lesson: that those who have a heart must crush out its love before they can go through life in peace! Dolores — it seemed like an atonement to call her so; but would I had not given her the fatal name. God will help her to forget — as He has given me peace."

The darkening eyes, straying far out over the waters, seemed for a moment ready to belie the boast of her lips, so restless and uneasy was their light; but the discipline of half a lifetime asserted its power, and she went from the room, calm and self-possessed as ever.

Little did she dream of the cause of what she deemed Lola's uncomplaining resignation. The girl had seen her lover, and, unspeakably wretched as he was, she could say no word to comfort him, but held his hand in hers, with all the love her heart contained beaming from her glorious eyes. Only once did he clasp her to his heart in a passionate embrace: she had sealed the promise to be his, with a kiss. They would enter on their new life together at the beginning of the year. They would be wedded to each other on New-Year day — but the priest who received their vows should be Death, and their marriage-bed the bottom of the bay.

Charlie's name was never mentioned in the Wheaton mansion; the events of Christmas morning seemed banished from the memory of the three people who had participated in them. There was nothing to indicate that a change of any kind had taken place or was likely to take place. Once only in the course of the week Miss Fanny remarked laughingly, that she thought Lola was preparing to elope, because all her books, dresses, and trinkets were so neatly packed together. But as no one seemed to join in Miss Fanny's pleasantry, the young lady betook herself to her usual pastime — the novel and the lounge.

During the week the weather changed, and heavy storms swept over land and sea, stirring to the depths the waters on which Lola gazed for many a half hour with a kind of stony satisfaction. She had not seen Charlie since the first day of the week, and she often muttered to herself, "Far better death than a life without my love."

At last New-Year's morning dawned clear and bright, like a morning in early spring. At an early hour the Wheaton mansion became the scene of great rejoicing. There was a vigorous pull at the bell, and when the door was opened a robust young fellow made his way very unceremoniously into the breakfast-room, and a fresh Irish voice with its rich brogue burst out:

"Plaize, mam, and it's a splendid b'y; and nurse says I'm not to stay a minit, but you're to come right aff."

Mr. Wheaton threatened to go off with joy this time, his face turned so red.

"A boy, mother — think of that!" he shouted, forgetting for once in his life what he deemed his dignity, and for the first time calling his wife anything but Mrs. Wheaton in the presence of strangers or servants. "Pat, my boy, here's something to drink his health [Thank 'ee, sur; — and it's a half aigle, shure], but not now; mind you, go right back and stay there till I come, or I'll skin you alive."

After this unprecedentedly familiar and jocular speech, he turned Pat out of doors, kissed his wife frantically and rushed up-stairs to dress, as though the boy's life and safety depended on his taking immediate charge of him. In the meantime the door-bell had been rung again, and Mr. Wheaton stopped when halfway up the stairs, there was something so frightened and excited in the manner of the lady who entered the hall-door.

"Miss Lola is at home, I think," said the servant in answer to her question; and Mrs. Wheaton, crossing the hall at this moment, turned to look at the strange woman.

A little scream, and Miss Myrick — for it was she — asked of Lola, who stood white and ghostly in the doorway, "Is that your mother, Lola? Oh, then I understand it all. Poor Charlie? The woman who could —"

Mrs. Wheaton stepped quickly forward. "Stop, Augusta Myrick; not one word more before my child."

Mr. Wheaton had descended the stairs, and sprung to his wife, who seemed ready to sink, but Lola, unheeding both, clutched Miss Myrick's arm.

"Charlie?" she gasped.

"Oh, Lola! he's gone; his room is empty and all his papers have been stolen or destroyed. My poor, poor boy."

"Gone — to his death without me! How cruel — but I am coming, Charlie; I will follow you."

Her eyes were wandering, and she broke from Miss Myrick's grasp.

"Hold her," cried Miss Myrick, "hold her. Charlie is dead and she is crazed. Help!"

Mr. Wheaton was beside himself, and Mrs. Wheaton flung her arms about Lola, who was struggling to free herself. At last her father's strong hands bore her to a sofa in the nearest room, and as he laid her down the weary eyes closed and the fainting head drooped back.

"Not dead," he groaned. "Oh, God, not dead!" and as the mother and the strange woman bent low over the prostrate girl, a tall, manly form broke into the room, as though led there by an unerring instinct.

"Oh, my darling," and he knelt beside the sofa, chafing her hands and kissing her cold brow; "wake up; you are mine, and we will not die, but live together. Open your eyes, darling; nothing more will part us now. See, I am rich once more, and no one shall come between us. Look up, darling. Come back to me."

Slowly his kisses brought a faint color to her brow and cheek; and when she opened her eyes and he pressed warm kisses on her lips, there was none to say him nay. Papa Wheaton was occupied with his handkerchief — he seemed suffering from a fresh-caught cold, and Mrs. Wheaton stood with clasped hands watching her daughter's motionless form.

Miss Myrick alone had noticed the graybearded, sun-burned man who had come into the house with Charlie. The stranger had gazed silently on Mrs. Wheaton till a mist gathered in his eyes, and he said softly to himself, "*Dolorosa!*" Then the name has been a prophecy, and my poor Annie went through life — Dolores.

Lola moved at last, and as Charlie lifted her tenderly in his arms, no one stepped forward to separate them.

"She is mine now!" he cried exultingly, and he held up to Mr. Wheaton's view a morning paper. "It was false about the Golden Lamb, and I am worth a hundred thousand to-day."

"And besides," the stranger introduced himself with a courteous bow to Mr. Wheaton, "Charles Somervale is my nephew and will be my heir. I am a total stranger to you, so I beg to refer you to the house of Daniel Meyer & Co."

At the sound of the voice Mrs. Wheaton had hastily scanned his features; then she staggered against the wall with a look on her face that spoke so plainly of a life-long sorrow, of a pain for which there is no remedy on earth, that Miss Myrick, forgetting all the hard feelings she had shown at first, sprang forward and passed her arm around the falling woman.

"The excitement has been too much for her," she said; "leave the room, all of you, and I will bring her to herself."

But Mrs. Wheaton's was a strong nature.

"It is nothing," she said, and she turned slowly to the stranger. "Let your coming to this house on a New-Year's morning — though you knew not who its inmates were — be an earnest of your kind feeling for them, and let us be united in the wish for the happiness of my child and the child of your dead sister."

The stranger had advanced and raised Mrs. Wheaton's hand for a moment to his lips.

"To-morrow I take ship to return to the far Indies; but my wishes and prayers shall always be for the happiness of these children, and — the peace of mind of Annie — my Dolores loved and lost."

The last words were spoken in a husky whisper, and none saw the tear that fell on Mrs. Wheaton's ice-cold hand. Her own eyes were dry; and though she had not lowered them, she *felt* the tear burning its way into her very soul.

Mr. Wheaton's cheery voice roused her.

"The boy, children — have you all forgotten about the boy? Matilda's son, sir," shaking Charlie by the hand, "a fine, healthy boy. One of the family now, Charlie — come and see."

But who can blame Charlie for declining to go? His uncle had left the house, and Aunt Myrick had gone with Mrs. Wheaton up-stairs, there to renew the friendship broken off years ago, because of the lonely man who was standing at this moment, gazing far out on the restless, ever-changing sea.

We could not be indiscreet enough to play eavesdropper after everybody but Lola and Charlie had left the parlor, but we have it on good authority that Uncle Barton is to be present at the wedding ceremony before taking ship again for the far Indies.

IT OCCURRED AT TUCSON.

WELL, perhaps it is n't much of a place, after you get there, though harder to describe than many a town of fifty times its size and importance. But it is the capital of Arizona, and a fair representation of the whole Territory. Could you be lifted from the midst of civilization, and "let down" in Tucson over night, you would know at once what the rest of Arizona is.

How like a *fata morgana* it looks when you first see it in this enchanted atmosphere: the intensely blue sky overhead, the plain about it covered with sparse grass and fantastic cactus, that hide the sand and make the earth look verdant; the low, white dome and the picturesque buildings clustering about it; the *adobe* garden-walls, with arched gateways, sometimes whitened, sometimes left in their native mud color, toned down by age and the glare of the sun; a tall mesquite-tree or a group of cotton-woods striving heavenward from among the *adobe* houses; Saddle Mountain, with its ever-changing tints and its strong lights and shades in the far distance, and Sugar-loaf or Sentinel Hill to the immediate left. On the plain between town and the Sugar-loaf, the ruins of what, in any other country, I should pronounce to have been a monastery, lift themselves from the fresh, dewy green — venerable, gray, and stately — some wild vine creeping stealthily in at the frameless window, and out again at the roofless top.

Having purposely avoided a close inspection of this spot, for fear of being compelled to see that the ruins were only coarse mud-walls, standing in a wilderness of hideous sand

and clay, flecked with stiff bunch-grass, the contemplation of it, with my mind's eye, is one of the pleasures of memory to me, even at this day. Could I have avoided passing through the streets of Tucson, perhaps I could think of it, too, as a charming and delightful place. There are gardens down on our left, as we come in from this side, that "blossom as the rose," and are overshadowed by just such beautiful, waving trees as we see in among the houses yonder; and, from these "indications," we are justified in supposing that we will find *parterres* of flowers in the gardens surrounded by those high walls. But we have forgotten to take into account that a stream of water flows along those fields; that gardens don't flourish here without water, and that water in the town can only be had by digging deep down into the hard ground.

The *élite* of the Spanish population pride themselves on their gardens—flower-beds in the inclosed court-yards; flower-beds raised some three or four feet from the ground and walled around with stones—but if the flowers that grow on these elevations are "few and far between," they make up in color and fragrance what they lack in numbers. The court-yard is usually flagged, like the best room in the house, and the whole is kept cool and fresh by continual sprinkling and irrigating. This, however, is correct only of a very few houses; the average Mexican, even though his family consist of twenty head, lives in a single dark *adobe* room, without window or fireplace—the hard, dry, yellow clay within a continuation of the hard, dry, yellow clay without—not divided even by a jealous door. In summer, the family live inside the house, rolling around on the bare floor, or the straw matting spread in one corner—careful not to venture into the sun that bakes the barren ground by their *casa* harder and harder every day. In winter, the day is passed on the outside, the different members of the family shifting their position with the sun — huddling together, flat on the ground, with their backs against the wall that is warmest from its rays. What they do for a living, I don't know: could they harvest nectar and ambrosia, instead of wine and bread, from the land surrounding their miserable houses, they could not be induced to till it; and, as for trade or handicraft, they have never flourished in Tucson. The only thing that swarthy, black-eyed lad there will ever learn, is to lasso his starved *bronco*, or shoulder his lockless gun, and start out with the pack-train, just loading for Sonora, in front of the largest store in town. If he returns from there without losing his scalp, he will never rest till the last *paso* has been spent with his *compadres*, at the *baila*, or the new American bar and billiard saloon at the corner. Nor will he begrudge his sister, or any other lass to whom he is attached, the many-colored shawl in the show-window of the American dry-goods store at the other corner; and, should anything be left then, he will conscientiously devote it toward promoting the bull-fight that is to come off next Sunday.

"Miserable people, a miserable place, and a miserable life!" came from between the set, white teeth of a little personage at the window of a house lying on something of an eminence, in the "fashionable" quarter of the town, as she absently gazed on the fields, bright and alive with the stir and the sun of this pleasant July afternoon.

The fact of the house having windows, and the windows being set with glass, marks it as one of the "aristocratic" houses, though the man who built it, only two years ago, had come empty-handed and broken in heart and spirit from scenes of desolation and wretchedness in the Southern States. If ever a man buried hope, ambition, and life-energy with the Lost Cause, that man was Oray Granville. Even before the rebellion broke out, he had lost his all through the North (as he reasoned); for all that life seemed worth living for, was the woman he had loved. A wealthy Northern man had led to the altar the queenly form which to him had been an embodiment of all that is graceful and divine. The form, life, and soul seemed to have fled from the eyes into which he had gazed just once after the binding words had been spoken.

When the war broke out, he was among the first in the field; and, though fighting for what he deemed his rights, he asked, at the end of each bloody affray — as did St. Arnaud at the Crimea — "And is there no bullet for me?" And after each such day did the look he had caught from those sad, black orbs settle down deeper into the shadows of his own gray eyes. Returning to the home of his youth once more, before starting out on his dangerous journey over the plains to Arizona — where he was to join an older brother — he found domiciled at his father's house his cousin, a young girl of eighteen.

In Miss Jenny's eyes, the vague rumor that Cousin Ray had been "crossed in love" lent an additional charm to his handsome presence, and the melancholy, half-reserved air that made him almost unapproachable. Though there was apparently little in common between the world-weary, disappointed man and the little elfish creature that looked so joyfully out upon the world with her light-blue eyes, he unconsciously fell under the influence of her restless, but most cheerful spirit. Not that her temper was always sunny and even — far from it: but too often her eyes would flash fire, and the quivering flanks of the fine-chiselled nose distend and almost flatten in the hot, flushed face. Just so her Cousin Ray's nostrils were wont to spread when angered or excited — only that his face would grow white and more marble-like than usual.

On what ground these two spirits met, I cannot say; but when Oray Granville finally left his southern home, it was in company with his wife, Mrs. Jenny. Nor can I recount, at length, how love worked wonders, and the petted, white-fingered little lady learned to take thought for the morrow and the comfort of her lord and master; and though often flying into one of her sudden fits of passion, when a batch of "sad" bread was the reward for all her pains and patience, or a burn on her wrist or fingers, she never once breathed a word of regret at having come with her husband. Her husband never attempted to subdue her temper or soothe her ruffled feelings; but if, when worn out with the day's toil (of which he bore his honest share), she crept up beside him, he had most always a kind word for her; or, if more chary of words than usual, a soft pressure of the little hand that had stolen into his, told her that her affection was felt and appreciated.

Shortly after their arrival in Tucson, he was prostrated by the horrible fever which this place has in store for most strangers. The *petite* frame of the wife resisted the enemy to whom the stalwart man was forced to yield; and with untiring devotion she watched by him through the long days and the lonely nights. He needed sleep, the doctor said; and she crept about like a little mouse. But, hanging over him, and listening to his low, irregular breathing, such a terror would seize her that, bending close to his ear, she would plead, "Ray— Cousin Ray— are you alive? Speak to me, please." Then the heavy eyes would open for a moment, and she remain quiet, till her fears got the better of her judgment again. But never a look of reproach came into the weary eyes, and never a word from the white lips, though his life had nearly been a forfeit to her loving, but impatient spirit.

Nor did she once fly into a passion during the long days of his convalescence; but when he had quite recovered, she proved that she had not left her temper behind her in the South, where he, according to her accusation, had left his tongue. There were days in which he seemed to live only in a dream, so silent were his lips; but the office which had been bestowed upon him, almost against his will, was ably and faithfully filled — though a bend of the head or a single terse sentence was given, where other men would have deemed volumes of speech necessary. It was no wonder that his wife flew into a rage, when, as sometimes happened, she had recounted to him the troubles and trials of the day — which were not few — and found, at the end of an hour's harangue, that he had neither heard nor understood a word of what she had said, but seemed to waken from a trance at the little pettish shake she gave his arm. Then she would accuse him of not loving her, bewail her sad lot, and vow to grow silent and unloving like himself. After a season of storming on her part, and utter silence on his, she would creep back to her old place beside him, to find her kiss returned, and any cunningly devised question, calculated and shaped toward reconciliation, answered by him, kindly and calmly as ever.

One afternoon, while Cousin Ray sat in his office — silent, preoccupied, and moody as usual — the din and confusion of an extensive dog-fight disturbed his reveries. A cloud of dust and dogs rolled up to the office-door, and the next moment the attorney of the Territory stood in the street, a club in one hand and a "rock" in the other. A few well-aimed blows soon freed "the under-dog in the fight" from his half-dozen assailants; and with a half-sneaking, half-confident air, the little ugly thing — part cur, part *coyote*, with a slight tinge of sheep-dog — followed his deliverer to the office. When evening came, the dog shyly, but persistently, followed his newly-elected master home; and Mrs. Jenny, after first bitterly railing both at her husband and the dog, proceeded to set supper before them with equal care and conscientiousness. Next morning she found occasion to anathematize Arizona in general and Tucson in particular; and, her eye falling on the new acquisition, she instantly attacked him.

"Get away with you! Of all things in creation you're the ugliest, and *your* name should be Tucson, too."

And Tucson it was, from that day out. The dog soon learned to understand Mrs. Jenny as his master did, only he could not be brought to endure her bursts of temper with the same gentlemanly calmness. His meals were as well and regularly provided as though he had a well-founded claim to the best of treatment; and of an evening, when Cousin Ray was absent, he was left at home, and admitted to the sitting-room, where a small piece of Mrs. Jenny's dress-skirt was tacitly admitted to be his privilege during his master's absence. But only during his absence: as soon as his footstep was heard approaching from the street, Mrs. Jenny seemed suddenly to discover the dog's proximity, and with a threatening "You get out!" the dress-skirt was quickly withdrawn, while Tucson, made wise by experience, would spring to a safe distance, and there flash defiance at her, with his white teeth and his glittering black eyes.

Last night, however, the edge of the dress-skirt had been carefully gathered up from the floor, and Tucson, on growling his dissatisfaction, had been turned into the cold, open hall, where he met his master with a little whine when he came home, late, and more moody and buried in thought than ever. Nevertheless, he stooped to pat the dog's shaggy head, before entering the room, with a half-drawn sigh. Mrs. Jenny had well merited the reproach she always flung at her husband, this night, so silently and noiselessly she moved around the room. Cousin Ray cast on her just one look — that said more than all the words she had spoken for years; but she did not heed it, and, with another sigh, at the remembrance of the letter signed "Margaret," which she had found in his pocket that morning, he sought the couch where neither sleep nor peace came to the two. Early the next morning he had gone to the office, but returned before noon, and mounted his stout *bronco*, being accompanied by a small number of Americans and an old Mexican guide.

It was not the first time Mrs. Jenny had helped equip and furnish a cavalcade of this kind, for a prospecting or mining expedition; and, unbidden, she brought out her husband's warmest wraps and her best stores from the larder. For a moment her cheeks blanched, as, from a few chance words she caught, she was led to believe that the object of the journey was the finding of the firmly-believed-in Jesuit, or Hidden Silver-mine. But her husband volunteered no explanation; and she would show him, for once, that she could refrain from asking questions. As he approached and bent over her to bid her good-by, the fatal white envelope that had so angered her yesterday, again gleamed from an inside pocket; and, hastily drawing back, she spoke sharply in answer to his cordial words:

"You need *never* come back to me with that letter in your pocket. Never — never!"

And, passing in through the hall-door, she saw Tucson quenching his thirst eagerly, as preparing for a long run, at his basin on the floor. Quick as thought she had caught him up in her arms, and, carrying him to the door, she flung him with all her force against Cortez, who was just moving off, with his master on his back.

"Go along with your master, you ugly brute. *I* never want to see you again — never, never!" and the heavy door closed with a loud bang.

Then she went back to her household duties, never heeding that the sun had reached the meridian, and never pausing till material and strength together were thoroughly exhausted. At last, after obstinately brushing down the curls that would as obstinately spring up again, she drew near to the window. She never knew how long she stood there; but when the women by the *acequia*, in the tree-bordered field, away down from the house, packed the linen they had made a pretence of washing all day, into their large, round baskets to carry home for the night, Mrs. Jenny—uttering her verdict on the people and the place — turned sharply on her heel, and opened the box containing her outdoor garments. Her hat was soon tied on, and a heavy shawl thrown over her arm, to guard against the cool of the night that might overtake her. Pleasantly returning the greeting that all who met her offered, she went unmolested on her way till she reached the last huts of the Papagoes — who burrow here, half underground, at a respectable distance from the better class of Mexicans. From the door of a stray *adobe*, that looked like an advance-post of rude civilization among these wicker-huts, a female voice, in the musical language that the roughest of these Mexicans use, called after her:

"Holy Virgin, *señora*, are you not afraid of the Apaches?"

But, like the youth who bore "the banner with the strange device," she passed on, heedless and silent, to all appearances, but saying, within her stubborn little heart, "Indians or no Indians, *I'm* going to Cousin Will's."

In less than an hour's time, the barking of dogs fell on her ear, and, though no trace of fence, orchard, or barn could be seen, she knew that in and beyond that grove of mesquite-trees lay Cousin Will's possessions — counted one of the finest farms in the Territory. Directly she turned from the road into an open space, where a low, solid *adobe* house and two or three dilapidated *jacales* represented a comfortable farm-house and extensive out-buildings, to the right of which a large field of waving corn stretched downward to the river. Back of the house blossomed a little garden, the scarlet geranium covering almost the whole wall; from the garden the ground fell abruptly to the water, where a clump of willows and cotton-woods shaded a large cool spring. But the most surprising feature of this Arizona scene was a spring-house, which, though built of *adobe*, looked just as natural, and held just as rich, sweet milk as any spring-house found in the Western States.

Mrs. Jenny, however, had no time to advance to this spot, even had such been her intention. The barking of the dogs had called a dozen or two of swarthy little Cupids from the *jacales* and other resorts of the *peones*, who, with a simultaneous shout, had rushed in a body to the house of the master, announcing the coming of the unexpected visitor. Cousin Will and his wife — one of those grand, black-eyed women, with the bearing of a princess, whom we find among the old Spanish families—met the sister-in-law long before she reached the house. Cousin Will's wife greeted her sister-in-law cordially as "Juana;" while Mrs. Jenny held to the more formal "Doña Inez," which she had never yet dropped — perhaps on account of a fancied likeness between her and Margaret, of whom she had secretly begged a most minute description from one of the younger brothers in her uncle's house, at home.

"Why did Brother Ray let you come out here alone?" asked the older brother, almost indignantly.

Doña Inez, who understood English, smiled a good-humored, but expressive smile; noticing which, Mrs. Jenny supplemented, without the least resentment: "And, besides, he wasn't at home to try. He started out this morning with Blake, and Goodwin, and old Pedrillo."

"To look for the Hidden Mine of the Padres? Oh, the foolish, foolish boy! Had I known how determined he was to go, I should not have left him last night. Will he never stop dreaming and chasing after shadows?"

Cousin Will was full twenty years his brother's senior; and it was, perhaps, the recollection of the almost fatherly love he had always shown for the younger brother that made Mrs. Jenny suddenly, when Doña Inez had left the room, fling her

23*

hat on the floor, herself on the lounge, and give way to the tears that had gathered in her heart all day. Cousin Will knew her too well to offer a single word of comfort or consolation; but when her convulsive sobs had ceased at last, he told her, in answer to her quick, impatient questions, all he knew of the letter, its contents and consequences.

In the old archives of Tucson, to which Ray, by virtue of his office, had access, he thought he had found sufficient proof of the existence of the old silver ledge, and sufficiently clear advices of its location, to warrant him in making a search for it. Fully aware of the many dangers to which any party he might organize for that purpose would be exposed, he had long hesitated — hesitated, too, partly on account of his wife's violent opposition, and partly because there were few, whom he would select, willing to go with him, where hundreds had already perished from the Indian's arrow and the want of food and water. Three days ago, the letter from Margaret had found its way to him. She was not long for this world, she said, and, poor and in distress — abandoned by her husband, who had been beggared by the war — she pleaded that Ray should care for the two children she must leave to the cold charity of strangers, if she died.

"What will you do about it?" his brother had asked. And then Ray had unfolded to him what the brother called one of his day-dreams. He would find the mine, load Jenny with the treasures its discovery would bring, and send her back to the States, to find Margaret, or the children (if she were dead), while he remained behind to develop and finally dispose of the mine, before joining his wife. He knew what Jenny had undergone in this country, for his sake; he knew how well she loved him, and he trusted that, with her noble instincts, she would aid him in carrying out his projects in regard to Margaret and her children — neither of whom he ever intended to see.

Since she had once given way to softer feelings, Jenny's better self arose against the hard, cruel spirit that had prompted her to turn from all of Ray's attempts at kindly explanation. Bitterly she regretted the harsh words she had uttered when her eyes first fell on that miserable letter; and, like serpent's fangs, the words she had called after him on parting, struck again and again into her own bleeding heart. Restlessly she tossed on her bed all night — the first to discover the approach of a band of Apaches, from the uneasy stamping and the frightened wickering of the mules — she was the only one who insisted that Tucson's bark could be heard among the gang of *coyotes* that made night hideous with their howls. With the first gleam of the coming day she was up; and, in spite of all her brother-in-law could say, in spite of the suspicious footprints that marked the ground in the neighborhood of the mule-*corral*, she started for home, alone and unprotected, as she had come the night before.

The gorgeous sunrise had no charm for her; unheeding, her eye passed over the landscape, that was like the smile of a fair, false woman — soft and alluring to the eye — a bright mask only, veiling death and destruction from those who were blinded by it. When near the town, a small, ragged-looking object came ambling swiftly toward her.

"What — Tucson?" and then, apostrophizing the dog, who crouched in the sand at her feet with a pitiful whine: "You mean little deserter! Could n't you hold out as long as your master? And I know your master has not come back yet." Nor *had* he — though she entered the house with an insane hope that she might meet the grave eyes peering out from the gloom of the darkened hall. After another sharp reprimand, she prepared Tucson's breakfast from a part of her own; and then flew into a passion and drove the dog from the house, because, instead of tasting a mouthful, he insisted on dragging her to the door by the dress-skirt, and barking and howling in turn, when she refused to come.

Later in the morning, when she had occasion to go "down town" for something, she recounted how the dog had shrunk from the fatigues of the prospecting-trip, and had returned to his comfortable quarters at home. "But I drove him from the house; and I guess he has gone to overtake his master now — I don't see him around any more."

He *had* gone to overtake his master — but not alone. The dog's strange bearing had excited suspicion — here, where people are always on the alert for danger and evil of all kinds. Before the sun was well up, a little band of well-armed citizens was on the trail that Oray Granville and his friends had travelled but the day before.

Well for Jenny that her eye never caught the meaning of the looks thrown on her as she passed through the straggling streets back to her own home; well for her that the soft-voiced *señoras*, who came to her in the dusk of the evening, could check the word of sympathy that rose from the heart to the lip. Ah, me!

And in Jenny's voice there was a new tone; a new light was in her eye, and — a new greeting in her heart for Cousin Ray. If he would only come soon! Of course, he could not return for a day or two; perhaps not for a week; but when he did come —

"Petra," said Jenny, "you must play me Oray's favorite air to-night" — and she hastened to the corner where the harp of the girl, who was a pet of Mrs. Jenny's, and Ray's too, was generally kept.

"No, *señora* — no; not this night," remonstrated the girl. "The wind howls so dismally — and there is no moon in the sky; and then, you know, I cannot sing."

Petra was whimsical, and what she said was true: the wind passed with a low, sobbing sound through the bare, wide hall, and swept up to the door, where it shook the lock as with living fingers.

Mrs. Jenny drew back the curtain and laughed.

"In our country, people don't like to own that they're moon-struck; but you are right — the night is black as ink, and — why — there is quite a company coming up the hill toward us, with lights and torches. Going to the governor's house, probably; but who can they be?"

"We can slip out of the back-door, directly, and look over to the house: then the men cannot say that we have undue curiosity," suggested Anita, desperately; and Mrs. Jenny dropped the curtain.

Petra's blanched face drooped low, over a book she had snatched up from the table; and Anita's hands were clasped in a silent prayer to the Holy Virgin. But the train came nearer, and — "Hark! they stop here — at this door — it is Ray — Cousin Ray!" And Jenny was on the threshold — where half a dozen gloomy, earnest faces met her gaze.

There was a horse there, too — stamping with a half-frightened motion, and a low, shivering neigh; and as she sprang forward with a shriek — a terrified question rising unconsciously to her lips — a dog flew at her with an angry howl, tearing at her garments, and making frantic efforts to prevent her touching the motionless form on the back of the horse.

To Jenny's ear the dog's wild yells spoke terribly plain her own cruel "Never — never — never!" but among the men there was a hasty murmur that the beast had gone mad, from running so long without food and water. There was a flash and a sharp report — Tucson's career had come to a close. And Jenny lay fainting in the arms of the sobbing women.

S

A BIT OF "EARLY CALIFORNIA."

THAT many strange and wonderful things happened in early times in California, is so trite a saying that I hardly dare repeat it. As my story, however, is neither harrowing nor sentimental, I hope I may venture to bring it before the reader.

Long before the great Overland Railroad was built, there entered one day one of the largest mercantile establishments in San Francisco a handsome, athletic man, whose fresh, kindly face showed a record of barely five-and-twenty years, and whose slender fingers belied the iron strength with which he could hold and tighten the threads forming the net into which malefactors are said, sooner or later, always to run. If he *was* a detective officer, he had friends, because he had a warm heart; and in spite of all the dark phases of life that were brought to his notice every day, he had not learned to disbelieve in the bright side, or the better instincts of humanity.

The chief clerk of this establishment was Captain Herbert's (the detective officer's) most intimate friend, and he had come to bid him good-bye — perchance to charge him to guard the "fatherless and the widowed," should the trip on which he was about to start out end disastrously to him. "Early Californians" realized, better than any other class of people, the uncertainty of life — particularly with those who had to cope with the desperadoes of that time; and the captain intended to start out as usual — with the determination to do or to die.

"By-the-by," said young Taylor, laughing, to the senior partner of the firm, studying the morning paper in the counting-room, "Mr. McDonald has been silent for so long that I think it would be a good job, and an economical one, to commission the captain to hunt up the junior partner of this firm, at the same time, and bring him in with the absconding cattle-agent."

The old gentleman took off his glasses, and folded the paper.

"Yes; it's time Harry was home. I'm really getting uneasy about him. They may have tempted him with the prospect of a whole string of wives as he passed through Salt Lake — whereas here he can have only one."

"Give me his *carte-de-visite*, or the color of his hair and eyes, height, breadth, and weight, and I'll bring him, sure!" laughed the captain.

"Thank you kindly, captain; but I don't know whether Mr. McDonald would appreciate your kind attentions; particularly," continued the old gentleman, "if enhanced by those little steel bracelets you bring into requisition sometimes."

Twenty-four hours later the captain was hurrying, as fast as the stage-horses could run, to Salt Lake City, where, it was surmised, the dishonest cattle-agent would be found. A few hours' vigorous hunt convinced the captain that the object of his search was not there — circumstances pointing backward to one of the smaller places he had passed on his journey thither; — and the next stage that left had the captain for its occupant again. The only other passenger beside the captain and his one man, was a rather slender, well-built person, who, like himself and assistant, had both hands full, literally, to keep from being buried by the sides of bacon with which the stage was filled almost to overflowing.

When night set in, the coats of the captain and his man,

and the woollen shirt of their travelling companion, seemed all to have been made of the same material, thanks to the equalizing gloss which the tumbling sides of bacon had spread over everything; but they fought the pork as valiantly as ever true-believing Israelite had done. There was little rest for them through the night, and no sleep; the treacherous bacon-sides, that had been closely packed to serve as pillows, would unexpectedly slip away from under their weary heads; and the bacon barricades, laboriously built, would descend like an avalanche of blows and hard knocks, when left unguarded by the drowsy travellers.

Luckily the bacon was left, the next morning, at a little town where it was wanted more than in the stage coach; and the captain, who had passed nothing on the road without casting on it at least half of his keen, official eye, gathered enough information here to feel confident of finding his game in one of the little new places springing up on the mail-line in Nevada. They reached the place next day at nightfall — it was near the border of California — and the captain saw at a glance that it would be warm work to cage any of the ill-favored birds who flocked about this place. Warm work it would have been under any circumstances: but made more difficult by the fact that the man in question had absconded from his employers in British Columbia somewhere, had merely passed through San Francisco with his plunder — some thirty-six thousand dollars — and could have defied all the law officers in California, if they came, as the captain did, with only the commission of the victimized cattle-owner, but without the authority that the existing relations between British Columbia and the United States made necessary.

Among the gamblers and roughs loafing about the hotel, the captain's quick eye had soon lighted on the right man; and after quietly taking his supper with his companions, he proceeded to arrest him. Of course there was an outcry and a hubbub among the patrons of this hotel, and the captain, who knew where his customer came from, gave the guilty man to understand that lynching a man who was no better than a horse-thief, was nothing unusual in California and Nevada; but that if he, the prisoner, would promise to remain quietly up-stairs in the room with the captain's man, he himself would go back into the bar-room and try to persuade the people to desist from carrying out any horrible plans they might have formed. The prisoner seemed to feel weak in the knees; asked permission to lie down, and sadly but gently extended his hands to the alluring steel wristlets which the captain persuasively held out. Returning to the bar-room, the latter singled out the head bully, approached him confidentially, and whispered that on him he must depend for assistance in keeping his obstreperous prisoner from breaking away; that he himself and his assistant were so tired out with a three-nights' ride and the fruitless chase, that they could hardly keep their eyes open; and that after seeing the landlord he would return and consult how they had best manage to keep their man safe.

From there the captain went straight to the room of the stranger who had come in the stage with him; to him he told all the circumstances of the case, and asked for his help. He was not mistaken in the man; and the stranger at once expressed his determination to aid the side of the law and the right. Proceeding together to the room of the prisoner, the captain's assistant was instructed to procure, as secretly as possible, a conveyance for himself, the stranger, and the prisoner, to the next town — already in California — some thirty miles away. Then there were more dark fears expressed concerning mobs and lawless proceedings, and hints thrown out, suggestive of the contempt in which horse-thieves and the like were held, and a clump of trees was spoken of, that stood close by the hotel and had been found convenient for hanging purposes before this. The stranger was left to guard the prisoner, and the captain made his way to the bar-room, where he was examined in the most friendly and patronizing manner, concerning "that little affair;" how much money the man had taken, whether the captain had yet recovered it, and what he meant to do next. Not a cent of the money had been recovered as yet, the captain said (with thirty-five thousand dollars neatly tucked away about his person), but he hoped that with good help — winking at the most ill-favored among them — he would get both the man and his money safely into California. He was not sparing in treats, and had the crowd drink the health and success of everybody and everything he could think of, till at last, apparently overpowered with sleep, he beckoned the rowdy he had spoken to before to one side. Familiarly tapping him on the shoulder, he said, trustingly:

"Now, old fellow, remember, I depend on you, should any of these rascals here make an attempt to assist my man in getting away from me. I'm tired to death, and if you'd sit up for an hour or two longer, while I take a short nap, I'd take it as a great kindness. At all events, I shall handcuff my prisoner and myself together, so that he cannot leave the bed without my knowledge."

The man swore a thousand oaths that he'd see the captain out of this, and then returned to his companions — to plot the release of the thieving cattle-agent, who, he felt certain, still had the stolen money about him. Tired out and sleepy, the captain certainly was; and, after barricading the door with as much noise as possible (having previously nailed boards across the window with a great deal of hammering), he lay down, and was soon in a sound sleep. Sometime after midnight he was aroused by loud, heavy blows on the door. Of course, the captain knew who was there, and what they wanted, just as well as though each member of the rowdy delegation had sent in a card with name and object of the visit engraved thereon. After considerable parleying, and some "bloody" threats, the barricade was slowly removed, the door opened, and the captain discovered, admiring a very handsome six-shooter in his hands. His confidential friend, the bully from the bar-room, was spokesman of the gang; and, after some hard staring and harder swearing, the truth dawned on the minds of these worthies, and they withdrew from the room to search the rest of the house before taking farther measures.

The captain resumed his broken slumbers, never dreaming that they would carry proceedings any farther; but next morning, seated on the stage beside the driver, he saw on the road the wreck of a turn-out, and grouped about it a number of the would-be liberators of the night before. They had "raised" a team somewhere, and had started in pursuit of the fat prize, hoping to outwit and outride justice for once. The night being dark and their heads very light, they had run full tilt against a tree in the road, which had the effect of killing one horse, stunning the other, and scattering the inmates of the wagon indiscriminately over the ground. Bully No. 1, and two stars of lesser magnitude, insisted on mounting the stage; and, on arriving at the next town, the captain, fearing that the local authorities would interfere on the representation of these men, had his prisoner on the road again before they had time to take any steps, either legal or illegal.

The horror of the prisoner can be imagined when he learned that these terrible men, who were trying to get him out of the captain's hands in order to mete out justice on their own account, were actually pursuing him — probably with a rope ready to slip around his neck at the first opportunity. He earnestly besought his protectors not to abandon him; for the captain had told him that he had no right to hold him as prisoner, and should have none until certain formalities had been gone through with in San Francisco.

On they flew — without rest — still pursued by the three roughs, who seemed to have gotten their spunk up when they found that the captain was determined to escape from them with the man and the money they wanted so much. At last Sacramento was reached, and with it the highest pitch of danger. The prisoner was informed that the men were still following him, and that they would probably make an attempt to take him on the way from the hotel to the boat that was to carry them to San Francisco. All this was strictly true. Captain Herbert had only omitted to mention the fact that there would be among the number of captors a member of the Sacramento police, to which both the roughs had applied, setting forth that the man was illegally restrained of his liberty, etc. The prisoner shook in his boots, and probably wished in his heart that he was safely back in British Columbia, with the cattle unsold, and his employer unrobbed. What was to be done? Time was flying, and he *must* be gotten on to that boat, or he might never see San Francisco; so feared the captain as well as his prisoner.

Again it was the intrepid stranger and travelling companion who came to the rescue. The captain's plan was "hatched" and carried out in a very little while. With a pair of handcuffs clasped on his wrists, and his arms securely tied behind, the obliging stranger was led to the boat by the hard-hearted captain, who handled this free-will prisoner very roughly — while the guilty cattle-agent was slinking along with unfettered hands by the side of the captain's assistant, to whom he "stuck closer than a brother." Just as the captain was hustling his prisoner on to the gang-plank, a policeman stepped from the crowd, laid his hand on the man's shoulder, and, amid the cheering of the roughs and the angry protestations of the captain, led him to the office of the nearest justice. The *bonâ fide* prisoner in the meantime slipped unnoticed on board, and was taken out of the cold, and kindly cared for on reaching San Francisco, by the proper authorities, who had been summoned to meet the boat, by a telegram from the captain.

An excited crowd had gathered around the door of the

office into which the stranger had been brought. The intense disgust of the roughs can be better imagined than described when their eyes and ears convinced them, very much against their will, that their benevolent purposes could not be carried out, and that *this* "prisoner at the bar" had never absconded with anybody's money. They listened in dogged silence to the man's declaration that, far from being restrained of his liberty, he had come with the captain "just for fun," and had worn the handcuffs because they were just an easy fit.

"And what is your name!" thundered the enraged justice.

"Henry Fitzpatrick," was the quiet reply, "merchant, from San Francisco. I fell in with the captain at Salt Lake, where I was stopping on my way home from the States; and as he's a mighty clever fellow, I thought I'd go all the way with him. Sorry you detained us, gentlemen — we both had urgent business in San Francisco."

He went his way in peace, though the real sinner — the thieving cattle-agent — had never been in as much danger of coming to harm at the hands of these men as was this inoffensive person.

The captain saw no more of him till a day or two after his return to San Francisco. Entering the store of his friend Taylor, to tell him of his safe return, he was surprised to see the stranger, Mr. Henry Fitzpatrick, in the counting-room. The senior partner greeted him with:

"Well, well, captain, so you brought Harry home with a pair of handcuffs on, after all! Allow me to introduce my partner, Mr. Henry Fitzpatrick McDonald."

"Happy to meet you again, captain. It *was* fun, wasn't it, though? But I didn't think it was necessary to give those inquisitive chaps at Sacramento the benefit of my full name. I did not want them to say, in case I should ever run for office, that 'McDonald had been led through the country with a pair of handcuffs on.'"

HER NAME WAS SYLVIA.

"SAN MATEO! Stages for Pescadero and Half-Moon Bay!" shouted the conductor, and a dozen or two of passengers left the uncomfortably crowded car.

Some of them entered the handsome equipages in waiting, to carry them to luxurious country residences; a few sought their cottage in the suburbs on foot; others, armed with satchels, shawls, and field-glasses, clambered into and on the stage. Among these, a young lady — whose glossy braids and brilliant eyes were not altogether hidden by a light veil — stood irresolute, when the polite agent addressed her, " Have a seat outside, Miss — with the driver? Very gentlemanly person, Miss; ladies mostly like to ride with him." Her indecision was abruptly ended by the gloved hand of the driver, reaching down without more ado and drawing her up, with the agent's assistance, gently, but irresistibly, out of the crowd and confusion below.

For the first five miles the young girl saw nothing and knew nothing of what was on or in the stage; her eyes were feasting on the scenery, new to her, and fascinating in its beauty of park-like forest-strips and flower-grown dells, where tiny brooks were overhung by tangled brush and the fresh foliage of maple-tree and laurel-wood. The sunshine of a whole San Francisco year seemed concentrated in the bright May morning; and the breeze stirred just enough to turn to the sunlight, now the glossy green side of the leaves on the live oaks, then the dull, grayish side — a coquetry of nature making artistic effects.

At Crystal Springs our friend suddenly became aware that she had thrown aside her veil, and a deep blush covered her features when she saw a wonderfully white hand reaching up with a cluster of roses, evidently meant for her acceptance. The rustling of the trees, the sound of water splashing, the sight of birds, coming in flocks to drink at the fountain, had so held her senses captive, that she did not even know how long they had been stopping at this place; but the bunch of roses, and the deep blue eyes looking up into hers, recalled her to reality. Had she not looked into these eyes before? Had not the stage-driver just such a long, tawny moustache? And was this he, offering the flowers with all the courtliness and easy self-possession of the gentleman? All these thoughts flashed through her brain in a second, and she shrank, momentarily, from what seemed a piece of presumption on the part of the man. But a glance at the sad eyes, and the barely perceptible play of sarcasm around the firm-closed lips, induced her to bend forward and accept the offering, with a grace peculiarly her own.

Not a word was exchanged after he had remounted his seat; but since her veil was dropped she noticed that there were others on the outside of the stage beside herself. There was a female with a brown *barège* veil, and a big lunch-basket on the seat back of her, who had been most intent on studying how the young lady could possibly have fastened on those heavy braids, that they looked so natural; whereas hers were always coming apart, and showing the jute inside. And there were the two tourists — English people probably. They had never disturbed her yet by a word of conversation. Then her thoughts travelled to the inside of the stage, and her eyes rested uneasily for a moment on her neighbor, the driver. Had she only dreamed of the white, well-shaped hand? Large, heavy gloves were on his fingers, and covered the wrist with a stiff gauntlet. Just as stiff was the brim of the light-colored hat; and it was so provokingly put on that nothing was visible from under it but the end of the long moustache.

But she was soon lost in thought again, and in contemplation of the placid blue ocean, that suddenly shone out beyond the low hills, away off to the right.

"Das Meer erglänzte weit hinaus—"

She turned with a start, to see whether she had dreamed this too, or whether a voice at her elbow had really hummed it — and was just in time to see the driver gather up the lines of the six horses closer, while he strove hard to banish the guilty color from his face.

A stage-driver, who offered her roses with the air of a cavalier of the *ancien régime*, and sang snatches of German music. It made her more thoughtful than ever; and when they reached Spanishtown, and had taken dinner, she had decided on what course to pursue. The driver was on hand to assist her back to her lofty perch, but she said, with perfect *sang-froid*:

"I think I should prefer to ride inside for the rest of the way; the sun is too hot outside."

Perhaps she had feared to see an expression of wounded feeling on the bronzed face, but it was rather a quizzical look that shot from his eyes as he answered:

"No sun after this; fog from here out — depend upon it."

Her face relaxed. "I don't know that I want to be enveloped in a fog-cloud, either;" but she placed her foot on the wheel, and, without another word, she was assisted back to her old seat. The ice was broken, and the fog that soon rolled in on them did more to thaw it away between them than the sunshine of the morning had been able to do.

After awhile she told him that she was on her way to visit an uncle and aunt, who had taken up their residence at Pescadero, and that she meant to make them many a visit, as she was fond of them, and they petted her to her heart's content. And she liked the country, too. Then he told her of the pebbles to be found on the beach near Pescadero, and of the attractions of the sea-moss, at a point more distant; and he hoped that he might always have the pleasure of carrying her through the country, whenever she came this way.

"Uncle shall surely let you know when I am coming back, so that I may come with you," she said; "but what is your name?—so that he can find you out."

"Jim!" he replied, grimly, pulling his hat far down over his eyes, apparently indifferent as to the impression his abbreviated appellation might make on her. Then, with a touch of sarcasm in his voice, he asked, "And yours?"

"Stella," she answered simply; and they both laughed, and she fastened the roses in her hair before they came to the end of their journey, which had on the whole passed off so pleasantly.

So pleasantly that Stella reverted to it when in Aunt Sarah's comfortable sitting-room, where Uncle Herbert was allowed to smoke his after-dinner cigar.

"I should like to go back with the same driver; his name is Jim. Do you know him, uncle?" she continued, with the most innocent face, in which a sharper eye than Uncle Herbert's would nevertheless have detected a somewhat heightened color.

"They have nicknamed him 'The Duke,'" he replied, knocking the ashes off his cigar with a thoughtful look, "and they say he is quite a character. Proud and unapproachable, but the best driver on the road, and, so long as no one interferes or asks questions about himself, perfectly obliging, and courteous in his manners."

After the usual round of dissipations, consisting of a sea-bath for the more venturesome, a visit to the pebble-beach, a more extended tour to gather sea-moss, Stella was ready to return to San Francisco. To both aunt and uncle she imparted her design of soon revisiting Pescadero, for the purpose of exploring the distant hills, with their dark forests, where the redwood was said to reach a circumference of sixteen feet, which the wise little lady would not believe till her own eyes had proved it. The old couple were without children, and nothing could be more welcome than the niece's prospective visits.

Stella thought she could see a sudden light flash over the gloomy face with the sunburnt moustache when she came out of the waiting-room to mount the stage, for she naturally wished to view in the light of the morning sun the scenery on which the evening shadows had lain when she came. Not that she saw much of it, after all; the fog prevented her from seeing what her veil did not shut out. But the sun breaking through the fog suddenly and driving it back, the sky became clear, her companion said, "heaven smiled once more;" and while he spoke he was careful to manipulate the veil she had dropped, in such a manner that it found its way into his coat-pocket, from where, he was determined, it was not to be unearthed till the steeples of San Mateo should come into sight.

He listened with such an air of interest to Stella's recital of all she had seen, that it did not strike her till after a long while that she had really sustained conversation altogether on her side; and when she grew quite still after this, he made no effort to draw her on or speak himself. But when they approached the long, steep bridge across the Toanitas, and rolled along close by the sea, where the waves dashed against the crags with angry roar, through which there wept and moaned a bitter grief and sighed a forlorn hope of peace to come, he pushed his hat back with an impatient motion, and, gazing moodily into the waters, he muttered:

"Bleib Du in Deinen Meerestiefen Wahnsinniger Traum."

"Do you really read Heine in the original?" she asked, quickly.

"And only a stage-driver," he returned, with the old sarcasm, seeing that she hesitated. "Yes; I read Heine in German — or did. I read nothing now. I drive stage."

There was painful silence; an apology would have made matters worse; but seeing the grieved expression on her face, he continued, in his gentlest voice, "You say you are coming this way again in the course of the season — coming with me — in my stage? You wonder how I came to be stage-driver; when we are better acquainted, and you think it worth while to remind me of my promise, I will tell you my story."

"And forgive me now?" she asked, extending her hand. The glove came off his right hand, and the fingers that clasped hers were not less white and soft, but strong they looked — strong as iron. "Thanks," she said; and he felt, somehow, that she wanted her veil just then, and he pretended to discover it, by chance, on the seat.

In the course of the season she came again — more than once — coming always when she knew she would meet his stage at the San Mateo depot.

One bright day in October, when, after the drought of the long summer, the earth had been refreshed by generous autumn showers, Stella again sat beside him, high up, on the driver's seat. The same azure was in the sky, the same deep blue on the waters; it was all as it had been the day she first saw the tangled wildwood by the brook, the spreading live-oak by the roadside — only, the foliage on the brush had changed its colors to deep-red and yellow.

"You once said," began Stella, timidly — for she had learned that his temper was very uneven — "that if I reminded you of your promise when we were better acquainted, you would tell me your story."

He turned and looked steadily into her faltering eyes a

moment, then drew his hat down over his brows, and commenced, without further preliminaries:

"Her name was Sylvia — and her eyes were as deep as a well; so deep that I don't think I ever quite fathomed them. When my mother died, she said we were both young, and we must not be married until at least a year had passed over my mother's grave. I was touched with the sympathy she displayed on this sorrowful occasion; so was my father. I was his only son, and would undoubtedly fall heir to his wealth — great wealth — after his death. I had grown up as rich men's only sons generally grow up; had visited schools, colleges, universities; was called good-looking, a clever fellow generally, the best driver of a four-in-hand, the best shot — in short, a great catch for any girl to make. Sylvia told me so herself often. But, after all, I was only the son, you see, and my father might live for twenty years longer, and if Sylvia married me, she married only a prospect — whereas, if she married my father, she was the wife of a wealthy man at once. I had not been brought up to business habits, as Sylvia pointed out, and if my father ever became displeased with me — of which he showed strong symptoms about this time — I should be thrown on the world with a wife as helpless as myself, and as poor. For Sylvia, though brought up among aristocratic relatives, was as poor as a church mouse. What need to make many words? She married my father before the year was out, and I left home secretly on the morning of their wedding-day, with never a cent of the riches which had bought my best-beloved to be my father's bride — never a dollar of all the wealth I had been taught to look upon as my own.

"For years I read in every Eastern paper that happened to fall into my hands the promises of reward to any who might bring tidings of me — dead or alive — to my father; but I never could tell: Was it his own heart that urged him to this long continued search, or was it she that felt some slight compunction at having driven the son from the father's house? There are officious people everywhere — greedy people — who will do anything for money. One of these soul-sellers, worming himself into my confidence when sick and broken from unaccustomed labor, strung together what might have passed with others for the ravings of a delirious patient, and wrote my father of my whereabouts and occupation. Before I had recovered, my father was with me, urging me with much kindness, I must say, to go with him, if not to his home, at least to the city, where he proposed to set me up in business for myself, in case I was too independent to live under his roof.

"His wife's health, delicate since her marriage, had been so much benefited by the climate of California that she advocated their remaining here, and he intended to settle in San Francisco. I thanked him for all his kindness — I did, indeed; he is a weak old man, but he had been an over-indulgent father to me in my boyhood, and why should I harbor an unkind feeling against him? But I would not go with him. He said I was taking a cruel revenge on him. That is not so, however — or do you too blame me for being a stage-driver?" He bent down toward her quickly and raised her face with his hand. There were tears in her eyes, and his arm stole around her as gently as though he had forgotten about the six horses he was guiding with his other hand.

Don't be shocked, reader; there was no one on the outside of the stage but these two. And supposing even that he had pressed her head to his breast and kissed her forehead; no one saw it, or made remarks about it, except the sea waves, and they seemed rippling all over with good nature and laughter, and rejoicings at the new light in the man's eyes, and the tears and the smiles in the woman's.

For a long while neither spoke; but when the stage halted he lifted her down so tenderly, and she looked up into his face so confidingly, that words seemed unnecessary between them. Then he went his way, and Stella knew that she must not expect to see him again till she should be ready to return to the city; for neither Uncle Herbert nor any one else in the place had ever succeeded in enticing him to visit their homes.

But when he assisted Stella into her usual place on the morning of her departure for San Francisco, his eyes told her that his thoughts had been with her all the days since relating to her "his story." He had not encouraged any one else to ride on the outside; and once clear of the town, he touched Stella's hand with his lips, drew it through his arm and pressed it, very much, I am afraid, as any ordinary lover might have done. But when the fog rolled away, he sent out his clear baritone to greet the sun-kissed ocean, and the burden of his song was once more:

"Das Meer erglänzte weit hinaus!"

And the hat was not drawn down over his face when she turned to him, and his eyes were like the ocean, dark-blue, and a sunny light laughing in them.

"It is my farewell to the sea," he said, gayly. "I am never coming back again. I am going to San Francisco, turn 'gentleman,' put on 'store clothes,' and enter the ranks of respectable business men."

She laughed as he straightened himself and put on a severely sober face, and he relaxed and urged his horses on with a smart cut of the whip, as though he could not enter the state of a "respectable business man" soon enough. When they came to Crystal Springs he brought a bunch of red roses once more, and held them up to her with a roguish smile on his no longer gloomy face. She took them with a little blush at the remembrance of his first attempt at gallantry; and when he sat beside her again, he fastened them with his own hands in her shining braids. They were as merry as children out for a holiday; and only when they drove up to the depot at San

Mateo did the old gloom come back into his face as he lifted her from her elevated position.

"After three days, if in the land of the living, I will come to claim you for my bride"—what more he said was lost in the din and racket of the approaching train.

She saw nothing of him after she had watched the supple figure at the last moment springing lightly on the platform of the last car. But she knew he was near and was happy.

Early the next forenoon, in the counting-room of a mercantile firm on Front street, sat one of the principals, enjoying his Havana, when the door was darkened by the shadow of a tall figure standing in it.

"Jim—old fellow!" he cried, seizing the newcomer by both hands. "Welcome — thrice welcome! Have you come to stay, vagabond and rover? Say at once — I read something in your face that tells me you are unbending at last. Are you in love, my dear boy?—or what hath wrought this change?"

"How you do run on, Luke. You have not changed, at least. Yes, I am the prodigal son, returning to his father to be — set up in business. And — no — I'm not in love; I have simply learned to worship the dearest, noblest girl, and will make her mine — or die," he added, in a lower tone.

"Why not accept my offer, Jim? The desk at my elbow is always kept vacant for you. Your father, poor man, is not the only friend you have, remember." He laid his hand impressively on his friend's arm, and looked with frank affection into his face.

Their interview was a lengthy one: friend Luke seemed averse to parting with his old chum, and the son seemed in no great haste to greet his father. But as we need not intrude on their first meeting, we can rejoin father and son as they ascend the broad stairs in front of the family residence, whither the father has taken his son in the first flush of happiness.

"You will love little Willie, I know; he is a brave boy, with long flaxen ringlets just like my — like his mother." For the first time something like hesitation came into his speech, and even the son's heart beat faster for an instant as the door swung open in answer to the old man's ring. He preceded him through the corridor, threw open a door and called out, "Jim has come home, my dear; we are going into the library, and will be ready for lunch after a while."

She had known of their coming just a moment before they entered; he felt it, for she had snatched up the boy, and half hid her face in his dress. Very faded she looked; her cheeks, softly rounded once, were thin, and the pink and white of her complexion had grown sallow. The "long fair ringlets," too, were but limp, stringy curls, that hung without grace or fulness down her back. The eyes, pale blue, though radiant once with health and happiness, were weak and expressionless — save that a dumb terror was written in them now.

A smile, half contemptuous, half pitying, flitted over the young man's face as he passed through the room, with only a silent bow to the woman.

When they had vanished she stood like a statue, till the prattling of the boy on her arm recalled her to herself.

"He spoke not one word to me," she said, as she put the boy down, "not one word. Oh, to hear the tone of his voice once more — only once more." The door was open through which they had passed, and her burning eyes seemed to pursue the form last vanished through it. She silently rose, like one in a dream, and walked slowly, slowly along the corridor that led to the library.

Little Willie pulled over mamma's willow work-stand first, and then found harmless amusement in winding a spool of crimson embroidering-silk around and around the legs of a convenient table.

What was it that turned his little beating heart and his puny white face to stone all at once? Was this really a Medusa on which he looked? The long ringlets seemed serpents, indeed; every one of them instinct with the wild despair the bitter hatred pictured on the face that looked so meek and inoffensive but a while ago. "His bride!" — the serpents hissed it into her ears — "His bride! Never — never. She shall die — and he? I will murder him with these hands, first. His bride — and I am to be a friend to her — ha! ha! ha! The dotard." Every one of the serpents echoed the mad laugh, as the woman threw back her head and clinched her hands in wild defiance. The child broke out into shrill complaining cries, and she sprang toward him, seized him and shook him by the shoulders till his breath failed. But in the midst of her mad fury the door opened, after a soft knock, and a female servant entered the room.

"Is Master Willie troublesome?" she asked. "Dear heart; let me take him, mum."

"Leave the room instantly, nurse; Master Willie is naughty and will remain with me."

Two little arms were stretched out imploringly; but nurse had to withdraw — with her own opinion of Master Willie's naughtiness, and "Missus' temper."

But the furies were banished, and when father and son entered the room some time after to say that they would take lunch down town, "Sylvia," as the old man addressed her, came forward quietly, leading the child by the hand, and spoke words of welcome to him, in his little brother's name. And she gave him her hand as she said "good-by," to the old man's unspeakable joy.

Poor old man! He fondly dreamed the gods were propitiated, the furies appeased; that the son whom he really loved had been restored to his rightful place, and would be guardian at some future day to the child of his old age — the son his idolized young wife had given him.

Yet he had not strength to battle against the storm that the idolized young wife called up — the storm that was to sweep from him again the long-lost, bitterly mourned son. Ah! well; it is not hard to fancy how she strained every nerve to wrest from another the happiness once within her own reach. Had she not bartered away her peace when she ruthlessly deserted the man she loved? And should some other woman be happier than she? No! Let them all be wrecked together. What cared she? Her husband; bah! Her child, yes; she strained him to her breast, and bemoaned him, and caressed him, and said that he was to be robbed by that wicked, wicked man, who had come to disturb their quiet happiness. That his unnatural father was about to squander on his undutiful older son, who had deserted him and disgraced him for years, the fortune she had been so sparing of — knowing that she would be left alone in the world some day, with no one to provide for herself and her child. And she would take her child now — a fresh burst of hysterical grief — right now, and start out into the cold world to earn her daily bread, or beg, for her child — for it would come to that, now that this cruel, hard-hearted man had undertaken to provide for his profligate, vagaband son.

And the child, little knowing how useful a tool he was in his mother's hands, wept with her, and would not be comforted by the distracted father, but clung to his mother's neck, crying, when she made a feint of leaving the house at the dead of night. Then the old man in his anguish promised to abandon his "vagabond" son, and was but too happy to have peace restored to his troubled home at this price. After all, the boy had lived away from him so many years; had never troubled himself about him; then why should his father heap all this trouble on his own head for what might be only a passing whim of the boy's?

The third day had dawned since the long-lost son's return. Friend Luke again sat in his counting-room, in company with his early Havana, his meditations were disturbed by a boy, who was shown in by one of the clerks. "A note for you, sir," and he had vanished.

But the young merchant seized his hat when he had glanced at the contents, and repaired, breathlessly, to his friend's hotel. Cold sweat stood on his forehead when he knocked at the door, and it was opened by a stranger. One glance at the bed and at those standing around it was sufficient.

"I was his friend," he said, and they respectfully made room for him.

He touched the cold hand, and gently lifted the cloth that hid the rigid face. His friend had always been a good shot, and Luke groaned as he replaced the cloth.

"Poor girl, poor girl — and I am to break the news to her!"

The doctor who had been called in, a shock-headed, spectacled German, looked at him, first from under his glasses, then over them, and at last through them. "Aha!" he said, with evident satisfaction, catching at Luke's words, "now we have it. It vas a voman who made dis misfortune, after all."

"A woman" — Luke repeated, softly; "yes, but her name was Sylvia."

CROSSING THE ARIZONA DESERTS.

HEAD-QUARTERS DEPARTMENT OF CALIFORNIA,
SAN FRANCISCO, CAL., March 11, 1868.

MY DEAR MADAM: — The next steamer for Wilmington is advertised to sail on the 14th, but as she is not yet in, her departure may be delayed a day or two.

I enclose letters to the commanding officers of Drum Barracks and Fort Yuma, and am,
My dear Madam,
Truly yours, E. N. PLATT.

It was my intention to visit quite a remote part of Arizona; and, although an officer's wife, having no personal acquaintance with any of the officers stationed in the Territory, the letters the colonel gave me to the commanding officers of both these posts, through which I should have to pass, were very acceptable. As I was quite alone, the commanding officer of Drum Barracks was particular to give me reliable people for my long journey. Phil, the driver, was a model, and in many respects a genius, while the two soldiers — who had been in the hospital when their comrades had started for Arizona, two months before, and who were sent by the post commander to protect "Government property" (the ambulance) — were attentive and good-natured, as soldiers always are.

With so small an escort, it was possible — nay, expedient — to make the journey very rapidly. We were unincumbered by tents or baggage — my only trunk and what provisions we carried were all in the ambulance, which was drawn by four large mules. I had decided, being alone, to stop at the forage-stations, whenever we could reach them, expecting to take my meals there and to find quarters for the night. Luckily, the quartermaster and Phil had made arrangement and provision to have my meals cooked by one of the soldiers, in case the "station-fare" should not agree with me; and my ambulance was of such ample dimensions that it was easily turned into a sleeping apartment for the night: so that Phil, who had all the merits and demerits of such places by heart, had only to give an additional nod of the head to induce me to say to the station-keeper, who would always invite me to enter his "house" when Phil drove up to the *corral*, "No, thank you: I can rest very well in the ambulance." Then there were days' marches to be made when no station could be reached, so that we were compelled to camp out; and on such occasions Phil would appear in the full glory of his well-earned reputation. He boasted that he had brought fully one-half the number of officers' wives who ever visited Arizona to the Territory himself, and that he had always made them comfortable. Knowing, of course, before, whenever we should camp out, he would go to work systematically. His carbine was always by his side, and early in the morning he would commence his raid on the game and birds abounding, more or less, throughout the Territory. Slaying sometimes five or six of the beautifully crested quails at one shot without moving from his seat, he would send one of the soldiers to gather up the spoils, and then set the men, placed one on each side of him, to pick the birds. That this was thoroughly done he was very sure of, for he watched the operation with a stern eye. Not the smallest splinter of wood, or anything combustible, was left ungleaned on the field over which he passed on such a day; fifty, ay, a hundred times, he would turn to his right-hand man, or to his left, with the admonition:

"Miller, we've six birds to cook, and bread to bake, to-night: pick up that stick."

Down would jump Miller, trusting to his agility, and the gymnastics he might have practised in younger days, for safety in vaulting over the wheels; for never a moment would Phil allow the ambulance to halt while this wayside gathering was going on.

I always preferred camping out to "bed and board" at the roadside hotels of Arizona, for Phil, with all his sagacity, would sometimes go astray in regard to the eligibility and comfort of the quarters furnished. As, for instance, at Antelope Peak, where my mentor assured me I should find a bedstead to place my bedding on, and a room all to myself. I *did* find a bedstead; but after the family (consisting of an American husband, a Spanish wife, sister-in-law, brother-in-law, and three children) had removed their bed-clothes from it, to make place for mine, it looked so uninviting that I requested Phil to spread my bed on the floor. I had a room all to myself, too; but, on retiring to rest, I found that the whole family — again consisting of husband, wife, sister-in-law, brother-in-law, and three children — had spread their bed on the floor of the adjoining room, which, being separated from my apartment only by an old blanket, coming short of the ground over a foot, and hung up where the door ought to be, enabled, or rather compelled me to look straight into the faces of the different members of this interesting family. As it grew darker, and the danger of being stared out of countenance passed over, another serious disturbance presented itself to my senses. All my friends can bear witness to the fact that I consider Mr. Charles Bergh the greatest public benefactor of the present age (the woman who founded the hospital for aged and infirm cats not excepted), and that, with me, it calls forth all the combative qualities lately discovered to lie dormant in woman's nature, to see any harmless, helpless animal cruelly treated; but if I could have caught only half a dozen of the five hundred mice that nibbled at my nose, my ears, and my feet that night, I should exultingly have dipped them in camphene, applied a match, and sent them, as warning examples, back to their tribe.

Only once after this, toward the close of the journey, did Phil entice me to sleep under a roof. It was at Blue-water Station; and the man who kept it turned himself out into the *corral*, and made my bed on the floor of the only room the house contained. There was no bedstead there, but the man gave his word that neither were there any mice; so I went to sleep in perfect faith and security. When I woke up at midnight, I thought the Indians must have surprised us, scalped me, and left me for dead. Such a burning, gnawing sensation I experienced on the top of my head that almost unconsciously I put up my hand to see if they had taken *all* my hair. But I brought it down rapidly, for all the horrid, pinching, stinging bugs and ants that had ensconced themselves in my hair, during my sleep, suddenly fastened to the intruding fingers, and clung to them with a tenacity worthy of a better cause.

But these experiences were not made until I had crossed the greater part of the Arizona deserts; and I considered them rather as pleasantly varying the solemn, still monotony of the days passed, one after one, in a solitude broken only, at long intervals, by those forlorn government forage-stations.

The first desert we crossed was still in California — though why California should feel any desire to claim the wilderness of sand and rattlesnakes lying between Vallecito Mountain and Fort Yuma, I cannot see. We had passed over the thriving country around San Bernardino, and through the verdant valley of San Felipe; and striking the desert just beyond Vallecito, it seemed like entering Arizona at once.

Could anything be more hopelessly endless — more discouragingly boundless — than the sand-waste that lay before us the morning we left the forage-station of Vallecito! For days before, Phil had been entertaining me with stories and accounts of travellers who had been lost in sand-storms on the deserts. Not a breath of air stirred — not a cloud was to be seen in the sky on this particular morning; nevertheless, I watched for the signs that precede the springing up of the wind with a keen eye, as the ambulance rolled slowly and noiselessly through the deep sand, and I listened attentively to Phil's stories. The road we followed was but a wagon-track, at best; and I could well believe that, in ten minutes from the time a storm sprang up, there would be no trace of the road left. Then commence the blind wanderings, the frenzied attempts to regain the friendly shelter of the station, on the part of the inexperienced traveller — ending, but too often, in a miserable death by famine and starvation. The sand, flying in clouds, conceals the distant mountains, by which alone he could be piloted; and, straying off, he finds himself bewildered among piles of sand and tattered sage-brush, when the storm has blown over. The remains of human beings found by parties going into the mountains have proved that such poor wretches must have wandered for days without food, without water, till they found their death, at last, on the wide, inhospitable plain. Their death — but not their grave; for the *coyote*, with his jackal instinct, surely finds the body of the lost one, under the sand-mound mercifully covering it, and, feasting on the flesh, he leaves the bones white and bleaching in the pitiless rays of the sun.

"Phil," said I, interrupting him, "you told me the mules would not get a drop of water to-day: what is that lake before us, then?"

He looked up to where I pointed.

"It is *mirage*, madame. *You* cannot be deceived by it; I am sure you must have seen it on the plains, before this."

"Yes," I said, stoutly, "I have seen *mirage;* but this is water — not *mirage.*"

"We shall see," said Phil, equally determined to hold his ground.

But I was sure it could not be *mirage* — it must be water — for did I not see each of the few scattering bushes of *verde* and sage that grew on the border, and farther out, all through the water, reflected in the clear, slightly undulating flood? The bushes seemed larger here than any of the stinted vegetation I had yet seen on the desert, and every bush was clearly reflected in the water; but it was strange that as we approached the water receded; and if I noted any particular bunch of sage or weeds, I found that, as we neared, it grew smaller, and I could no longer see its image in the water.

Phil was right — it was the *mirage;* and this *Fata Morgana* of the plains and deserts of our own country became a most curious and interesting study to me. I could write a volume on the "dissolving views" I have seen. Leaving camp one morning, I saw, on turning, that a narrow strip of short, coarse grass had been suddenly transformed into a tall, magnificent hedge; and a single, meagre stem of *verde* would as suddenly grow into a large, spreading tree. Out of the clouds, on the horizon, would sometimes loom up, majestically, a tall spire, a heavy dome, or a vessel under full sail; and changing into one fantastic shape after another, the picture would slowly fade into vapor at last. Whole cities have sprung up before my eyes: I could have pointed out which one of the different cupolas I supposed to be the City Hall, and which steeple, according to my estimation, belonged to the First Presbyterian Church; and could have shown the exact locality of the harbor, from the number of masts I saw across the roofs of the houses yonder. Even Phil was deceived one morning. I asked him why he stopped the ambulance, and allowed the mules to rest at so unusual an hour in the day? He pointed to a mountain I had not noticed before, which stood almost in front of us, and was steep and bare, of a light clay-color.

"There ain't a man driving government mules knows this road better 'n I do; but I'll be derned if ever I saw that mountain before."

He asked the men if they thought it could be *mirage*, but they hooted at the idea — it was too substantial for that, altogether; it was a mountain — nothing else. But while we were, all four, so intently gazing at it, the scene was shifted; the mountain parted, leaving two steep banks — the space between apparently spanned by a light bridge.

For days we continued our journey through the desert, making camp generally near one of the numerous wells indiscriminately scattered between Vallecito and Fort Yuma. There are Indian Wells, Sacket's Wells, Seven Wells, Cook's Wells, which, on close inspection, prove to belong to the dissolving views, of which Arizona possesses such a variety; an old well-curb or muddy water-hole generally constituting all the claim these places have to the distinction of being called wells. But no; at Cook's Wells, we *did* find a good, clear well of water; nor is this the only object of interest connected in my mind with the place. The station-keeper told me that a tribe of friendly Indians, not far from here, the Deguines, were to celebrate the funeral rites of a departed warrior the following day. The spirit of the "brave" was to find its way up to the Happy Hunting Grounds from the funeral-pyre on which the body was to pass through the process of incremation — this being their mode of disposing of the remains of deceased friends. A novel spectacle it would be, no doubt; but I decided not to witness it. I could already see Castle Dome looming in the distance, and I knew that I should be able to reach Fort Yuma in the course of the following day. So we left Cook's Wells early in the morning, and reached the crossing of the Colorado some time in the forenoon.

The Colorado river was "up," Phil said; and I was prepared to agree with him when I saw an expanse of muddy water covering the flat, on the other side, to a considerable distance. The old scow, or flat-boat, manned by two dirty-looking Mexicans, had no difficulty in coming up close to us, where we were waiting on the shore: the difficulty lay in our getting on the crazy thing without breaking through the rotten planks. Perhaps the two Mexicans looked so dirty because all their "clean clothes" were hanging out to dry, on two lines of cowhide, stretched on either side of the flat-boat, which the wind kept blowing into the mules' faces, causing them to "back out" twice, after our *entrée* to the ferry had been almost effected. There was no railing around the boat (the four posts from which the clothes-line was stretched having evidently been erected at the four corners for that purpose), and, as it was only just large enough to afford standing room for the ambulance and the men, it was anything but soothing to a woman's nerves to see the mules rear and plunge every time the wind flapped one of the articles on the line into the animals' faces. I had remained in the ambulance, and in my usual corner, but as the shore receded, and an ocean seemed to stretch out on every side of me, I found it hard to stay there. I had suggested to Phil, in the first place, to cut down those miserable clothes-lines, if the Mexicans refused to gather in their week's washing, but he had quieted me by saying that our men would hold the mules. However, when the current grew swifter, and the Mexicans found some difficulty in managing their craft, the men were directed to take the long poles, of which there was an abundant supply, and help to steer clear of the logs floating down the river.

Now came the difficulty; for the refractory mules would not listen to the "Ho, there, Kate; be still — will you?" with which Phil admonished the nigh leader, but persisted in rearing every time a piece of "linen" struck them, till the old scow shook with their furious stamping, and I grew desperate in my lone corner. "Phil," I cried at last, with the energy of despair, brandishing an enormous knife I had drawn from the mess-chest, "unless you come and quiet the mules immediately, I shall get down, cut the harness, and let them jump into the river!"

An hour's drive brought us to Fort Yuma, where we rested a day or two, before resuming our journey. The country here has been described again and again; its dry, sterile plains and black, burnt-looking hills have been sufficiently execrated — relieving me of the necessity of adding my quota. Fort Yuma — grand in its desolateness, white and parched in the midst of its two embracing rivers — needs but the Dantean inscription on its gateway to make it resemble the entrance to the regions of the eternally damned.

It was by no means my first glimpse of the "noble savage" that I got on the banks of the Colorado, or I might have been appalled at the sight of a dozen or two of barely-clothed, filthy-looking Indians, squatted in rows wherever the sun could burn hottest on their clay-covered heads. The specimens here seen were different from those that had come under my observation on the Plains. That Indians can be civilized William Lloyd Garrison would not doubt, could he but see with what native grace these dusky belles wear their crinoline. Nor can they be accused of the extravagance of their white sisters in matters pertaining to toilet and dress: the crinoline (worn *over* the short petticoat, constituting their full and entire wardrobe, aside from it) apparently being the only article of luxury they indulge in, except paint — and whiskey, when they can get it. But grandest of all were the men — the warrior-like Yumas — arrayed in the traditional strip of red flannel, an occasional cast-off military garment, and the cap of hard-baked mud above alluded to. I had never seen these before, and thought them very singular as ornaments; but Phil soon explained their utility in destroying a certain parasite by which the noble red man is afflicted. During the summer months he seeks relief in an application of wet mud to the part besieged — his head. The mud is allowed to bake hard, in the course of weeks, under the broiling sun; and when quite certain that his enemy has been slaughtered, he removes the clay until another application becomes necessary.

Following the course of the Gila river for some time, we struck the desert again, beyond Gila Bend. What struck me as very surprising was, that the desert here did not look like a desert at all: the scattering *verde*-bushes and growth of cactus hiding the sand from one's eyes, always just a little distance ahead — the cacti growing so thickly in some places that, when they are in blossom, their flowers form a mosaic of brilliant hues. Some of them are very curious — particularly the "monument cactus," a tall shaft, growing to a height of over thirty feet, sometimes with arms branching out on either side, more generally a simple obelisk, covered with thorns from three to four inches long.

We were now nearing Maricopa Wells and the Pimo villages. Phil was the pearl of all drivers; and he recounted traditions and legends belonging to the past of this country that even Prescott might have wished to hear. Phil had studied the history of the country in his own way, and had evidently not kept his eyes closed while travelling back and forth through Arizona. Halting the ambulance one day, he assisted me to alight near a pile of rocks the most wonderful it was ever my fortune to behold. He called them Painted Rocks, or Sounding Rocks; and his theory in regard to them was, that this had been a place where the Indians had long ago met to perform their religious rites and ceremonies. Rocks of different sizes — from those not above a foot high, to others that reached almost to my shoulders — all rounded in shape, were here, in the midst of the plain, gathered together within a space of twenty or thirty feet. They were black — whether from the action of the weather merely, or from some chemical process — and covered on all sides with representations from the animal world of Arizona and Mexico. The pictures had been engraved, in a rude manner, on the black ground, and embraced, in their variety, snakes, lizards, toads; also, four-footed animals, which I could conscientiously recognize neither as horses nor antelopes. Were they horses, it would go to prove that these pictures had been made by roving bands of Indians, any time after the conquest, as it is held that horses were first brought to this country by Cortez. Did the pictures represent antelopes, it would almost tempt me to believe that it was a specimen of the picture-writing of the Aztecs. The sun was also represented, with its circle of rays, which, in Phil's estimation, was proof conclusive that the heathens had come here only to worship, particularly as there was no water in the neighborhood, and they could not have lived here for any length of time. What the character of the rocks may be, I am not geologist enough to know; but when struck they emit a peculiarly clear and ringing sound, like that produced by striking against a bell or a glass. None of the tribes now to be found in that part of the country appear to claim any knowledge of the origin of these rocks.

If either the Pimos, Maricopas, or Yumas are descendants of the Aztecs, they have most wofully degenerated. On one point their traditions all agree: namely, that the three tribes were not always at peace with each other, as they are now. Long, long ago, when the Pimos were sorely pressed by the more powerful Yumas, they allied themselves with the Maricopas; and when they still found themselves in the minority against the common enemy, and had been almost exterminated, they flew to the white man for assistance, and never broke the treaty made with him.

But the shimmer of romance and poetry one would willingly throw around them, is so rudely dispelled by the sight of these lank, dirty, half-nude creatures, with faces exhibiting no more intelligence than (perhaps not so much as) the faces of their lean dogs, or shaggy horses. Yet, again, I must confess that even these Indians are susceptible of a high degree of refinement and cultivation. Two of them, mounted on a horse whose diminutive size allowed their four feet to touch the ground at every stride, dressed, or rather undressed, in a manner to strike terror into the soul of any well brought-up female, rode close up to the ambulance one day, as it passed through the Indian villages, one of them shouting, "Bully for you!" at the top of his voice, while the other whipped up the horse at the same time, as though anxious to retreat the moment their stock of polite learning had been exhausted.

Meeting at Maricopa Wells with the captain of the infantry stationed at La Paz, we visited the interior of the Pimo and Maricopa villages together, on horseback. We rode through the field the Indians cultivate, and irrigate from the Gila river, by means of *acequias* dug through their lands in all directions. Some of their huts on the roadside were deserted by their owners, who had removed to very airy residences, constructed of the branches of cotton-wood and willows, growing on the banks of the Gila, located where they could overlook their possessions on all sides. As these residences consisted simply of a roof, or shed, it was no such very hard matter to keep a lookout on every side. That they do not trust a great deal in each other's honesty, was evident from the way in which they had fastened the doors of their city residences when exchanging them for their country-seats: they had firmly walled up the entrance with *adobe* mud. However, they are quiet and peaceable, I am told, unless, by any chance or mischance, they get whiskey — of which they are as fond as all other Indians.

In the mountain around which we had passed on the last day's journey from Gila Bend, is to be seen, plainly and distinctly, the face of a man, reclining, with his eyes closed as though in sleep. Among the most beautiful of all the legends told here, is that concerning this face. It is Montezuma's face, so the Indians believe (even those in Mexico, who have never seen the image), and he will awaken from his long sleep some day, will gather all the brave and the faithful around him, raise and uplift his down-trodden people, and restore to his kingdom the old power and the old glory — as it was, before the Hidalgos invaded it. So strong is this belief in some parts of Mexico, that people who passed through that country years ago, tell me of some localities where fires were kept constantly burning, in anticipation of Montezuma's early coming. It looks as though the stern face up there was just a little softened in its expression, by the deep slumber that holds the eyelids over the commanding eye; and all nature seems hushed into death-like stillness. Day after day, year after year, century after century, slumbers the man up there on the height, and life and vegetation sleep on the arid plains below — a slumber never disturbed — a sleep never broken; for the battle-cry of Yuma, Pimo, and Maricopa that once rang at the foot of the mountain, did not reach Montezuma's ear; and the dying shrieks of the children of those who came far over the seas to rob him of his sceptre and crown, fall unheeded on the rocks and the deserts that guard his sleep.

Two days more, and Phil pointed out to me, at a distance of some two miles away, the ruins of the Casas-Grandes, sole remnant of the Seven Cities the adventurous *Padre* had so enticingly described to the Spaniards. I could not induce Phil to allow me a nearer view, as we were in the Apache country, and had no escort save the two soldiers in the ambulance with us. From this distance the houses looked to me like any other good-sized, one-story, *adobe* buildings; but the material must have been better prepared, or differently chosen, from that which is now used in erecting Mexican houses, or it could not have resisted the ravages of Time so far.

On we journeyed, not without some dread on my part, and a great many assurances on the part of Phil that I was a very courageous woman. But nearing Tucson, where the danger was greatest, we were not always alone. Mexican trains bound for, or coming from Sonora, sometimes fell in with us, and I did not despise their company, for I knew that only "in strength lay safety" for us. Some of these trains consisted of pack-donkeys only, bearing on their bruised backs the linen and cambrics which are so beautifully manufactured in Sonora and other Mexican provinces; others consisted of wagons heavily laden, their drivers armed to the teeth, and well prepared to defend them against attacks the Apaches were sure to make on them, sometime and somewhere between Sonora and Tucson.

One of these trains belonged to Leopoldo Carillo, a Mexican merchant of Tucson, who paid his men one hundred and fifty dollars for every Indian scalp they delivered to him. Phil asked one of the Mexicans, driving a wagon drawn along by some twelve or sixteen horses, if he had taken any scalps on the trip. The Mexican nodded his head in silence, and turned away. The teamster belonging to the next wagon — an American — told us how the Indians had "jumped them," just after crossing the border, and how two of them had held the Mexican, just spoken to, at bay, while two others killed and scalped his younger brother. They all together, some seven or eight of them, had taken three scalps from the Indians on this trip; but he was willing to lose his share of the prize-money, the man said, if the "pesky devils had n't taken the boy's scalp;" for the brother, he averred, cried and "took on about it" *just like a white man.*

DOWN AMONG THE DEAD LETTERS.

STRANGERS visiting Washington, and admiring the style and architecture of the General Post-Office building, would never know that there are numbers of ladies seated behind the plate-glass of the second-story windows. Indeed, few people residing in the capital are really aware in what part of the building those female clerks are stowed away. I had passed on every side of the building — morning, noon, and night — but never had seen anybody that looked like a "female clerk," till I found myself of their number, one morning; and then I discovered the right entrance to the Dead Letter Office. It is on F street, so close to the Ladies' Delivery that any person entering here would be supposed to be inquiring for a letter at that delivery. There is another entrance on E street, but it is not much patronized by the ladies until after fifteen minutes past nine o'clock; for punctually at that time, the door-keeper is instructed to lock the ladies' door on F street, and those who are tardy are compelled to go up the gentlemen's staircase, or pass in at the large public entrance on E street. Crowds of visitors walk through the building, day after day, but not one of all the ladies employed here do they see, unless they request to be shown the rooms of the female *employés*.

In this department, working hours are from nine o'clock in the morning till three o'clock in the afternoon. Ladies are not allowed to leave the office for lunch, nor do they waste much time in discussing the lunch they may have brought, as it is only in consideration of their industry and close application that they are allowed to leave the office at three o'clock, instead of four.

This Dead Letter Office is one of the most complicated pieces of machinery in the "ship of state." I will try to explain and elucidate as much of it as came under my observation. Letters left "uncalled for" at the different post-offices throughout the country are sent to the Dead Letter Office, after a certain length of time. Letters not prepaid, or short-paid, through neglect or ignorance of the writer, also find their way here; and so do foreign letters, from all parts of Europe, which have been prepaid only in part, and therefore come here, instead of reaching their destination. Sometimes mails are robbed, and the mail-bags hidden or thrown away, but are afterwards searched for, and their remaining contents brought to this office. Then again, a vessel at sea, homeward-bound, brings letters from ships meeting it, of sailors and passengers, who send their letters in firm faith that they will reach their anxious friends at home; but if our Government happens to have no treaty or contract with that particular government to which the writer belongs, of course, the letters cannot be forwarded, but are laid at rest here. These letters are carefully preserved for a number of years. They are sometimes called for, and found, a long, long time after they were written; in fact, only "dead" letters are destroyed.

Though I wish to speak more particularly of the duties and labor performed by the ladies employed in this department, I must begin by saying that all letters pass through the hands of, and are opened by, a number of gentlemen — clerks in the department — whose room is on the ground floor of the building. A great number of letters contain money, valuable papers, and postage stamps. These are sent to the superintendent's room. Letters without contents are folded, with the envelope laid inside the letter, tied in bundles, and sent up-stairs for directing. Money, drafts, and postage-stamps, however, are not the only articles considered "mailable matter" by the public. One day I looked over a box filled with such matter, taken from dead letters and parcels in the opening room, and found in it one half-worn gaiter boot, two hair-nets, a rag doll-baby, minus the head and one foot, a set of cheap jewelry, a small-sized frying-pan, two ambrotypes, one pair of white kid gloves, a nursing-bottle, a tooth-brush, a boot-jack, three yards of lace, a box of Ayer's pills, a bunch of keys, six nutmegs, a toddy-stick, and no end of dress samples. This matter is allowed to accumulate for three months, and is then sold at auction; but a register is so carefully kept, that the person mailing the doll-baby without prepaying can follow its progress from the little country town where it was mailed to the end of its career under the hammer at the Dead Letter Office, and here can claim the amount it brought at auction.

Every clerk, male or female, has his or her letter, from A to Z, and beginning again with A A, when the alphabet "runs out." Before the ladies take their places at the desk in the morning, the messenger has already placed there the number of envelopes each lady is expected to direct in the course of the day; and large baskets filled with bundles of letters, sent up from the opening room (the bundles marked with the letter of the clerk through whose hands they have passed), are brought into the rooms. The envelopes are stamped in one corner with the lady's letter, in red; so that the ladies are spoken of, by the superintendent or the messengers, as Miss A, B, C, D — not as Miss Miller, or Mrs. Smith. Fifty of these envelopes are contained in one package, so that it is easy to calculate whether any of them are wasted by misdirecting or blotting. The work looks simple enough, when you see a number of ladies seated at their desks, writing addresses on envelopes, with the greatest apparent ease. "And then," as a gushing young lady said to me one day, "how romantic it must be to listen to the outpourings of love and affection that these letters must contain in many cases, and the dark secrets that others disclose." She thought it rather a cruel restraint, when I told her we were allowed to read only so much of a letter as was necessary to discover the name of the writer, and to read no part of it, if the name was signed clearly and distinctly at the end. Let the lady reader pause a moment and ask herself, "Do I sign my letters so that one of these clerks could return them from the Dead Letter Office, without going over the whole of their contents?" By the time you have finished reading this paper, I hope you will have formed the resolution to sign your name "in full," and just as it is, to every letter you send by the mail. Don't sign your name " Saida," when it is really Sarah Jones " in full ; " and if you call your father's brick house on Third street, " Pine Grove," because there are two dry pine-trees in the front yard, don't neglect to add " No. 24, Third Street, Cincinnati, Ohio." The greater number of letters passing through this office are badly written and uninteresting; many of them so perfectly unintelligible that no human being can read or return them; not that the greater portion of our community are uneducated or unintelligent people, but that they are either reckless or careless. Letters directed with any kind of common sense are most always sure of reaching their destination without visiting the Dead Letter Office. Not only do people, in a number of cases, neglect to prepay their letters, but frequently, letters without direction or address of any kind are dropped into the letter-boxes. In writing to individuals residing in the same city with them, people think it is necessary only to mention the name of the individual; the " post-office man " is expected to know that the letter is not to go out of the city. The post-office people are, if not omniscient, at least very obliging. I have found a letter directed to " Carrolton, in America," and the letter had been forwarded to, and bore the post-mark of every Carrolton in the United States before it was sent here.

The work of the ladies falls under two heads: "Common" and "Special." We will get the best idea of what "Common" means, in contradistinction to "Special," by watching Miss A, on "Common" work this morning. Taking one of the bundles of letters from the basket, she opens it and takes up the top letter; spreading it on the desk, she finds the envelope inside; it is directed to "William Smith, Philadelphia, Penn.," and the words "uncalled for," stamped on the envelope, show why it was sent here. Now, the signature is to be looked for: it is here—"John Jones;" next, where was it dated?—"Somerville, Ohio;" but does the post-mark on the envelope correspond with that? Yes, it is post-marked from where it was dated; so, "John Jones" will receive his letter back again: his friend, "W. Smith," may have left Philadelphia, or may have died. "John Jones'" letter is returned to him in a coarse, brown "P. O. D." envelope, stamped with the letter A in one corner, and he pays three cents for the privilege of knowing that his friend "Smith" never received his letter. The next is a delicate pink affair, dated, "White Rose Bower"—signed, "Ella;" "only this, and nothing more;" so the letter is hopelessly dead, and thrown into the paper-basket at Miss A's side. The epistle following this is signed, "Henry Foster," and could be returned if it had not been dated at "White Hall" and post-marked "Harrisburg." On looking over the Post-office Directory, we may or may not find a White Hall in Pennsylvania, but there is nothing in the letter to show whether "Henry Foster's" home is in Harrisburg or White Hall; consequently, that letter is dead, too. Here is one, signed plainly and legibly, but the writer has omitted to date it from any particular place. From the tone of the letter, it is plainly to be seen that he lives where the letter was mailed — but where was it mailed? The post-mark on the envelope is so indistinct that any lady not employed in the Dead Letter Office would throw it aside as "unreadable;" but ladies here learn to decipher what to ordinary mortals would be hieroglyphic, or simply a blank. After consulting the pages of the Post-office Directory beside her, Miss A passes the envelope to Miss B. "Can you suggest any post-office in Indiana beginning with M, ending with L, with about four letters between?" Miss B scrutinizes the envelope closely. "The post-mark is not from Ind. (Indiana), it is from Ioa" (Iowa), is her decision. Misses C, D, and E, at work in the same room, differ in opinion, and at last Miss A steps across the hall to the room of the lady superintendent, where a "blue-book" is kept, and, with the assistance of this lady and the book, Miss A discovers the place in Indiana, directs the letter, and continues her work. When she has directed fifty letters, she ties them (with both envelopes — the "P. O. D." and original one — inside each letter) carefully together, and the messenger carries them into the folding-room, where other ladies, employed in this branch, fold and seal them. Of these "Common" letters, every lady is required to direct from two hundred to three hundred a day — a task by no means easy to accomplish.

"Special" work is generally disliked by the ladies, and is of a somewhat "mixed" character. Letters held for postage — consequently not "dead" — come under this head. They, too, are sent back to the writer, if the signature can be found, and the place from which they are dated corresponds with the post-mark; if not, they are assorted according to letter and put away into "pigeon-holes," marked with the letter corresponding. Foreign letters, such as I spoke of before, come under this head, too. Then there are official letters — in relation to military and judicial matters — short-paid, and, therefore, brought before this tribunal. These require minute attention, as three and four documents are inclosed in one envelope sometimes, making it difficult to discover who is the proper person to return them to. Again, there are letters with postage-stamps to be returned, and money letters containing not over one dollar: those with larger amounts are directed in the superintendent's room. Ladies directing stamp and money letters keep account of them in a book, submitted, together with the letters, to the superintendent, at the close of office hours, every day. Money letters are marked with red stars, stamp letters with blue. Stamps taken from dead letters are destroyed by the proper authorities. Then, there is copying to do — orders and circulars, rules and regulations, to be transmitted to the different local post-offices; and translations to be made of communications received from foreign post departments. All this is "Special" work. A large proportion of the letters passing through the office are German letters — some French, Italian, Norwegian, and Spanish; but two German clerks are constantly employed, while one clerk can easily attend to the letters of all the other different nationalities together.

Sometimes it comes to pass that the superintendent visits one room or the other, with a number of letters in his hand; these have been misdirected or badly written. The red letter stamped on each letter guides him to the desk of the lady who has directed it; and very sensitive is each and every lady to the slightest reproach or reprimand received, because of the universal kindness and respect with which they are treated by all the officials with whom they come in contact.

If the task of poring over these epistles of all kinds, day after day, is, on the whole, tiresome and wearing, there are certainly many incidents to relieve the tedium of the occupation. Incidents, I say; letters, I should say. The deep respect we entertain for a well-known army officer was justified to me by the insight his own letters gave me into his character. It is against the rules of the post-office department to read any part of a letter, unless it is necessary to do so in order to discover the correct address of the writer; but, as the general's handwriting is a little hasty and peculiar, and his military honors and titles were not appended to these letters I speak of, it was natural that they should be read by the clerks, in order to ascertain whether they could be returned to the place they were written from. One of these letters had been written to an old lady (I judged so from the fact of his inquiring about her son and grand-children) somewhere in the South, who, it appeared, had entertained the general at her house, one day during the war, when the general was very much in want of a dinner to eat. He had not forgotten her kindness and hospitality, though it was now after the close of the war; but the old lady had probably removed from the little village to which the letter was directed, or, perhaps, she had died: so the letter came into our hands, and was returned to the general. Another was to an old friend of the general's. They had played together as boys, perhaps, but his friend had not risen to fame and fortune, like himself; he was giving words to his deep sympathy with a misfortune or bereavement that had befallen his friend — sympathy expressed with such tender, true feeling, that we felt as though it were another bereavement that he should have lost this letter of the general's.

The remark was often made among us that the Dead Letter Office afforded the very best opportunities for making collections of autographs of celebrated people — only the authorities could not be made to see it in that light. It was always with a sigh of regret, I must confess, that letters signed by such names as Bancroft, Whittier, Beecher, Grant, Greeley, were returned to their rightful owners. The most interesting accounts of foreign travel were sometimes contained in the dead letters — accounts more interesting than any book ever published. These were, as a general thing, written by ladies — and that sealed their doom. Gentlemen writing letters almost always sign their full name; but a lady will write a dozen pages, telling her friends all about the Louvre and the Tuileries, the Escurial and London Tower, in one long letter, and then sign Kate, or Lillie, at the end, thus precluding all possibility of having her letter returned, though we know from it that she has returned to her home in Boston. It is almost incredible what a large number of letters passing through our hands are "finished off" by that classically beautiful verse — "My pen is bad, my ink is pale; my love for you will never fail" — and it is impossible to believe in how many different ways and styles these touching lines can be written and spelled, till you find them dished up to you a dozen times a day, in this office. Eastern people don't appreciate this "pome" as Western farmers do. Missouri rustics are particularly addicted to it. What the predilection of the Southern people might have been, I cannot say; it was just after the close of the war, and their letters were pitiful enough. Of course there was not a Federal postage-stamp to be had in any of the Southern States; and no matter how deeply the contents of some of these letters affected us, we could not forward them to the people they were addressed to. These letters from the South portrayed so terribly true the bitter, abject poverty of all classes, at that time, that the Northerners to whom they were written would not have hesitated to assist these friends of "better days," could they have received the letters; but, even had we been allowed to forward them, the chances were extremely slender that people were still in the same position and location after the war as before the war.

Not these letters alone were sad; for sometimes a whole drama could be read from one or two short letters. One day we found among the dead letters a note written in a feeble, scrawling hand. It was by a boy, a prisoner and sick, in one of the penal institutions of New York — sick, poor fellow! and imploring his mother — oh, so piteously! — to come and see him. He was in the sick ward, he said, and if he *had* been wicked, and had struck at his step-father when he saw him abuse his mother, would she not come to see him, only once, for all that? She must not let his step-father prevent her from coming; he was dreaming of his mother and sister every night, and he knew his mother would come to him; but she must come soon, for the doctor had said so. Perhaps the letter had not reached the mother because the step-father had taken her out of the son's reach; for, in the course of a day or two, we found another letter addressed to the same woman, by one of the prison officials: the boy, Charley, had died on such a date — about a week after his letter had been written — and he had looked and asked for his mother to the last.

About letters written by German people I have noticed one peculiarity: they never omit to write the number of the year in some part of the letter, or on the envelope, outside. Sometimes it is written where the name of the country or the State should be found on the envelope, so that the direction would read, "Jacob Schmied, St. Louis, 1865;" or they write it at the bottom of the letter, instead of signing their name, and then write their name at the beginning of the letter, as though they were writing the letter to themselves. Everything is heavy and clumsy about their letters; they never indulge in joke or sentiment; and through the negligence of one of the German clerks, the most serious trouble had almost been brewed in a German brewer's family, at one time. It happened in this way:

A substantial German brewer had written to Hans Biersöffel, dunning him for money, owing on several barrels of *lager*. Hans must have left the city — at any rate, the letter came to our office, and was returned to the brewer; but, unfortunately, a very sentimental letter, containing a copy of some love-sick verses, written by a German lady, and held in the office as a curiosity for a little while, had (by mistake, of course) found its way into this letter. The honest Dutchman had meant to return this piece of property to our office at the first opportunity, and therefore carried it in his pocket-book, where his wife discovered it, seized it, and held it over his head, as the sword of Damocles, forever after — as he could not prove to her satisfaction that the letter and verses had *not* been sent to *him* by the writer.

At the time I belonged to the corps of dead letter clerks, there were three rooms fronting on Seventh street, fitted up as offices for the lady clerks, and one very large room on the other side of the hall. A straw mat was spread on the stone floor in our room; one office-chair was furnished for each lady, and desks barely large enough for two ladies to work at, without elbowing each other; and in one corner, wash-stand and water. In the large room some twenty ladies were writing, while four or five folders had their desk in the same room. Of the other rooms, one was occupied by the lady superintendent, together with whom were from four to six ladies; the next room also accommodated six ladies, and the last one, which had the look of a prison, from a high grating running through it, afforded room for four others. There were old Post-office Directories, boxes containing printed matter, and such like valuables, kept behind this grating; and one day, when a party of sightseers came unasked into our room, the youngest lady there — whose spirit had not yet been broken by the weight of the responsibilities resting on her shoulders — explained to the gaping crowd that behind this grating were kept the silver and household furniture of General ——, — the assistant postmaster — boxed up, while he was recruiting in the country. This was a twofold revenge, the young lady said to us: it was punishing the visitors for their inquisitiveness, and "old ——" for having the grating put up there. Several years have passed since I last saw the post-office building; the ladies of room No. —— were then petitioning to have this grating removed. Whether their petition was granted, I have not learned.

MARCHING WITH A COMMAND.

FROM Carlisle Barracks, Pennsylvania, we were ordered to Fort Leavenworth, Kansas, there to join General Sykes' command, then fitting out for the march across the Plains. General Sykes commanded the Fifth Infantry, while my husband belonged to the Third Cavalry; but as the latter regiment was to take up the line of march from Little Rock, Arkansas, through Texas, the lieutenant, as well as some three or four other officers of the Third, were well satisfied to be assigned to the infantry command, and sent in charge of recruits from Washington and Carlisle, to join General Sykes at Fort Leavenworth.

The two regiments (Fifth Infantry and Third Cavalry) were to rendezvous at Fort Union, New Mexico, where General Carleton was to meet the troops, and assign them to the different forts, camps, and stations in his department. This was immediately after the close of the war; and these eight hundred men of the Fifth Infantry and the Third Cavalry, under Colonel Howe, were the first regulars sent out to the Territories, from whence they had been called in to do some of the hard fighting when the rebellion broke out — volunteers and colored troops taking their place on the frontiers.

It was early June — the sky radiant, the earth laughing. Birds of the western prairies warbled their greeting from out the rose-trellises and sweet-scented flowers of the little enclosures in front of the officers' quarters, which, surrounding the well kept parade-ground, gave the place the look of one large bright-blooming garden. For days there had been at the fort signs and sounds as of a swarm of bees preparing to leave the hive. The carriage of the general flew back and forth between the town and the fort; the quartermaster dashed through the corrals, and by the workshops on his handsome sorrel; females of all shades and colors were interviewed and interrogated by officers' wives, who meant to provide themselves with luxuries for the journey; and new faces were seen and scanned in the mess-room every day.

The first day out from Fort Leavenworth we made but a few miles; the general seemed bent only on getting his command away from the barracks, for, though warned for weeks of the day of starting, there were those who seemed as little prepared for the march now as they had been two weeks ago. Well I remember the camp we made that first day — amid grass so high that we felt and looked like ants moving among the blades — and the confusion in our own establishment and that of our neighbors. The advantages of having secured the services of an old army-woman became apparent at this early stage. Without having at all consulted me, Mrs. Melville had boiled a ham, and stowed bread, cheese, and sardines, where she could readily lay hands on the articles, in the mess-chest. Coffee was quickly cooked, and we could sit down to our meal and invite others to it, before we had fairly realized the discomforts of a first night in camp.

A good woman was Mrs. Melville, but dreadfully tyrannical — domineering ruthlessly over myself and her husband, and only in awe of the lieutenant when he insisted on having his own way. They had always served in the cavalry, and had now again enlisted (I mean the husband, who drove our carriage, had enlisted) in the Third; and as Melville was the only cavalry recruit with the command, it had been a matter of some difficulty to appropriate him and his wife. It was not till the second day, when we made camp, that I saw how large the command was; and I remember thinking that it had taken since yesterday for the "tail-end" of the train of wagons, mules, and horses to leave the corrals and get into camp. When we left our camping-ground in the morning and returned to the highway, there was a broad road with deep ruts behind us, and hundreds of acres of prairie-land made bare and torn up, as though a city had been swept away, where the day before no sign of human life had been and the tall grass had waved untouched over the soft, black soil. Fancy the tramp of eight hundred men, the keen, light-turning wheels of a dozen or two of carriages, and the heavy, crunching weight of two hundred army-wagons, drawn each by six stout mules! No wonder the grass never grew again where General Sykes's command had passed!

Besides the twelve hundred mules in the wagons, there were some two hundred head extra, and a number of horses for the officers. All of these animals had been drawn from the government corrals at Fort Leavenworth; but I never realized how many there were, till one evening about four days out from the fort.

Elsewhere I have spoken of my white horse, Toby, who had so quickly become domesticated that he *would* insist on returning to our tent, no matter how emphatically he was told that he must be turned out, and stay with the rest of the herd. The mules had been accustomed to follow the lead of a white "bell-mare" in the corrals; and as Toby was the only white horse in the outfit, they became greatly attached to him, and would follow him in his vagaries wherever he led. Unfortunately, when he took his way back to the camp and to our tent this evening, the herders were not on the alert as usual, and before they could turn the tide there was a stampede, and a perfect overflow of mules in the camp. Such yelling and bellowing as those animals set up, when they found themselves floundering among the tents, and belabored with clubs, ropes, and picket-pins by the enraged soldiers, was never heard before nor since. Even Toby's serenity was disturbed, and he stood half-way in the tent, trembling, and looking as though he knew that the wagon-master was making his way to our settlement. Though I could forgive the man's rage, as he pushed the horse to one side and passed into the tent, neither the lieutenant nor myself took kindly to his offer to "shoot the horse the next time he undertook to stampede the herd;" and I held close on to Toby till the mules were driven back, and the wagon-master's wrath had cooled.

Truth to tell, before the next forty-eight hours were over, I was wellnigh converted to the belief that we had drawn the meanest stock the government-stables had ever contained. I forgot to say that each of the officers had been assigned a company of the recruits, and as they marched with them, we ladies were left in our carriages alone. No sooner was the command fairly on the road this morning than Molly and Jenny, a pair of green mules drawing our carriage, fell to jumping and kicking on a rough piece of ground, and a moment later the carriage was laid prone on one side, while I quietly clambered out on the other. A chorus of little screams went up from the rest of the carriages — expressing more horror, I think, at my getting up without the assistance of the doctor, who came flying up on his square-headed bay, than at the accident itself.

This was not enough of evil for the day. We made camp early (the general made not over fifteen miles a day when first starting out with the recruits), and Molly and Jenny, fastened to each other by a light chain around the neck, followed Toby through the camp, where they had come to be accepted as standing nuisances. Away up near the general's tent, Toby must have fancied there was good grazing, for he went there, the two mules *en train*. What followed I learned from the grinning orderly, who rapped at our tent soon after, holding the mules by the chain, and saying that "the general sent his compliments to the lieutenant, and he'd shoot the mules, and the white horse too, the next time they pulled the tent-fly down over him."

I looked stealthily out, and saw Toby in the distance, contemplatively switching his tail, and half a dozen men at work re-erecting the general's tent. The story was too good to keep; and the general himself told how, lying asleep on his cot, under the tent-fly, where it was cool, he had been waked up by Toby's nose brushing his face. Raising himself, and hurling one boot and an invective at the horse, he was surprised at seeing the two mules trying to stare him out of countenance at the open end of the fly. The other boot was shied at them, but there was no time to send anything else. The chain fastening the mules together had become twisted around the pole holding up the fly, and the precipitate retreat of the long-eared pair brought the heavy canvas down on the general's face.

Would I could end my "tale of woe" right here; but a love of truth compels me to say that the meanness of that horse seemed endless, and his capacity for wickedness was such that portions of it fell on Molly and Jenny, when a particularly rich harvest rewarded his efforts at deviltry. When Toby came to the tent-door, early next morning, I noticed a strangely bright polish on his fore-hoofs, and a suspicious greasiness about his nose and face. Molly and Jenny had greasy streaks running all over them, and seemed so well fed that I wondered to myself which of the officers' horses had to suffer last night, and go supperless to bed. Toby sniffed disdainfully at the bread I offered him, and turned to walk off very suddenly when he saw Melville coming toward the tent. I must explain that the tents were always pitched in the same order—the lieutenant's on one side of us; Captain Newbold's on the other; the baggage-wagon assigned to each officer drawn up behind the tent; the mules, of course, turned out with the rest of the herd. Melville pointed to the wagon behind Captain Newbold's tent, where a knot of men were gathered, bending to the ground; but he seemed too full for utterance. Almost instinctively I knew what he wanted to tell me. Newbold had brought two large jars of butter with him from Leavenworth, and Toby had encountered them last night, wiping his mouth on Molly and Jenny when he found the butter not to his taste. Over and above that, he had hauled six or eight grain-sacks out of the wagon, opened the sacks with his teeth, and scattered the grain for the two mules to eat.

I wanted to kill Toby on the spot; for the Newbolds were the best of neighbors, sharing with us, through the whole of that journey, the milk their cow (the only one with the whole train) was pleased to give. Not a word of complaint was heard from the captain or his little wife; but I did hope honestly that the miserable white horse might die of his extra feed of butter and oats.

In the evening Colonel Lane gathered the ladies together, led us to the top of a hill, and pointed out where Fort Riley lay, like a grand fortress, with long, white walls, rising on a green eminence. We reached it next day by night-fall, and though camped several miles outside of it, there were so many things which we found we actually needed, and which could only be had at this, the last post of any importance, that the greater number of officers were constantly to be seen between the sutler-store and the saddler-shop, the quartermaster's office and the corrals.

After a rest of three days, we took up the line of march again through prairie-land, dotted with farms and broken by forests and streams, through which (after having crossed the Kansas river at Manhattan, on a pontoon-bridge, before reaching Fort Riley) the soldiers seemed to think it rare sport to wade, barefooted, carrying shoes and stockings in their hands.

The country grew wilder and more desolate; and passing a farm-house one day, near which there were buffaloes grazing in the pasture with oxen and cows, it seemed nothing extraordinary, though, of course, we did not see the buffalo in his native freedom till some time after. At Ellsworth (now Fort Harker) we halted again for a day, and then gradually entered the wilderness. Fort Zarah seems to have grown where it is, only to help make the country look sadder and more desolate; but the well they have is splendid. I think so at least, for I was *so* thirsty when we turned in there at noon, though we continued the march and did not make camp. The general seemed to consider the feet of his men fully seasoned by this time; and they certainly made some hard days' marches before they reached Fort Union. The days' marches were harder for them than they were for us, on the whole; though many a time, creeping slowly over the tediously level ground, did I wish that I could march with them, or help drive mules, or lead horses — anything rather than sit in the carriage for hours, the sun beating down in just the same direction, the men in front moving along in just the same measure. But there was something grand about it at the same time — a forest of bayonets in front of us, an endless train of wagons behind us, moving silently through the solemn wilds; hosts of red-winged black-birds fluttering along with us, the rarer blue-jay flying haughtily over their heads.

There was always something to see; the prairie-flowers were so dazzlingly colored some days, or the rock lay in such odd strata; and in one place we saw the remains of some rough fortifications built of the rocks — thrown up hastily, perhaps, one day when the party of brave emigrants spied "ye noble savage" bearing down on them. In camp everything looked pleasant and cheerful. The general had traversed the country more than once, knew every spring on the road, and had the camping-ground kept so neat that we could have stopped in one place a good many days without any discomfort. Beyond that, he was courteous and thoughtful of our comfort, as only a soldier can be; and there was not a lady "marching with the command" who would not have voted him a major-general of the United States army, or into the Presidential chair, if he had preferred it.

At Fort Dodge, where officers and men burrowed half under ground (at that time), I had not the least desire to remain. However, a few miles back, where the river makes the bend, there is a singular grandeur about the country, with nothing to break the utter loneliness, save the sad, heavy murmur of the water. And now we are out on the plains again; day after day we travel over land that lies so level and so still that not a being but the lark seems living here beside us. How hot and fierce the sun glares down on the slowly-winding column—a serpent it seems, with its length outstretched, as it moves over the bare, brown prairie. The spirit grew oppressed, and the heart fainted in the noon-day sun; the command to halt was always received with joy; and more than once we had to make forced marches to reach water. Yet we lost but one man out of the eight hundred, and he died the day we struck the Arkansas again—died in the road almost—and we carried him with us to camp; and at night, when the stars had come out and tear-drops hung in the eyes of the flowers by the river-bank, they carried him to his lonely grave. I went to the tent-door when I heard the muffled drums, and stood outside, in the dark, where I could see the short procession passing. Lanterns were carried in the train that moved ghostly away from the camp-fires and the white-looming tents. The grave was not far, and when they had lowered the coffin I saw the form of a man bowing over it, as though in prayer, and then the earth was shovelled back. The soldiers returned with measured tread, and left their comrade on the wide, lone prairie, with only the Arkansas to sing his dirge.

I went to sleep with tears in my eyes; but we were to make an early start in the morning, and before daybreak we were all awake and astir. Sadness could not live in the heart those early mornings, and I thought sometimes the general had *reveille* sounded so early purposely, to show us how beautiful Nature was at sunrise.

Sunrise on the plains! Is there anything in music, in painting, in poetry, that can bring before eyes that have never beheld it, the passing beauty of such a scene? There are strains in music which bring a faint shadow of the picture back to me; no art can ever reproduce it. How balmy the faint breath of wind that seems to lift upward the light, gray clouds, to make way for the rosy tints creeping athwart the horizon! Watch the clouds as they rise higher in the heavens; see how the sun-god has kissed them into blushes as bright as the damask-rose, sending a flood of yellow light to cover them with greater confusion. Now they float gently upward till they reach the clear, blue sky, from where the yellow light has faded; and, watching bevies of other clouds, still dancing in the light above the first rays of the rising sun, the color fades from them, and they waft hither and thither — white clouds on deep blue ground — till the morning breeze bears them away from our sight. But words are weak and tame; and the yellow-breasted prairie-lark alone, rising high in the sun-bright air as the day begins, gives fit expression to her thanks for the glories of creation, in the wordless song she sings forever.

We were always far on the day's journey before the sun was fairly up; it was very early, to be sure, and often as the tents were struck when the *générale* was sounded, the families occupying them could be seen tumbling out, the children only half-dressed; and it happened sometimes that carriages were left behind, when not ready to fall into line when the march was beaten. In times of danger from Indians, of course, this would not have happened; but at that time there was thought to be no danger, except at night.

Mrs. Melville had developed into an unmitigated tyrant, and one of her victims was an Englishman, a raw recruit, who had been given the lieutenant as servant. His name was either Ackley or Hackley, Ockley or Hockley. If he insisted it was one, Mrs. Melville said it was the other; and so completely cowed was he at last that he no longer dared to assert his right to any name. I often thought it was a national revenge she was wreaking on the poor fellow (she and her husband had sprung from the Emerald Isle). He had to do all the work that should have fallen to her share, and he never had a moment to spare for the lieutenant or myself. From the first day of starting, I had detected, among the detail of men sent to pitch our tent, a countryman of mine, a poor Dutchman, the greenest of his kind. I electrified him one day by speaking German to him, and ever after his pale, worn face would brighten, and his eyes light up, when I asked of him any little service or assistance. The general, knowing me to be a German, allowed the man to wait on us; and Mohrman was happy as a king when he could fondle Toby, or put our tent to rights, and fix things comfortably for me in the carriage. He was a cabinet-maker, and the camp-table he made for us was the envy of the whole camp. The poor fellow was weak in the chest (something unusual for one of his nationality), and a big Irish corporal, who was a good enough fellow otherwise, had always imposed on Mohrman, because he was ignorant of the language, and could make no complaint to his officer. He continued to bear with Stebbins's petty persecutions like a saint, till one morning he made his appearance at the tent-door, with tears in his eyes, and complained that the corporal had deprived him of the last thing he had left, coming from the "Fatherland" — his *Gesang-Buch*, which his mother had given him on the day of confirmation.

I stepped outside, where Corporal Stebbins with his detail stood, waiting to strike the tent at the sounding of the *générale*. There was a lurking grin on the corporal's face, as he approached at my summons.

"Corporal," said I, "have you Mohrman's book?"

"Sure, ma'am, and is it his prayer-book the poor b'y wants? Ye see, he complained yesterday that his knapsack was so heavy that he couldn't pack me blankets; so I thought I'd carry this for him a while;" and, amidst a half-suppressed snicker, he solemnly drew forth from his capacious pocket a big black hymn-book, substantially German-looking, about ten inches in length by five inches across.

"I'll take that book," said I, looking severe, and turning very quickly to hide my face.

After this Mohrman seemed to have more peace; and we journeyed on serenely till we reached Fort Lyon, Colorado, the first human habitation we had laid eyes on for many weeks. Sterile and rock-strewn as the country is, it was the boast of the post commander that he had as fine a company-garden as could be seen, twenty miles away from here; to which his wife added, "the only pity was that the vegetables should always be dry and wilted before they reached the garrison."

I was well pleased to think that our destination lay beyond Fort Lyon; though there were those among the ladies who so dreaded the crossing of the Arkansas just before us, and the passage of the Raton Mountains later, that they would have remained here, where no flower could be coaxed into blossom, rather than have gone on. The Arkansas river was to be crossed at Bent's òld fort, where the overland mail-stage also had its crossing. The carriages were discreetly sent a mile or two above the fording-place, for the soldiers — poor fellows — had to swim across, their clothes, knapsack, and gun in one hand, while with the other they held to the stout ropes stretched from shore to shore. Not a man of the eight hundred was lost. There were mounted men in the river, ready to lend a helping hand at the first cry for aid, and they all crossed safely, though many, I dare say, in fear and trembling. When the men were over, the married officers were permitted to join the ladies, and we were ferried across in the skiff belonging to the stage line, for which little water-excursion we paid two dollars a head to the Overland Mail Company. Carriages and wagons were brought over by the wagon-master and teamsters; and when the whole train was on the other side, we thought we had spent rather a pleasant day.

Like sailors scanning the edge of the horizon for land, so the soldiers had for days been watching the nearer approach of the Spanish Peaks looming faintly in the distance, and breaking the grand monotone of the level, changeless plain, verging, where the eye could see no further, into limitless space. Those who had been out this way before commenced talking of the "Picketwire," and the beautiful valleys we should see, and the big onions the Mexicans would bring to the camp to sell. After a while I discovered that the "Picketwire" was a little river — the "Purgatoir" or "Purgatory" — along whose banks the Mexican raised vegetables and fruit, of which I saw specimens, later, in the big onion spoken of. I had not been in California then, and the onions produced there, of the size of a large saucer, certainly had a stunning effect on me.

I am not prepared to say why the little river was called Purgatory. For the most part the country was good enough — lovely, even; and sometimes grand. One or two days seemed rather purgatorial though, come to think of it. On one occasion we passed through steep, barren hills, strewn all over with little cylindrical pieces of iron, that looked exactly as though they had been melted in that place just below purgatory, and thrown up here to cool. Another day we marched along the bed of a river, over boulders from three to six feet high; if *we* did not think it purgatory, the horses and mules certainly did. But the worst day of all remained.

It broke at last — the dreaded day in which the Raton Pass was to be attempted. The horrors of the Pass, however, must have been less vivid in the eyes of the general than in the minds of the ladies belonging to his command; for, contrary to all hopes and expectations, he allowed none of the married officers to remain with the carriages. It was a "steep" pass, undeniably. To this day I have not forgotten the sound of the grating of the wheels on the bare, unmitigated rock, as the carriage made ascents and descents that were truly miraculous — one wheel pointing heavenward sometimes, while the other three were wedged in below; scraping along a rock wall, bounding from rock to rock, with the pleasant prospect, on the other side, of a launch from a jagged, well-deep precipice, into eternity.

The crowning point to our terror, and to the grandeur of the scene, was a fearfully inclined plane of solid rock, with a frowning bank on one side, a gaping drop-off on the other, and a dark, heavy wall rising square in front of us; against which, to all appearances, the mules must dash their brains out, for neither bit nor brake was of the least avail on this road. Just where the crash against the wall seemed inevitable, there was a narrow curve, and the road ran on in spite of the seeming impossibility. True to the saying, that there is but a step from the sublime to the ridiculous, I fell to laughing here, so that Melville turned in surprise to see whether fear and terror had robbed me of my sober senses; but I had seen in passing, painted on that dreadful wall of frowning rock, the cabalistic words and signs: " Old Cabin Bitters; S — T — 1860 — X — ; " and below this, "Brandreth's Vegetable Pills."

These horrors past, there lay before us valleys, hills, crags — that formed as picturesque a landscape as tourist's eye was ever gladdened by. At the foot of tall, straight pines, crowning the heights and covering the sloping hill-sides, was a carpet of short, soft grass, out of which laughed the merriest flower-eyes, and over which nodded the slenderest stalks, bearing blossoms that seemed exotic in their intensely bright hues. The balm-laden breath of the wind told enticing tales of the untrod velvet on the heights above, where the pine-trees bent and swayed in the passing breeze. We had come upon this all so unexpectedly that the lieutenant insisted on my mounting Toby to obtain a better view of the whole country. My saddle was in the wagon somewhere, and there was no time to hunt it up; but as I had seen Mrs. Lane start off on the colonel's horse and saddle sometime before, I clambered on Toby's back at once, into the lieutenant's saddle. By crossing some little low hills, which the command had to march around, I found myself pretty soon ahead of the train. Not aware that we were to pass any place where human beings dwelt, I kept bravely on — feeling all the more safe from seeing Captain Newbold's cow, with her guardian, just in front of me. When I saw a rude kind of gateway a little later, I could not resist the promptings of my curiosity, and quite forgot the command, which approached just then with beating drums and flying colors. Had I realized how near they were upon me, I think my native modesty would have prompted me to let General Sykes, with his command, pass in front of me; but seeing Captain Newbold's cow march through the gate, and an avenue of Mexican and Indian faces, I followed the lead, barely escaping the feet of the drummer-boys, who were close on my heels.

It was the residence of an old pioneer — old Wooten — a pioneer in the boldest sense of the word. In conversation with one of the officers, when Kit Carson was mentioned, he spoke of him as being a comparative stranger in these parts, having been in the country only some twenty-five or thirty years.

If, in the eyes of the straggling Mexicans gathered around, it was an honor to ride in front of the command — next after Captain Newbold's cow — that honor, and the privilege of riding in the lieutenant's saddle, was dearly paid for before night. Determined not to have the drummer-boys so close behind me again, I turned aside from the road, lured on by the magnificent fresh, soft grass before me. Toby seemed strangely averse to crushing the grass, for he stepped very gingerly, and made two or three attempts to turn back. Skygazing, I urged him on, till a sudden plunge he made had nearly thrown me out of the slippery saddle, and for the first time I saw that the fresh, treacherous green had only covered an ugly quagmire, in which Toby was wildly plunging about, getting in deeper at every fresh effort to raise himself. The command had nearly passed; only Colonel Bankhead lingered behind, picking the rare flowers for his wife — gallant man! — and my wild shouts caused him to look around. It was a slow job to rescue me; and by the time I was on dry soil, the colonel's clothing was very much the color of Toby's legs just then, for the frightened horse would not move a step, and Colonel Bankhead — I repeat my thanks to him now — had made his way into the horrible bog at the risk of his life almost. After this I could let Toby have the reins, and go anywhere — he never got mired again. But I took to the carriage that day, and never mounted Toby again till we reached Fort Union, some time later.

They were building very comfortable quarters at Fort Union when we got in, but that did us no good. General Sykes had his camping-ground assigned by General Carleton a mile or two outside the post; and our place was with the Fifth Infantry, until our regiment should get in. Now we used to strain our eyes looking for signs of "our regiment;" not that we were not well enough off where we were, but we used to congregate at the tent of some officer of the Third, and feel clannish, and speak of the delight we should feel when "old Howe" got in with the regiment — all out of sheer contrariness, I suppose.

One day Melville rushed wildly into the tent, and announced a great dust arising in the distance. We all rushed out, and a perfect fever took possession of the camp — cavalry and infantry, officers and men. Tables and mess-chests were brought out and spread; bottles were uncorked, and fruit-cans opened; dried-apple pie (a great luxury, I assure you) and salt pickles, raw sliced onions and raspberry jelly, were joyfully placed side by side.

Nearer rolled the dust — slowly — slowly; a snail might have moved faster, I thought, than this regiment, famed once as the Rifles, and blessed with the reputation of being very unlike a snail in general character. Mrs. Melville needed no stimulant to do her best; affection and ambition prompted her alike — she had served with the Third before, and was now again of them — and she worked like a beaver to have the table well spread for the expected guests. The slow, heavy tramp of the approaching troops shook the earth like far-off thunder; but the dust was so thick that it was hard to tell where the soldiers left off and the wagons commenced, while the train moved. At last there came the sudden clanging of trumpets, so shrill and discordant that I put my hands up to my ears, and then the command halted near our camp.

Let no one dream of a band of gay cavaliers riding grandly into the garrison on prancing steeds, and with flying banners! Alas, for romance and poetry! Gaunt, ragged-looking men, on bony, rough-coated horses — sun-burned, dust-covered, travel-worn, man and beast. Was there nothing left of the old material of the dashing, death-daring Rifles? Ah, well! These men had seen nothing for long weeks but the red, sun-heated soil of the Red River country; had drank nothing but the thick, blood-red water of the river; had eaten nothing but the one dry, hard cracker, dealt out to them each day; for they had been led wrong by the guide, had been lost, so that they reached Fort Union long after, instead of long before, the Fifth Infantry.

Their camping-ground was assigned them quite a distance from the Fifth, and we rode over the next day to visit the ladies who had come with the command. The difference between the two camps struck me all the more forcibly, I presume, because General Sykes was famed for the order and precision he enforced; and when we rode up to his tent two days later, to bid him good-bye (the officers of the Third having received orders to join their regiment), I exclaimed, in tones of mild despair:

"Oh, general, can you not come with us, and take command of the Third?"

He shook his head solemnly, looking over to the cavalry camp.

"Nothing would give me greater pleasure, madame, than to accede to your wishes; but really in this instance I must decline. *There are too many unruly horses for me in that camp.*"

I hope the general meant only what he said; I hope too the Third will forgive me, when I say that an old soldier in the ranks, a German, once told me in confidence that every member of that regiment could pass muster for the Wild Huntsman, so well known in the annals of terror in German fable-history.

II.

It was a novel court-martial, whose last sitting was held at the dead of night, between Fort Union and Los Vegas, in New Mexico. Let no one think that a love of the romantic induced the general commanding to order this assembling at the "witching hour, when church-yards yawn," but dire necessity — "the exigencies of the service," as they have it. General Sykes, who was president of the court, was under orders to take up the line of march with his infantry, on the day following, for Fort Sumner, while Colonel Howe, with five companies of cavalry, was to proceed to Fort Craig; and as General Carleton understood no joking in regard to orders once issued, and as the board had not been able to finish up the business brought before it while convened at Fort Union, this midnight session was agreed upon — the command to separate and march in opposite directions, as soon as the court adjourned.

Of the prisoners at the bar, the lieutenant was one, though I have forgotten for what heinous crime arraigned; doubtless the charges against him and the other unfortunate wights were very grave and serious in the eyes of their superior officers, though trivial they might be in the estimation of civilians. Just as the gray dawn crept up the horizon, the lieutenant entered the tent, where I was waiting, fully dressed for the march, knowing that the tents would be struck as soon as the court was over.

Slowly the long train arranged itself, and lumberingly it wound its way out of the camp, entered only at a late hour the evening before. The blast of the bugle seemed fairly to cut the crisp morning air, and the horses neighed and stamped, while here and there a mule couple — part of the six attached to each wagon — would begin frisking and jumping, till called to order by the blacksnake of the irritable driver. As the lieutenant was under arrest, he was relieved from duty; and as this state of things was likely to continue until the proceedings and findings of the court had been sent to Washington and returned, we set out with the intention of enjoying the journey as well as was possible under the circumstances. We were expected to march with the command, but in the rear of the cavalry, and preceding the army-wagons. The dust, however, was anything but pleasant here, and as, altogether, Uncle Sam holds the lines of government somewhat slacker in these frontier countries, the lieutenant was allowed to take his carriage, the orderly, and the wagon containing our tent and camp furniture, to the end of the entire train. In this way we could make a halt, or an excursion into the neighboring country, whenever we felt inclined, and could catch up again with the command by the time it went into camp — where I was an object of envy to the other ladies, whose husbands were not under arrest.

Toward noon we reached Los Vegas, the first Mexican town I had seen — Fort Union being but the entrance to New Mexico. The country around Los Vegas is flat and uninteresting, but by no means barren, though only a small portion of it is cultivated. A little stream, the Gallinas, runs by the place, emptying later into the Rio Pecos; but the Mexicans are not content with this water-course alone — they have dug irrigating canals, which look again like little streams where grass and wild flowers have sprung up on the banks. It is the only branch of art or industry cultivated anywhere in New Mexico — this digging of irrigating ditches — and in it the Mexicans surely excel. Wherever we see a patch of green, we may be certain of finding canals on at least two sides of it; and they can lead the water where a Yankee, with all his ingenuity, would despair of bringing it.

The houses of Los Vegas, though looking very much so to me then, are not so hopelessly Mexican as those I found later along the Rio Grande and farther in the interior. The houses were one story high, the roofs of mud, of which material were also mantle-shelves, window-sills, walls and floors. But the little enclosed fire-places, with overarching mantle, were smooth and white, as were the walls; and the more pretentious houses, and where Americans lived, were set with glass. In the houses of the Mexicans I noticed that a width of red or yellow calico was tacked smoothly up around the wall, at a distance of three or four feet from the ground. The use of this drapery is just as incomprehensible to me as what benefit the trunks derive from being placed on two chairs, while the members of the family and visitors are requested to be seated on the floor. But then it is not every New Mexican family that can boast of having a trunk; and those who have one, and no chairs, build a kind of platform or pedestal for it to rest on.

The troops, while we were sight-seeing in Los Vegas, were not allowed to halt at all, but marched on toward Puertocito, where camp was made. At Fort Union a new driver had been assigned to our baggage-wagon — a little monkey-faced old man, Manuel — who had addressed me in Spanish, early that morning, praying that we should allow him to stop at Los Vegas, where his wife and his "pretty little girls" were living. I understood no Spanish, but his eyes looked so beseechingly when his request was made known to me, that I was glad to tell him we should stop there. The man was to go with us to the end of our journey, and it might be a long time till he could see his people again.

When the lieutenant sent the orderly for Manuel, with directions to move on and overtake the command, I saw the old man tumbling out of a little low house near by, his faithful wife and "pretty little girls" tumbling out after him — half a dozen of the scrawniest, most apish-looking specimens I ever saw of Spanish or Mexican people. For miles the "pretty little girls" followed the father and the army-wagon, and wherever we passed a house on the road, one or more women would come to the door — large-eyed and sweet-voiced — wishing good-day and good-journey to old Manuel. As far as my Spanish goes, *Puertocito* signifies little gate, or entrance. It should be Grand Gate, so majestically do rocks and boulders arise from out of green meadows and tree-covered hillocks.

Large flocks of sheep are herded here, and the whole is

said to belong to a Spanish·widow lady, living either in Mexico or Spain. In the course of my travels through the country, I met with accounts of this or some other widow, owning fabulous stretches of land, mines, and treasures, so often that I came to regard this widow-institution as a myth or a humbug; but the people living here were always very earnest in their assurances to the contrary. However this might be, it was a beautiful, romantic spot, such as we came upon time and again in this strange country. Well do I remember the succession of little narrow valleys on the route between Fort Union and Santa Fé; the hard, smooth road, the tall gramma-grass on each side of it, and the shapely-grown evergreens bordering the lawn-like fields, till lines of taller trees, coming up close to the road, seemed to divide off one little valley from the other. Yet never a house did we see the whole of that day, though the garden for many a one seemed ready planted by kind mother Nature's hands. The land was but a desert, in spite of the waving grass and the dark green trees. There was no water to be found for long, long weary miles.

Before we had been long on our journey, an unfortunate circumstance brought us to doubt the honesty of poor old Manuel so seriously that it had almost resulted disastrously to him. We had made camp not far from San Jose, a place consisting of two and a half houses, on the Pecos river. We were to cross the river here; and in the morning, when the tents were being struck, and we were already seated in the carriage, waiting for the mules to be harnessed to it, these same mules were reported missing. The command moved on, of course, leaving our baggage-wagon, our cook, our orderly, and ourselves, behind; the old colonel chuckling to himself that as we were in the habit of looking out for ourselves, we might do so on this occasion too.

The mules were unharnessed from the wagon at once,

Charley mounted on one, Pinkan on the other, Manuel on the third, and the lieutenant on the fourth, all starting off in different directions to search for the truants, while I was left in charge of the other two mules and the rest of our effects. A long time passed before any of them returned; and when Charley came back, soon after the lieutenant, he said he had heard from a Dutchman in San Jose that two mules answering the description had been seen driven by a Mexican, just at daybreak, over the bridge near the town; and the supposition now was that Manuel had sold them to some of his countrymen, always going in gangs through the Territory. Manuel soon came in, without the mules. When the lieutenant told him of his suspicions his face fell; and when the vague threat of summary justice to be executed was added, his shrivelled, monkeyish face grew livid, and he turned to me trembling, and begging, for the sake of his "pretty little girls," that I should intercede, and assure the lieutenant that indeed, *indeed*, he hadn't stolen the mules. I felt sorry for the old man; but just when things looked darkest for him, Pinkan was seen in the distance driving up the runaways.

The reaction of the fright experienced by old Manuel had the effect of making him drunk when we got to San Jose (perhaps the *aguardiente* imbibed at the house of his *compadre* had something to do with it, too); and just as I was making my first trial of *chile-con-carne* in the low room of the Mexican inn, he came and spread before me, beside the fiery dish which had already drawn tears from my eyes, papers certifying that he had rendered good services as teamster in the Mexican war, under General Zack Taylor, and could be trusted by Americans. If it was laughable to see the air of pride with which he struck his breast, declaring in Spanish that he was "a much honorable and brave man," there was yet a touch of true dignity in the low bow he made while thanking me for having called him an honest man, while the rest had taken him for a horse-thief, a *ladrone* and *picaro*.

We easily caught up with the command at night, and laid our plans while in camp for the next few days to come. The troops were not to pass through Santa Fé, and, though we could have made the detour without the colonel's knowledge, it was not safe to run into the very jaws of danger, as General Carleton's headquarters were at Fort Marcy, and he had probably returned to Santa Fé from Fort Union long before this time, travelling with only an escort and the best mules in the department. We had letters to Doctor Steck, "running" a gold-mine about thirty miles from Santa Fé; and as the command passed near by, we started off into the mountains where the mine lay. Wild and rugged as the scenery was, it was not so dreary as I had always fancied every part of the Territory must be. In some places it seemed as if man had done a great deal to make the face of nature hideous. Great unseemly holes were dug here, there, and everywhere — the red, staring earth thrown up, and then left in disgust at not finding the treasures looked for. The company of which Doctor Steck was superintendent seemed to have found the treasures, however, for in their mill half a dozen stamps were viciously crushing and crunching the rock brought down from the mountains above on mule-back.

The doctor is a Pennsylvanian, and he tried to have his ranch look as much as possible like a Pennsylvania homestead. There were necessarily slight deviations, more particularly in the furniture of the dwelling-house, which here consisted mainly of double-barrelled shot-guns and repeating rifles. These were merely a set-off, I presume, to the chunks of gold he showed us (the size of a fist), each being a week's "clean-up." There was quicksilver used in gaining the gold (what I know about gaining gold is very little), and the doctor turned a stream of water on the plates under the crushers, and then scraped up the gold for me to look at.

I did not learn till months later — though I readily believed it — that this man could travel alone and unarmed through the midst of the Apache country; and did he ever miss his road or want assistance, he had but to make a signal of distress, when the savages would fly to him from their lurking-places, shelter him, and guide him safely back to his white brethren. This I learned first from an old Mexican guide at our camp, who said that the Indians stood in awe of him as a great medicine-man, and loved him for his uniform kindness to them.

Santa Fé Mountain behind us, there were no more hills save the sand-hills, that seem shifting and changing from day to day, so that very often in the neighborhood of the Rio Grande, the river itself is followed as a landmark, the land being more unreliable than the water. The big sand-hill opposite Albuquerque, however, seems to be stationary; people who had been here twenty years before remembered the location.

There is something singular about these Mexican towns or cities. You hear them spoken of as important places, where the law-givers and the dignitaries of the American *régime* reside, and where renowned families of the Spanish period had their homes; where large commercial interests lie, and where things flourish generally. When you approach them, a collection of what seem only mud hovels lie scattered before you. You look for order and regularity of streets, and you find yourself running up against square mud-piles at every other step; you look for doors and windows in these structures, and find a narrow opening, reaching to the ground, on one side, and high up in the wall a little square hole without glass or shutter. This is the first impression. But you are compelled to remain at such a place; and as the eye grows to shrink less from the sight of the hard clay and cheerless sand, you discover the tips of the pomegranate tree peering curiously over the high mud wall enclosing a neat *adobe* with well-cultivated garden. In astonishment you press your face to the railing of the rude gate, and directly the soft voice of a dark-faced woman calls to you from within: "Enter, *señora;* you are welcome!"

When you leave the garden, where peaches, grapes, and pomegranates have been showered on you, together with assurances of the kindest feelings on the part of your hostess, the whole place somehow looks different. There are streets and lanes which you did not notice before, where the broad, double doors of the houses stand hospitably open, and the large square windows, if not provided with sash and glass, are latticed in fanciful designs, as we see them in old Spanish and Italian paintings. And there is such a dreamy languor in the air; such a soft tint in the blue of the heavens; such a wooing, balmy breeze, that seems to float down from the mountain yonder. There is no necessity for keeping one's eyes fixed on the sand-hill that hid Albuquerque from us at first. Look over again to the mountain. Could artist with brush and pencil create anything more perfect than the gentle rise away off there, over which houses and vineyards are scattered, and which climbs up steeper and higher, till the faintest shadow of a passing cloud seems resting on the blue-green peak? And winding its way slowly from the foot of the mountain, comes a train of black-eyed, barefooted Pueblo Indian women, bearing on their heads home-made baskets filled to overflowing with well-displayed fruit — melons, peaches, grapes — in such perfection, and with such rich, ripe coloring, as are seldom found away from Mexico.

Of historical interest, too, there is much in Albuquerque. The daughter of a Spanish lady belonging to the old family of the Bacas, was married to an officer in our army, and with her I visited the house of General Armijo. The younger daughters alone received us, the older married sister being sick or absent. The house was furnished with elegant material — the heavy Brussels carpet spread out on the mud floor, flowers and figures running up and down, just as the carpet had been cut off at the length of the room, and then rolled back again and cut off at the other end. The breadths were laid side by side, but not a stitch had been taken to hold them together. Cushioned chairs were ranged along the walls of the room, the line broken only where marble-top tables, what-nots, and a Chickering piano were introduced among them — all set against the wall without symmetry or taste. On the walls hung pictures, in embroidery, water-colors, and oil, executed by the young ladies while in a convent school; but in vain I looked for a picture of General Armijo among them. It was here at Albuquerque that I saw for the first time — and alas! the last — Kit Carson, and the less renowned but equally brave Colonel Pfeiffer.

Beyond Albuquerque the road lies again over the sand-hills and through the valleys of the Rio Grande; and we lost our way among the hills one day, when the command had passed but a short distance in advance of us. For hours we toiled through the shifting sand, hoping that each mound we climbed might bring the marching column to our view. Fortunately, Manuel, with the wagon, had fallen in line with the train that morning, and only Pinkan, riding the lieutenant's horse and leading mine, was with us. The lieutenant was driving, and I could see from the way his eyes wandered over the interminable range of low sand-hills that he was completely bewildered. All at once we came on a house, which, from a distance, we had taken to be another sand-pile; and the Mexicans living here, after treating us to the best their house afforded — eggs, and the sweet, unsalted goat-milk cheese — piloted us to Los Pinos, where we were to camp for the night. Here the command crossed the Rio Grande — forded it, bag and baggage — and the next day remained in camp below Peralta, where the tents were pitched in a delightful grove of cottonwood trees.

It has been said that a Mexican is born with a lasso in his hand. The feat old Manuel performed with his was quite new to me. Wood was so scarce that not the smallest bit of a dry limb or broken twig could be found under the trees. The lower branches having been lopped off, and the soldiers forbidden to cut down any trees, our old Mexican at once went to work with his rope, throwing it so dexterously over the brittle limbs that a snap and a crash followed every excursion of the rope.

We made a flying trip to Peralta the next morning, while the command was marching in the opposite direction. The place, with its pretty church and scattered houses, surrounded by walled-in gardens, made quite a pleasing impression. Then we turned back and joined the command.

The road now was one continuous level, with hills, uniformly bare and brown, in the distance. Bare and brown as they look, thousands of goats are herded on them, and, to judge from the milk and cheese we got on the road, find pretty good picking till such time as "Lo! the poor Indians" think proper to drive off the herds for their own use, when they are in most cases generous enough to leave the herders behind — dead. And the sun, smiling down so placidly on the river and the little towns lying near its banks, seems never to heed the death-cry of the helpless *peon* or the lonely wayfarer laid low in the dust by the prowling savage, but goes on lighting up the cloudless sky-dome, and bringing into strong relief the different features of scenery, life, and customs, that make a journey through New Mexico resemble a sojourn in the Holy Land. Through all those towns along the Rio Grande do we see the daughters of the land, barefooted, their faces half hidden by the oriental-looking *rebozo*, the earthen *olla* poised gracefully on the head, going at eventide to the well for water. Belen, Sabinal, Polvedaro — here are the low-built houses, the flat roofs, the gray-green olive here and there; even the wheaten cake, the *tortilla*, is set before the stranger when he comes. Then this dead, dead silence! The barking of the dogs as we come through the villages, the drawling sing-song of the children, calling to each other at the unusual spectacle we present, seem hardly to break the slumber of the mid-day air.

So wearying as the one color — clay — grows to the eye! the ground, the houses, the fence-walls, the bake-ovens, all, all the same color. Even where there are gardens, with the enclosing wall seems to terminate vegetation; never a vagabond grass-blade or a straggling vine can find its way outside. Bake-ovens are an institution and a marked feature in the landscape; every house has one, and as they are built with a dome-like top, they are more pleasing to the eye than the houses, and very often nearly as large. I remember seeing one day a dog and a little naked child (clothing is considered superfluous on children) mount from the mud fence to the top of the bake-oven, and from there to the house roof, with no more difficulty than we would experience in going up a flight of easy stairs. The bread that the Mexicans bake in these ovens is the sweetest and whitest that can be found.

Then came Socarro, where most of the officers spent the day, while the command went into camp some miles below. An English family kept a very pleasant house there, whose good cheer the old colonel had not forgotten from long ago. The garden back of the neatly-built house I thought one of the loveliest spots on earth; not from the fact alone that it contained flowers and some few tall trees, but from the view it afforded of the far-off mountain — probably of the Sierra Maddalena chain, but called Socarro Mountain here. There was the same dreamy haze that hung over the mountain near Albuquerque, and the same bluish-green tint that made it appear wooded to the top. A hot spring takes its rise in the mountain somewhere, and the tiny stream at my feet seemed hardly cold yet, though its waters had travelled many miles from its source.

Fort Craig, though an important military post, is not celebrated for the beauties or grandeur of the country surrounding. We crossed the Rio Grande here again — two companies only, the colonel, with the other three, having been assigned to Fort Craig. Toward the Jornada del Muerto we journeyed, making camp before entering the desert at Parajo, the Fra Cristobal of the Texan Santa Fé prisoners who were driven through here in 1842, on their long, weary journey to the city of Mexico. They had been captured, or rather tricked into a surrender, near Anton Chico, and, from Albuquerque down, I traced them all along the Rio Grande. They had been marched on the opposite side of the river, taking in their way Sandia, Valencia, Tome, Casa Colorada, and La Joya, crossing the river at Socarro, and recrossing probably near where Fort Craig now stands.

Such heart-rending tales as were told us of the sufferings and the diabolical treatment of these helpless men — mere youths, some of them, the sight of whom brought out all the native tenderness, the true charity there is in the heart of every Mexican woman! As in Albuquerque, the shadow of Governor Armijo — tall and stately, though with something of a braggart in his carriage, and the glare of a hyena in his eye — was ever rising before me, so in this wretched place did I seem always to hear the gentle, pitying *" Pobrecitos !"* of the kind-hearted women, who brought the last bit of *tornale*, the last scrap of *tortilla* that their miserable homes afforded, to these men who were so soon to be driven like cattle, and shot down like dogs, when their bleeding feet refused to carry them further on their thorny path. Had the horrible stretch of ninety-five miles of desert-land now before us not been christened " Dead Man's Journey " before these unfortunates passed over it, the baptism of the blood of those wantonly slaughtered there would have fastened on it that name forever.

Two companies of United States cavalry are not hastily attacked by ye noble red man, and we slept peacefully on the Jornada — though close to our tent, the first night, were two graves, dug for their murdered comrades years ago by some of the men now in the company.

A number of wagons had been loaded with water-casks, filled before entering the Jornada, so that we did not suffer; yet we were all glad when, on the third day, Fort Seldon was reached. After a rest of two days, we once more crossed the river, on a ferry-boat moved with a rope, leaving the other company at Fort Seldon, and proceeding alone, with the last company, to the farthest out-post of the department. At this place we disposed of our carriage to the post surgeon, as we were told that among the mountains in the vicinity of Pinos Altos we should have no use for it, while the officers of this garrison could make excursions to Donna Ana, Los Cruces, and even La Messilla, over the level and rather pleasant country.

The first day out, a heavy rain-storm came on, and I was glad enough to leave the saddle and seek shelter in the linen-covered army-wagon, where Manuel arranged quite a comfortable bed for me — seat it could not be called. And here let me say that, with bedding and blankets, spread over boxes and bundles underneath, there is more comfort to be found in one of these big wagons, where you can recline at full length, than in the most elegant travelling-carriage, where you have always to maintain the same position.

The stretch between Fort Seldon and Fort Cummings proved harder for us than the Jornada del Muerto. It was reported that large bands of Indians were hovering round us, and we could make no fires to cook by, but were hurried on as fast as possible. Many of the horses gave out and had to be shot; and my poor Toby was sometimes so tired from carrying me over the rough country, and up and down the rocky hills, that more then once he stopped and nibbled at my stirrup-foot—asking me in this peculiar language to dismount.

The soldiers were better off than we were, for they had their rations of hard-tack and salt bacon, which needed no cooking; while the dressed chickens and tender-steaks we had providently brought from Fort Seldon with us, uncooked, were going to decay in the provision-box, and we might have gone hungry had not the men divided with us. No one can think how sweet a bit of bacon tastes with a piece of hard-tack, when offered by a soldier whose eyes are shining with honest delight at being able to repay some trifling kindness shown him on the march.

The rock-strewn mountains of Cook's cañon frowned darkly on us as we made our way into Fort Cummings. The sable garrison, it is said, never ventured beyond the high mud walls with less than twenty-five in the party, were it only to bring a load of wood from the nearest grove of scanty timber.

At no post, I am fain to confess, have I seen a larger number of mementos of Indian hostility than at this fort. And the negroes had all the more cause to dread attacks from the Indians, as they had been accosted the first time they went out—a fatigue-party, to cut wood—by an Indian chief, who told them that he was their brother, and that it was their duty to come and join his band against their common enemy, the white man. The black braves refused, returning to the post without their load of wood; and since that time no fatigue-party ever returned that did not bring back at least one of their number dead or wounded.

The last thing we did before leaving this post was to stop at the large basin of water, Cook's Spring, there to drink, and let the animals drink, a last draught of the pure, clear flood.

How many a heart had this spring gladdened, when its sight broke on the longing eyes of the emigrant, before human habitations were ever to be found here! Just at the foot of the rough, endless mountain, the men who had come under protection of our train from Fort Cummings pointed out where the two mail-riders coming from Camp Bayard — our destination — had been ambushed and killed by the Indians only the week before. I had heard of these two men while at the Fort, one of whom, a young man hardly twenty, seemed to have an unusually large number of friends among men of all classes and grades. When smoking his farewell pipe before mounting his mule for the trip to Camp Bayard, he said: "Boys, this is my last trip. Mother writes that she is getting old and feeble; she wants me to come home; so I've thrown up my contract with Uncle Sam, and I'm going back to Booneville just as straight as God will let me, when I get back from Bayard. It's hard work and small pay, anyhow — sixty dollars a month, and your scalp at the mercy of the red devils every time you come out." The letter was found in the boy's pocket when the mutilated body was brought in.

It was no idle fancy when I thought I could see the ground torn up in one place as from the sudden striking out of horses' hoofs. One of the men confirmed the idea that it was not far from the place where the body had been found. The mule had probably taken the first fright just there, where the rider had evidently received the first arrow, aimed with such deadly skill that he fell in less than two minutes after it struck him.

This gloomy spot passed, the country opened far and wide before us; level and rather monotonous, but with nothing of the parched, sterile appearance that makes New Mexico so dreaded by most people. Trees were few and far between; but later, where the Mimbres river rolls its placid waters by, there are willows, and ash even, as I have heard people affirm.

But I must not forget the hot spring we camped by for an hour or two, the *Aqua Caliente* of the Mexicans. A square pond, to approach which you must clamber up a natural mud wall some two feet high, lay bubbling and steaming near the shade of some half dozen wide-spreading trees. That corner of the pond where the water boils out of the earth had once been tapped, apparently, and the water led to the primitive bath-tubs, made by digging down into the hard, clayey ground. A dismantled building showed that the place had at some time been permanently occupied, which was said to be the case by the Mexican family living under one of the trees, and who were sojourning here for the purpose of having life restored to the paralyzed limbs of one of the children. The people who had lived here were driven off by Indians, but I have heard since that the place had been rebuilt.

The second day after leaving Fort Cummings we came in sight of a lovely valley, enclosed on all sides by low wooded hills, with bold, picturesque mountains rising to the sky beyond. A clear brook — so clear that it was rightly baptized Minne-ha-ha — gambolled and leaped and flashed among the green trees and the white tents they overhung; and in their midst a flag-staff, at whose head the stars and stripes were flying, told me that we had reached our journey's end.

TO TEXAS, AND BY THE WAY.

I HAD not seen New Orleans since I was eight years of age, and to Texas I had never been; so I was well pleased with the prospect of visiting the southern country. To one coming direct from California, overland by rail, it seems like entering a different world — a world that has been lying asleep for half a century — when the great "pan-handle" route is left to one side, and Louisville once passed. Though we know that the country was not asleep — only held in fetters by the hideous nightmare, Civil War — I doubt if the general condition of things would have been in a more advanced state of prosperity if the old order of affairs had remained unchanged, as the march of improvement seems naturally to lag in these languid, dreamy-looking southern lands.

The line between the North and the South seems very sharply drawn in more respects than one. We were scarcely well out of Louisville before delays and stoppages commenced; and though the country was pleasant enough to look at in the bright, fall days, it was not necessary to stop from noon till nightfall in one place, to fully enjoy the pleasure. Another drawback to this pleasure was the reliance we had placed on the statement of the railroad agent, who told us it was quite unnecessary to carry a lunch-basket "on this route." Since we had found a lunch-basket, if not really cumbersome, at least not at all indispensable, from Sacramento to Omaha, we saw no reason why we should drag it with us through a civilized country, and consequently suffered the penalty of believing what a railroad ticket-agent said. In another section of the same sleeping-car with us was a party who had been wiser than we, and had brought loads of provisions with them. No wonder: they were Southerners, and had learned not to depend on the infallibility of their peculiar institutions.

The head of the party was a little lady of twenty-five or thirty years, with pale, colorless face, and perfectly bloodless lips. I should have gone into all sorts of wild speculations about her — should have fancied how a sudden, dread fright had chased all the rosy tints from her lips back to her heart, during some terrible incident of the war; or how the news, too rashly told, of some near, dear friend stricken down by the fatal bullet, had curdled the red blood in her veins, and turned it to ice before it reached her cheeks — had she not been so vigorous and incessant a scold. Now it was the French waiting-maid to whom she administered a long, bitter string of cutting rebukes, while the unfortunate girl was lacing up my lady's boots; next it was her younger sister — whom she was evidently bringing home from school — whose lips she made to quiver with her sharp words; and then, for a change, the mulatto servant was summoned, by the well-scolded waiting-maid, to receive his portion of the sweets meted out. An ugly thing she was, and so different from the Southern lady I had met in the hotel at Louisville — one of the most beautiful women I have ever seen — whose grace nothing could exceed as she handed me a basket of fruit across the table, when one glance had told her that I was a stranger and tired out with the heat and travel.

But, in spite of what I have said, I must confess that I accepted the sandwiches the little scold sent us, for the supper-station was not reached till eleven o'clock at night. As the conductor promised us another good, long rest here, the gentlemen left the ladies in the cars, and returned after some time, followed by a number of negroes, who carried a variety of provisions and divers cups of coffee. I thought, of course, that it was luncheon brought from some house established at the station for that purpose; but was told that the chicken the mulatto boy was spreading before us had been abstracted from his massa's hen-yard, and that the eggs the old negro was selling us had not by any means grown in his garden. Only the coffee, which was sold at twenty-five cents a cup, was a legitimate speculation on the part of some white man (I am sure his forefathers were from the State of Maine), who went shares with the negro peddling it, and charged him a dollar for every cup that was broken or carried off on the cars, which accounted for the sable Argus' reluctance to leave our party till we had all swallowed the black decoction and returned the cups.

We were to take dinner at Holly Springs, some time next day; and it *was* "some time" before we got there, sure enough. We had picked up an early breakfast somewhere on the road, and when the dinner-bell rang at the hotel as the cars stopped, we did not lose much time in making our way to the dining-room. The door, however, was locked, and we stood before it like a drove of sheep, some hundred or two people. Through the window we could see mine host, in shirt-sleeves and with dirty, matted beard, leisurely surveying the crowd outside; in the yard, and on the porch near us, stood some barefooted negroes, with dish-cloth and napkin in hand, staring with all their might at train and passengers, as though they were lost in speechless wonder that they should really have come. In the party with us was a Californian, some six feet high, who, though a Southerner by birth, had lived too long in California to submit patiently to the delay and inconvenience caused by the "shiftlessness" of the people hereabouts.

"Now, you lazy lopers," he called to the darkies, swinging the huge white-oak stick he carried for a cane, "get inside to your work. And if that door ain't opened in five seconds from now, I'll break it down with my stick."

He drew his watch; and, either because of his determined voice, or his towering figure, the darkies flew into the kitchen, and the landlord sprang to open the door, while the crowd gave a hearty cheer for the big Californian.

New Orleans seemed familiar to me; I thought I could remember whole streets there that I had passed through, as a little child, clinging to the hand of my father — himself an emigrant, and looking on all the strange things around him with as much wonder as the two little girls he was leading through the town. How it came back to me! the slave-market, and the bright-faced mulatto girl, hardly bigger than myself, who so begged of my father to buy her and take her home with him, so that she could play with and wait on us. There was nothing shocking to me, I regret to say, in seeing this laughing, chattering lot of black humanity exposed for sale, though my good father doubtlessly turned away with a groan, when he reflected on what he had left behind him, in the old fatherland, to come to a country where there were liberty and equal rights for all. I can fancy now what he must have felt when he spoke to the little woolly-head, in his sharp, accentuated dialect, which his admirers called "perfect English," as he passed his hand over her cheek and looked into her face with his great, kind eyes. He said he had brought his children to a free country, where they could learn to work for themselves, and carve out their own fortunes; and where they must learn to govern themselves, and not govern others.

Day after day, on foot or in carriage, we rambled through the streets, and I never addressed a single question to the driver or any of the party, satisfied with what information accidentally fell on my half-closed ear. I was living over again one of the dreams of my early days: the dream I had dreamed over again so often, among the snows of the biting, cold Missouri winter, and on the hot, dusty plains of Arizona, amid the curses of those famishing with thirst and the groans of the strong men dying from the fierce stroke of the unrelenting sun. Passing through the parks and by the marketplaces, I saw again the negro women, with yellow turbans and white aprons, offering for sale all the tempting tropical fruits which foreigners so crave, and still dread. And I thought I saw again the white, untutored hands of my father, as he laboriously prepared seats for us in the deepest shade of the park, and dealt out to us the coveted orange and banana. The cool, delicious fruit, and the picture of flowers and trees in the park; the black, kindly faces of the negro servants, and the laughing, white-clad children at play — how often I had seen them again in my dreams on the desert!

Canal street looked lonely and deserted, as did the stores and shops lining either side of the broad, aristocratic street. The material for a gay, fashionable promenade was all there; only the people were wanting to make it such. True, there were groups occasionally to be seen at the counters of the shops, but in most such cases a black, shining face protruded from under the jaunty little bonnet, perched on a mass of wool, augmented and enlarged by additional sheep's-wool, dyed black. One of these groups dispersed suddenly one day, vacating the store with all the signs of the highest, strongest indignation. The tactless storekeeper, who had not yet quite comprehended the importance and standing of these useful members of society, had unwittingly offended an ancient, black dame. She had asked to see some silks, and the shopkeeper had very innocently remarked, "Here, aunty, is something very nice for you."

"I wish to deform you, sir," replied Aunt Ebony, bridling, "that my name is Miss Johnson." With this she seized her parasol and marched out of the store, followed by her whole retinue, rustling their silks, in highest dudgeon.

On my way to the ferry, when leaving New Orleans for Texas, I saw something that roused all the "Southern" feeling in me. Two colored policemen were bullying a white drayman, near the Custom-house. I must confess I wanted to jump out, shake them well, take their clubs from them, and throw them into the Mississippi (the clubs, I mean, not the precious "niggers"). What my father would have said, could he have seen it, I don't know; the grass had long grown over his grave, and covered with pitying mantle the scars that disappointments and a hopeless struggle to accomplish purposes, aimed all too high, leave on every heart.

As the cars carried us away from the city, and gave us glimpses of the calm water, and the villas, and orange-groves beyond, there came to me, once more,

"The tender grace of a day that is dead."

It was just a soft, balmy day as this, years ago, when we lay all day long in a bayou, where the water was smooth and clear as a mirror, and the rich grass came down to the water's edge; and through the grove of orange and magnolia, the golden sunlight sifted down on the white walls and slender pillars of the planter's cottage. Stalwart negroes sang their plaintive melodies as they leisurely pursued their occupation, and birds, brighter in plumage than our cold, German fatherland could ever show us, were hovering around the field and fluttering among the growing cotton.

The graceful villa was still there, and the glassy waters still as death; but the villa was deserted, and the rose running wild over magnolia-tree and garden-path; the cotton-field lay waste, and the negro's cabin was empty, while the shrill cry of the gay-feathered birds alone broke the silence that had hopelessly settled on the plantation. Farther on, I saw the cypress-forests and the swamps, and I fancied that the trees had donned their gray-green shrouds of moss because of the deep mourning that had come over the land. The numberless little bayous we crossed were black as night, as though the towering trees and the tangled greenwood, under which they crawled along, had filled them with their bitter tears. But the sun shone so brightly overhead, that I shook off my dark fancies, particularly when my eyes fell on the plump, white neck and rounded cheeks of the lady in the seat before me. I had noticed her at the hotel in New Orleans, where I recognized her at once as a bride, though she had abstained, with singularly good taste, from wearing any of the articles of dress outwardly marking the character. I hoped, secretly, that I might become acquainted with her before the journey ended, for there was something irresistibly charming to me in her pleasant face and unaffected manner. My wish was soon gratified; for the very first alligator that came lazily swimming along in the next bayou so filled her with wonder, that she quickly turned in her seat and called my attention to it. Soon came another alligator, and another; and some distance below was a string of huge turtles, ranged, according to size, on an old log. As something gave way about the engine at this time, we could make comments on the turtle family at our leisure; and when the cars moved on again, we felt as though we had known each other for the last ten years.

I cannot think of a day's travel I have ever enjoyed better than the ride from New Orleans to Brashear. The dry, dusty roads and withered vegetation I had left behind me in California, made the trees and green undergrowth look so much more pleasant to me. The ugly swamp was hidden by the bright, often poisonous, flowers it produces; and though the dilapidated houses and ragged people we saw were not a cheerful relief to the landscape, it was not so gloomy as it would have been under a lowering sky or on a barren plain.

A steamer of the Morgan line, comfortable and pleasant as ever a steamer can be, carried us to Galveston — a place I had pictured to myself as much larger and grander. But the hotel — though my room did happen to look out on the county jail — was well kept; and some of the streets looked like gardens, from the oleander-trees lining them on either side. The trees were in full blossom, and they gave a very pleasant appearance to the houses, in front of which they stood. Some few of these houses looked like a piece of fairyland: nothing could have been built in better taste, nothing could be kept in more perfect order. Too many of them, however, showed the signs of decay and ruin, that speak to us with the mute pathos of nerveless despair from almost every object in the South. We planned a ride on the beach for the next day, which we all enjoyed, in spite of the somewhat fresh breeze that sprung up. The bride was anxious to gather up and carry home a lot of "relics" — a wish the bridegroom endeavored to gratify by hunting up on the strand a dead crab, a piece of ship-timber, and the wreck of a fisherman's net. Discovering that the driver was a German, I held converse with him in his native tongue, which had the pleasing effect of his bringing to light, from under the sand, a lot of pretty shells, which the delighted little bride carried home with her.

The following day we started for Houston. Eight o'clock had been mentioned as the starting hour of the train for that locality, but the landlord seemed to think we were hurrying unnecessarily when we entered the carriage at half-past seven. There was no waiting-room at the starting-point that I could see, and we entered the cars, which stood in a very quiet part of the town (not that there was the least noise or bustle in any part of it), and seemed to serve as sitting and dining-rooms for passengers, who seemed to act generally as if they expected to stay there for the day. But we left Galveston somewhere toward noon, and since we were all good-natured people, and had become pretty well accustomed to the speed of the Southern railroads, we really, in a measure, enjoyed the trip. The people in the cars — many of the women with calico sun-bonnets on their heads, and the men in coarse butternut cloth — reminded me of the Texan emigrants one meets with in New Mexico and Arizona, where they drag their "weary length" along through the sandy plains with the same stolid patience the passengers exhibited here, listlessly counting the heads of cattle that our train picked up at the different stations on the road. The wide, green plains looked pleasant enough, but I wanted to stop at the little badly-built houses, and earnestly advise the inhabitants to plant trees on their homesteads, as the best means of imparting to them the air of "home," which they were all so sadly lacking. The cattle roaming through the country looked gaunt and comfortless — like the people and their habitations.

Night crept on apace; and though I have forgotten (if I ever knew) what the cause of delay happened to be, I know that we did not reach Houston till some five or six hours later than the train was due. I was agreeably surprised to find vehicles at the depot, waiting to carry passengers to the different hotels. Our hotel-carriage was an old omnibus, with every pane of glass broken out; and the opposition hotel was represented by a calash, with the top torn off and the dashboard left out. Still more agreeable was the surprise I met with in the hotel itself — a large, handsome, well-furnished house, giving evidence in every department of what it had been in former days. Before the war, the step of the legislator had resounded in the lofty corridor, and the planter and statesman had met in the wide halls, bringing with them life, and wealth, and social enjoyment to the proud little city. Now, alas! the corridors were cheerless in their desolation, and the grand parlors looked down coldly on the few people gathered there. The proprietor had years ago lived in California; and of this he seemed unreasonably proud, as something that everybody could not accomplish. His wife was a Southern woman, and had not yet learned to look with equanimity upon the undeniable fact that her husband was keeping a hotel. I am sure that she had no reason to deplore the loss of her husband's wealth and slaves on that account; for both she and her husband were people who would have been respected in any part of the world, even if they had *not* kept hotel.

In the midst of a hot, sultry day, a fierce norther sprang up, chilling us to the bone, and causing us to change our original intention of remaining here for some time. The bride, too, and her husband, were willing to return to a more civilized country at an early day. Together we went back, and were greeted at the hotel we had stopped in, and by people on the steamer, as pleasantly as though we were in the habit of passing that way at least once a month. At New Orleans we parted, the new husband and wife returning to St. Louis, while I retraced my steps to Louisville, *en route* to New York.

In the cars I was soon attracted by the appearance of a lady and gentleman — evidently brother and sister — accompanied by an elderly negro woman. The gentleman seemed in great distress of mind, and the lady was trying to speak comfort to his troubled spirits. The negro woman would gaze longingly out of the window, shading her eyes with her hand, and then stealthily draw her apron over her cheeks, as though the heat annoyed her. But I knew she was crying, and the sobs she tried to repress would sometimes almost choke the honest old negro. The train went so slow — so slow; and the gentleman paced nervously up and down, whenever the cars stopped on the way.

Great sorrow, like great joy, always seeks for sympathy; and in a short time I knew the agony of the father, who was counting every second that must pass before he could reach the bedside of his dying child. A young, strong maiden, she had been sent by the widowed father to a convent, in the neighborhood of Louisville, there to receive the excellent training of the sisters of the school. Stricken down suddenly with some disease, they had immediately informed the father by telegraph; and he, with his sister, and Phrony, the old nurse of the girl, had taken the next train that left New Orleans. Both he and his father had been prominent secessionists, had been wellnigh ruined by the war, and had hoarded what little they could save from the common wreck, only for this daughter — and now she was dying. So slowly moved the train! Hour after hour the brother paced up and down the narrow space in the cars, while the sister poured into my ears the tale of his hopes and fears, their wretchedness and their perseverance during the war, and how, in all they had done and left undone, the best interests of Eugenia had been consulted and considered. The negro woman had crouched down at our feet, and was swaying back and forth with the slow motion of the cars, giving vent to her long pent up grief, and sobbing in bitterness of heart: "Oh, Miss Anne! Miss Anne! why didn't you let me go with my chile?"

To make full the cup of misery, we were informed next morning that our train would stop just where it was till six o'clock in the evening, when some other train would come along and carry us on. I don't think that the colonel (the father) did any swearing, but I fear that some of the Californians who were of our party did more than their share. Going to the nearest station, he telegraphed the cause of his delay to the sisters of the convent, and then waited through the intolerably long day. At nightfall the train moved on, slowly, slowly, creeping into Louisville at last, in the dull, cold, dismal day. Snow-flakes were falling in the gray atmosphere, settling for a moment on the ragged, shivering trees, ere they fluttered, half dissolved, to the muddy ground. The wind rose in angry gusts now and again, whirling about the flakes, and trying to rend the murky clouds asunder, as though jealous of the drizzling fog that attempted to take possession of the earth.

Breathlessly the colonel inquired for dispatches at the hotel. Yes; his child still lived! A buggy was ready, awaiting them at the door, and the brother and sister drove off, leaving Phrony to take possession of their rooms. I can never forget the heart-broken look of Phrony when the buggy vanished from sight.

"You see," said I, "there was no room in the buggy for you. If they had waited to engage a carriage, they might have been too late."

"Yes, Miss," said Phrony, absently, and turned away.

Toward the close of the day, when already hooded and cloaked for the onward journey, I was informed that Eugenia was dead: her father had received but her parting breath. The dispatch was sent for the information of those who had shown such sympathy for the grief-stricken father. I stepped over to the colonel's rooms, where I knew Phrony was. She was sitting on a little trunk by the fire, with her apron over her head, and her body bent forward.

"Then you know it, Phrony?" I asked.

"Yes, yes; knowed it all along, Miss. Had n't never no one to take care of her but her old mammy! Oh, my chile! my chile! my little chile! And she's done gone died, without her mammy! Oh, my chile! my chile!"

I tried to speak kindly to her, but my sobs choked me. I looked out of the window, but there was no light there. The snow was falling to the ground in dogged, sullen silence, and the wind, as though tired out with long, useless resistance, only moaned fitfully at times, when clamoring vainly for admission at the closed windows.

Was it not well with the soul just gone to rest? Was it not better with her than with us — with me — who must still wander forth again, out into the snow, and the cold, and the night?

"Oh, my chile! my chile!" sobbed the woman, so black of face, but true of heart; "if I could only have died, and gone to heaven, and left you with Massa Harry! Oh, Miss Anne! Miss Anne! what made you take my chile away from me?"

"It is only for a little while that you will be parted from her, Phrony," I said.

"Bress de Lord! Yes, I'll soon be with my little chile again. But she's dead now, and I can't never see her no more. Oh, my chile! my chile!"

I closed the door softly, for I heard the warning cry of the coachman who was to take us to the outgoing train.

MY FIRST EXPERIENCE IN NEW MEXICO.

ON a warm, pleasant afternoon in the latter part of August, 1866, our command reached the post to which it had been assigned — Fort Bayard, New Mexico. Our ambulance was driven to the top of a little hill, where I had leisure to admire the singular beauty of the surrounding country, while my husband was superintending the pitching of the tent.

The command to which we belonged was the first body of Regulars that had been sent across the Plains since the close of the war. Fort Bayard had been garrisoned by a company of colored troops, who were now under marching orders, and our soldiers were to build the fort, which, as yet, existed only in the general's active brain. The Pinos Altos gold mines were only twelve miles distant from here, and all the other mines — copper and gold — lying within a range of fifteen miles, had been prosperously and profitably worked, by Mexicans and Americans; but after the breaking out of the war, when the troops had been withdrawn from the Territory, bands of roving, hostile Indians had visited one mine after another, leaving in their wake mutilated corpses and blackened ruins. The news of the soldiery coming to this rich mining country was drawing miners and adventurers from far and near, and Pinos Altos promised to become a mining district once more.

Looking around me, I saw a number of officers approaching from where the One Hundred and Twenty-fifth Infantry was camped. They came to welcome us to the camp, and I should have liked to receive them "in style;" but all I could do was to smooth my hair with my hand. The tent was not yet pitched, and I certainly should not leave the ambulance, for I had observed hosts of centipedes crawling out from under the rocks that had been removed to make room for the tent-poles. The officers grouped themselves around the ambulance, and after congratulating us on our safe arrival, wondered how I had ever found courage to come to this place. "Did it not seem an age since I had parted with the last lady, at Fort Selden?" and "How would I like living here—the only lady in this wilderness—without quarters, without comforts of any kind?"

"Oh, I shall do nicely," I said. "I have not slept under a roof since leaving Fort Leavenworth, five months ago, and all the comforts we are in want of are commissaries; which of you, gentlemen, is quarter-master, by the way? I should like to send to the commissary to-day, though it is after issuing hours."

"Yes, certainly," said the quarter-master; "but our supply is limited just now. What do you wish for?"

"Sugar, coffee, tea," I enumerated; "canned fruit, rice—"

"Stop! stop!" hurriedly exclaimed the quarter-master; "all in the world we have in the commissary is soap, salt, and beans. We have taken our coffee without sugar since the Apaches captured the last train, and we rather hoped to get commissaries from your train."

Accustomed as I had become to live on "hard tack" and bacon occasionally, when it was dangerous to light fires, on account of "drawing" the Indians, this piece of information did not dampen my spirits in the least; but at night, while the cook was preparing our supper of coffee, bacon, and soda-biscuits, the orderly sergeant of the company made his appearance at the entrance of our tent, and, after the usual military salute, presented a large tin-pan filled with sugar, and a bag with coffee. "The men," he said, "had requested that their rations of coffee and sugar be delivered to the lieutenant's wife, till the next train should bring fresh supplies." The men had styled me "the mother of the company;" and this was only one of the many proofs of good-will and devotion I was constantly receiving, in return for some little trifling kindnesses I had shown one or the other, while crossing the plains and deserts of Kansas and New Mexico. A little piece of linen, to tie up a bruised finger; a cup of vinegar, a lump of white sugar, to change the taste of the wretched drinking-water, to some poor invalid, were held in sacred remembrance by these men; and some of them had risked their lives, in turn, to procure for me a drink of fresh water, when sick and faint, crossing Jornada del Muerto, that terrible Journey of Death.

Our tent looked cozy enough, when finished and furnished. A piece of brilliant red carpeting was spread on the ground; the bedding was laid on planks, resting on trestles; the coverlet was a red blanket; the camp-chairs were covered with bright cloth, and the supper — served on the lid of the mess-chest — looked clean and inviting. The kitchen, just back of the tent, was rather a primitive institution: a hole dug into the ground, two feet long, a foot wide, with two flat, iron bars laid over it, was all there was to be seen. Two or three mess-pans, a spider, and a Dutch-oven constituted our kitchen furniture; and with these limited means, an old soldier will accomplish wonders in the way of cooking. Before enlisting, one of our servants had been a baker; the other, a waiter at a hotel; and, between them, they managed the task of waiting on us very creditably. To be sure, my husband's rank entitled him to but one servant from the company; but then I was the only lady with the command, and our company commander was considerate of my comfort.

Reveille always comes early; but that first morning in Fort

Y

Bayard it came *very* early. The knowledge that we had reached "our haven of rest," after a five months' journey, made me want to sleep. I wished to feel sure that our tent was not to be struck directly after breakfast — that the bed would not be rolled up and tumbled into the army-wagon — that I should not have to creep into the ambulance, and ride, ride, ride, all that day again. But we had agreed to visit the great Santa Rita copper mines that day, in company with all the officers; and Charley was rapping at the tent, to say that breakfast was almost ready. We started directly after guard-mount: five officers, six men — who had been detailed as escort — and myself. We were all well mounted. My own horse, Toby — the swiftest and strongest of them all — was snow-white, with delicate, slender limbs, and tall, even for a cavalry horse. The camp was located in a valley, some four miles square; gently rising hills inclosed it on every side; beyond these, on one side, rose the San José Mountains, and, in an almost opposite direction, the Pinos Altos Range. All these hills and mountains were said to contain metal; copper and gold, and even cinnabar, could be found. And we were now making our way to the foot-hills, where the officers had promised to show us some rich leads they had discovered. We dismounted when we had reached the place; and some of the escort acting as guard against Indian "surprises," the rest were set to work, with picks and hatchets, to dig up specimens. They had not long to dig, for every rock they struck contained copper; and frequently the little specks of gold in it could be seen with the naked eye.

But it must not be supposed that these hills were barren, or destitute of verdure. On the contrary, as far as the eye could reach, even the highest mountains were covered with grass, scrub-oaks, and cedars; while in the valley, and on the hills, there was one bright carpet of grass and wild flowers. The white tents in the valley, with the flag-staff in the centre, and the flag just moving in the morning breeze, the dark-green trees shading the tents, the stream of water (called by the captain Minne-ha-ha) running around the camp — all this looked so refreshing, so beautiful, after those long day's marches among the sand-hills of the Rio Grande, and the weary tramps over the burning deserts we had lately left behind us, that my enthusiasm rose to the highest pitch.

"Why don't somebody claim this delightful country?— why don't people in the army resign, and own mines, and settle down here to live?" I asked — very irrationally, I am afraid.

"My dear madam," said the captain, leading me to the edge of the hill, and pointing downward, where, amid the long, waving grass and bright, laughing flowers, I discovered the charred logs of what had once been a miner's cabin, "neither the beauty of the country, nor the wealth of its minerals, has been overlooked; and hundreds of men have lost their lives, in trying to wrest from the Indian's grasp what would be a benefit and blessing to civilization."

I wanted to go near enough to touch with my hand two graves that were close by the burnt logs, but the captain refused to let me go. It was about fifty yards from where the guard was placed; and that, he said, was almost certain death. He promised, that as soon as the Mexican guide should return from Fort Craig, he would place him, with a sufficiently large escort, at my command, to visit the whole of the surrounding country. The guide — old Cecilio — had lived in this country before it had come into Uncle Sam's possession; had had many a narrow escape from the Indians, and knew the history of every mine and shaft in all that region. Pointing to the San José Mountain Range, the captain said there was a wagon-road leading along its foot to the Santa Rita mines, but that he knew of an Indian trail, which would take us there much quicker. Remounting, we resumed our journey.

New beauty surprised us every little while: sometimes it was a little silver rivulet, running over the most beautiful ferns; then a group of trees and red-berried shrubs; and again, a clump of rare flowers. But one thing weighed down the spirit like lead, in these wild regions: it was the death-like, uninterrupted silence that reigned over all. There was nothing of life to be seen or heard — no bird, no butterfly. The lizard slipped noiselessly over the rocks at your feet, and the tarantula gaped at you with wide-open eyes, before retreating to the shelter of her nest in the ground. But even the carrion-crow, following wherever human beings lead the way, never left the limits of the camp.

We had now reached a deep ravine. A shallow creek was running at our feet; dark, frowning mountains seemed to hem us in on every side; our horses looked tired, and the captain very unexpectedly announced that he had lost his way! He said he felt sure that this creek was to be crossed *somewhere*, but not here where our horses were drinking now. Old Cecilio had always accompanied him before this, and — and — in short, we were lost! Just then one of the men rode up to the lieutenant's side, and said something to him in a low tone. "Where?" asked he. The man pointed down the creek. The officers dismounted to examine the ground, and found the fresh tracks of eight or nine Apache Indians. To be sure, there were eleven men and officers on our side; but our horses were pretty well worn, and the camp twenty miles away, for aught we knew. The men looked to their fire-arms, while the officers consulted. If we were attacked here, the Indians, even if they could not take us, could starve us out before any party sent out from the fort could find us. Therefore, to proceed was our only chance. Perhaps, if we could succeed in reaching the top of the next mountain, we might discover some landmark showing us our way back to camp. Some one proposed to search again for the trail to the copper-mine; but the captain told us it was one of the favorite haunts of the Indians when in this part of the country, and this party had probably gone there now. At last we moved on, the escort so disposed that I was covered on every side. The mountain was steep, and covered with sharp rocks, cactus, and *chaparral*, which appeared to me moving and peopled with hideous forms. Every moment I expected to hear a savage yell, and see a shower of arrows flying around our devoted heads. Many a time a finger was raised and pointed silently, so as not to frighten me, to some suspicious-looking object; but all remained quiet, and we reached the summit at last, only to see that we were surrounded by mountains still higher and steeper than the one we had climbed. Giving our horses but short breathing-time, we made the next ascent, hoping then to see our way clear; but again we were disappointed. Never before, perhaps, had the foot of the white man left its impress on these solitary heights. There was untold wealth hidden under these sharp rocks, and in the crevices and clefts that looked so dark and treacherous in the afternoon sun; but even the mines of Golconda would have had but little interest for us just then.

We had now come to a mountain that we must descend some five hundred feet before we could make the ascent of the next. With trembling legs, the horses began the steep descent; the first horse stumbled and fell, and then the men were ordered to dismount and lead their horses. I wanted to do the same, but was told to remain in the saddle, as I could not mount quick enough, should the Indians attack us. When the horses found foothold at last, it was almost impossible to urge them on; so some of the men volunteered to reconnoitre in different directions, while the officers remained with me. At last, one of the men, having reached the summit, telegraphed to us that he had discovered some friendly post, and made signs how we were to travel round the mountain. Sundown saw us in camp again, worn out and hungry, but by no means daunted or discouraged. Santa Rita was to be abandoned until the old guide returned; but Pinos Altos was to be visited without him, in a day or two.

Poor Toby was tired and jaded after this exploit, so he was allowed to roam through camp, at his "own sweet will," without lariat or picket-rope; he could always pick out our tent from the rest, and he came to look into it, one morning, just as the cook had laid a freshly-baked loaf of bread on the mess-chest to cool. I had been in the habit of giving Toby a bite of our lunch whenever the command halted, and I could reach the lunch-basket; he was satisfied with anything I gave him—a bit of bacon, a piece of "hard-tack," a lump of sugar—and thinking now, I suppose, that he was being neglected, when I did not look up from my sewing, he quietly withdrew. The next moment I heard the men outside shouting, "Thief! you thief!" Stepping to the entrance of the tent, I saw Toby, the loaf of bread firmly between his teeth, making his way, at a two-forty gait, across the parade-ground. This made our bill of fare rather meagre for that day— "slap-jacks" taking the place of the bread. But, then, we would soon have eggs, the cook said; and he could do so many things with eggs. Now, these eggs were some that we expected certain chickens, then *en route* from Fort Cummings, to lay for us. An officer there had had some chickens brought up from El Paso, at great expense and greater trouble; of these, he had promised us three dozen, and they were now coming to Fort Bayard under escort of ten cavalrymen. I had made Charley promise, on honor, never to ask to kill one of these for the table, but to content himself with using the eggs they would, should, and ought to lay. Toward evening the escort with the wagon came in sight; all the men rushed down the road to meet it; and when the box containing the chickens was opened and the flock let loose, the whole company gave three cheers, and, for days afterward, the men could be heard, all over camp, crowing like roosters. They never seemed to get tired of feeding the chickens extra handfuls of corn, religiously bringing to our kitchen any stray egg a gadding hen had laid in the company hay.

The morning was cool and bright, when Copp and Toby, capering and dancing, as though we had never been lost in the mountains, were led up to the tent. The escort was already mounted, and every man of the twelve looked upon this as a holiday. They all had their curiosity to see Pinos Altos; but the clean gauntlets and white shirts had been donned in honor of this — to them — great event: escorting the first white lady, an officer's wife, into Pinos Altos. I can never tire of speaking of the magnificent scenery in this part of New Mexico. It was not New Mexico — it was a small piece of the Garden of Eden, thrown in by Providence, from above, in sheer pity for the Americans, when Uncle Sam made that Ten Million Purchase, known as the Gadsden. We galloped along a smooth road, made by the men for hauling fire-wood over, for a mile or two, till we crossed the Minne-ha-ha, and shortly after struck the Pinos Altos road. It had been a well travelled road at one time, though the Indian only had crossed it, in his wanderings, these three or four years past. Scrub-oak, and shrubs for which I knew no name, by the wayside; the aloe plant and cactus, *grama* grass and wild flowers, peeping out from under fragments of moss-covered rock; here and there a cedar, or pine, made the impression that we were inspecting extensive pleasure-grounds; the little stream — Whiskey Creek — that found its winding way down from Pinos Altos, was bordered by willows, and, though shallow, afforded us all a cool drink. The road rises almost from the time of leaving the fort, but so gently at first as to be hardly noticed. Part of the escort rode before us, for those romantic-looking hills, springing up here and there on our way, had many a time served as ambush for the savage hordes that infest all this country; and more than one grave by the road-side spoke of sudden attack, of sharp contest, and final defeat.

An officer alone would have thought it unnecessary to take so large an escort as ours, but the commanding officer had stipulated that the lieutenant must not undertake these rides with me unless he took twelve men. The Indians would risk any number of their braves, he said, to get an officer's wife into their possession; and then he would have to turn out his whole command to rescue me. So, to save him this trouble, we promised to obey orders.

There was one curious hill, that I never passed without counting from six to twelve rattlesnakes wriggling up the side of it. This rattlesnake hill was about half-way between camp and Pinos Altos; and a mile or two beyond, I saw the first tall pines, from which this region takes its name. They were giants, in fact; it made me dizzy to look up to the tallest point I could see, as the tree swayed gently to and fro against the deep-blue sky.

Our horses were walking now; the hills grew into mountains, and came closer around us; the road was hardly a road any more — I doubt that anything but Indian ponies or packtrains had ever gone over it, till the "boys in blue" came here — and the inconsiderate thorns caught and tore my "best" riding-habit at every step. We could now see the red earth the miners in this section liked so well to find; they had been prospecting all along Whiskey Creek, but had gone higher and higher, till settling in Pinos Altos proper, at last. Up, up, we went, till I thought we must be nearing the clouds. The air felt sharp and cool, even in the midday sun, but we had not yet reached the summit.

At last the advance-guard halted, and one of the men, turning, uttered an exclamation of wonder and surprise. The

Pinos Altos people had cut down the tall pines as much as possible on this side, because the Indians had always approached under cover of them when they had made their attacks on the place; and now, without hindrance or obstruction, we had a view, such as I have never enjoyed since. All the mountains I had thought so immensely high lay at our feet, and away beyond them I could see far into the country — for hundreds of miles, it seemed to me. To the right of us, we could peer into Old Mexico; the Three Brothers — three peaks very similar in appearance and close together — were pointed out to me; and over that way was Janos, they said — the first town after crossing the border — the place our deserters and fugitives from justice always tried to reach. Five minutes' ride now brought us in sight of Pinos Altos — a few straggling shanties, built of logs, brush, or *adobe*, just as it happened to suit the builder. Beyond Pinos Altos the world seemed literally shut in, or shut out, by mountains; there was snow on the highest peaks nine months of the year; no one had felt inclined to explore them as yet — indeed, it was all people could do to draw their breath comfortably here, I thought. The streets in this city had not yet been thoroughly regulated, as some of the inhabitants had found it convenient to commence mining operations in, or immediately outside, their houses; and, following a good lead they had struck, had sometimes continued these operations till some other miner, with six-shooter in hand, had declared no man had a right to dig "round his shanty." Some other miner had coaxed the waters of Whiskey Creek on to his "claim," situated on the other side of town, having dug for this purpose a ditch some five or six feet deep. Still another had sunk a shaft twenty feet deep, at his front door, so as to "hold that mine" for two years. But mining was not confined to the streets of the city, by any means; companies of five, six, or twenty men had ventured out as far as their number would permit. It would not have been a very safe occupation at the best; for even our men, when sent to cut hay within sight of the fort, had to work with their revolvers buckled on, and their carbines within reach. How much more, then, did these men risk, in lonely, out-of-the-way places, where no succor could reach them — where only the serene sky overhead, and the red demon inflicting the torture, could hear the last agonized cry that escaped the blanched lips of his writhing, helpless victim.

As we approached, the miners laid down their picks, and stared at us. Here and there a Mexican woman, who had followed the fortunes of her lord and master into the wilderness, appeared at the door of some shanty, her head covered with the inevitable *rebozo;* and, taking a quick survey of our party, would vanish the next moment to communicate the news of our arrival to her *amigos* and *compadres*. "Taking" the ditches, but carefully avoiding the shafts, we came to a house rather larger and better-appearing than the rest, and were invited by a mannerly Spaniard to alight and rest in his "house." His wife waited on us in the pleasantest manner; but the building we had entered consisted of only one room, which was store, sitting-room, kitchen, and all. The news of our arrival spread like wild-fire; miners from far and near hurried to Rodriguez' store; and the place being small, the circle around us was soon as close as good manners would allow of — and good manners they all had, Mexicans and Americans. Those who could not find room inside, were out by the door, patting Toby, examining my side-saddle, and asking questions of the escort. Señor Rodriguez was in the habit of weighing the gold the miners found in the course of the day, and buying it for greenbacks, or exchanging for it such provisions as he had on hand. A huge, bearded Mexican stepped up to the little counter now, and emptying his leather bag of its shining contents, selected the largest piece

— the size of a hazel-nut — and presented it to me, with an air of such genuine honesty, such chivalric grace, that I felt I could not refuse the gift without wounding the man's feelings. I could only say, "Thank you," in English; but having accepted this first offering, I could not refuse to accept from the rest the largest piece of gold each miner had found that day. The first piece had been the largest found.

Taking our departure when the sun was almost hidden behind the mountains, we could not shake off a nervous feeling as we picked our way through the labyrinth of rocks, trees, and shrubs, for this was the favorite hour for Indian attacks. They hardly ever attack a train or camp after night; their chosen time is just before dark, or early in the morning, before sunrise; of course, they are not particular as to what hour of the day they can appropriate your scalp, but they have seldom or never been known to attack the whites at night.

We could already see the camp-fires in the distance, when a number of stealthily moving objects in the road attracted my attention. Toby snorted as though an Indian were already clutching at the bridle; but a most discordant yelping, barking, and howling struck my ear just then like the sweetest of music: a pack of *coyotes* only had gathered around us. They followed us all the way to camp, and, surrounding our quarters, kept up their serenade till broad daylight. A band of equally musical wild-cats had chosen the infantry camp as the theatre for their performances; and an occasional roar from one of those long-built, panther-like animals called California lions taught me that there was life and animation in Nature here at night, if not in the daytime.

Old Cecilio having returned during our absence, we started out, the next morning, after guard-mount, on another exploring expedition. When the hills, shutting in the valley with the fort, had closed behind us, we halted for a moment to look down the road by which we had first approached Fort

Bayard. There, before us to the left, lay the San José Mountain Range, grand and stately, partly covered with cedars, pines, and firs. Winding along the foot of the range, the eye could follow the course of the beautiful, silver-clear White Water, bordered by willows, ash, and poplars. The most fantastic rocks rose abruptly out of the water, here and there, covered with moss and vines; an aloe plant or cactus generally adorning the highest point — growing where not a handful of earth could be seen, from which they might draw life and sustenance. To the right of us — ah! there was New Mexico, its barren hills, its monotonous plains, "the trail of the serpent" lying over all; for the Indians had only lately set fire to the grass, and it had consumed the scant vegetation.

An hour's ride brought us in sight of the ruins of the San José copper mines, on the side of the mountain. It was rather steep climbing to reach it; but the plateau, on which the works lay, must have been a quarter of a mile across. Placing sentinels, we inspected the old mill. Everything was rude and primitive, but huge in dimensions; and the different *jacals* that surrounded the *adobe* building corroborated the guide's statement that some fifty men had been employed here, "and they had fought bravely and sold their lives dearly," he said, "the day they were attacked by the Indians, three or four years ago."

"A white man," Cecilio continued, "a rebel, had led this band of Indians, and, adding his knowledge of the habits of the white man to the cunning of the savages, but few Americans or Mexicans could escape these fiends. This wretch never erred in the aim he took — a ball through the neck always sending his victim to his last account — but here, on this spot, he had found his match. Some American, whose name the guide had forgotten, had sent a bullet through his traitor's heart, at last; and the Indians, never resting until the brave man had been laid in the dust, then left this region, because, possibly, there was nothing more to destroy." Clearing away the brush and rubbish at our feet, the guide held up his hand —"And here, *señora*," he said,— pointing to two sunken graves marked by pieces of smoothed plank,—"here they are buried side by side: the rebel who led the Indians, and the white man who killed him." It was nothing uncommon to meet with nameless graves in this country; but a thrill passed through my heart, as I looked at these two mounds, where friend and foe slumbered so peacefully, "side by side."

It was dangerous to tarry long in one spot, the guide reminded us. The orderly brought Copp and Toby, and we pursued our way through the laughing, blooming valley. Nuts, grapes, and hops grew wild here; and peaches, Cecilio said, grew near the Santa Rita mines, but they had been planted there by the former inhabitants and employés of the mines. The mines originally belonged to a Spanish lady, to whose ancestors seven leagues of the country surrounding them had been granted by the Spanish Government, long before the territory belonged to Uncle Sam. Her representatives had worked the mines with a force of some two hundred men, till the Indians had overpowered them, and destroyed the works. The immense piles of copper-ore, on either side of the road, told us that we were nearing Santa Rita, at last; and there, just at the point of the San José Range, lay a large, strongly-built *adobe* fort. Buildings of different sizes and kinds lay clustered around this, which appeared to be furnace and fastness at once. Placing sentinels, we commenced exploring above ground; under-ground I refused to venture, in my cowardice. We found works of considerable magnitude; I counted twelve bellows, in a kind of hall, that must have been sixty feet high, but the rafters and beams overhead had rotted, and the weight of the mud, with which all roofs are covered in this country, had borne down the roof, and half covered an enormous wheel, some forty feet in diameter. Everything about this wheel that was not wood, was copper; not a vestige of iron, steel, or stone, was to be seen around here: it was copper, wood, and *adobe*. But copper was everywhere — copper-ore, so rich that the veins running through it could be scraped out with a pen-knife; copper just smelted; copper beaten into fantastic shapes, as though the workmen, in their despair, had meant to use these as weapons against the Indians, when attacked here, years ago. For the same band, with the white leader, had attacked these works; and Cecilio showed us the dents the Indian arrows had made in the little wooden door the men had succeeded in closing, when first attacked. But the families of these men had lived in the buildings outside the fort; and to rescue wife and children from death, and worse than death, they had abandoned their place of safety in the fort, and, with the superintendent leading them, they had fought the savages bravely, but had been defeated and slaughtered, at last. Leaving nine men with me, the lieutenant, guide, and three men descended into the shaft, went some five hundred yards, and, on their return, reported that everything looked as though deserted only yesterday.

Having confidence in old Cecilio, we now took the trail we had missed the other day, as this would enable us to visit the San José gold mine on our way back to camp. We could ride only "Indian file," but soon came to a mountain composed entirely of white flint. Sand and earth, carried here by the wind, and bearing grass and flowers, could be scraped aside anywhere, discovering underneath the same semi-transparent rock. Again we took the narrow trail, which brought us to what appeared to be the entrance to a cave, in the side of a hill; a wooden cross was fastened over it, and a road, built entirely by hand, led to the half-consumed remains of a number of buildings, on the banks of a creek. The guide and lieutenant entered the mine alone, leaving the men for my protection, but soon returned, as fallen earth blocked up the passage near the entrance.

"But oh, *señora*, the gold taken from this mine was something wonderful," the guide said, enthusiastically; "and there is still a whole 'cow-skin' full of it, buried in one of these holes"—pointing to different shafts we were passing on our way to the burnt cottages. "When the Indians came here the white men tried to take it with them, but were so closely pursued that they threw it into one of these places, intending to come back for it; but all they could do, later, was to bury their people decently, and the gold is still there —left for some stranger to find."

The eyes of the soldiers—gathered around the graves we had dismounted to see—glittered at the old guide's tale; but the sight of these lonely, forgotten graves could awaken but one thought in my breast: How long would it be before another group might bend over our graves and say, "I wonder who lies buried here!"

THE END.

www.ingramcontent.com/pod-product-compliance
Lightning Source LLC
Chambersburg PA
CBHW030357230426
43664CB00007BB/629